Carol + Danny

KING OF CHEER

STORIES OF SHOWING UP, GETTING UP AND NEVER GIVING UP FROM THE WORLD'S MOST ELECTRIFYING CROWD IGNITOR

CAMERON HUGHES

BIG Cheer to you! Love
your spirit + PASSION For
LIFE... But, I MISS You!
Thanks for your cheers!.

XO

"The first time you see Cameron do his thing is a moment you simply will not forget. He goes from random typical fan to a lightning rod of energy that gets the crowd pumping. His dancing skills may not win him any awards on Dancing with the Stars, but he is unmatched as a positive force that will get the crowd on their feet cheering. Cameron's story and passion will inspire many!"

Daniel Negreanu, 6-time World Series of Poker Champion

"I've seen Cam at the NBA Finals, Leafs games, Oilers games, the NHL Awards, etc. When I come home from these events and tell my teenage sons that Cam showed up again and did what he does best… inspiring fans and making people smile, they are always amazed and curious.

Why do I seem to always see him in my travels? I tell my boys it's simple… he hustles his butt off, he shows up and gives it his all. I know players really appreciate how much effort he gives to electrify and excite their respective arenas. Cameron brings us on a beautiful one of a kind journey of his career - I'm excited to have my boys hear how he did it."

Jeff Jackson, Executive Vice -President, Wasserman Hockey

"Throughout Cameron's many wacky adventures and the rollercoaster ride of a career, he's worked hard and hustled not just to take the path less traveled, but to actually create an exciting, creative, original path that is entirely his own. His story will inspire many others to live their dreams... and truly be themselves."

Thea Andrews-Wolf, Former ET Host, television personality

"Cameron is raw sunshine. He is positive energy personified - a man with so much magnetic, infectious joie de vivre, he single-handedly possesses the power to ignite an entire stadium of thousands. Cameron built himself by himself - personally and professionally - and I marvel at him."

Jill Leiderman, Executive Producer

"I've seen Cam in my playing days from the old Forum to the Staples Center to now in management and wow can he light it up. I admire his tenacity and heart each time I see him rocking the fans. Cameron's book is a great account of the behind the scenes fun at sporting events, shared by a guy who just wouldn't quit!"

Rob Blake, NHL Hall of Famer, LA Kings GM

"There's a difference between the atmosphere of stale organ music backing canned scoreboard graphics and one that boasts the idiosyncratic artistry of a 6'4" Canadian redhead wearing 11 t-shirts and dancing maniacally in the aisles to the delight of everyone around you. Cameron's presence changes the psychological environment in the arena or stadium; he creates new behavioral and emotional parameters for the situation that liberate fans to let go and join in the fun."

Sam Sommers, Tufts Psychology Professor, Situations Matter Author

"The first time I saw Cameron I thought he was going to get arrested, but then I found out he was part of the show. And thankfully because his energy and enthusiasm are unmatched making every show he works on superior."

Orny Adams, Comedian

"Cameron Hughes has truly used his smile, energy, and passion to change the world! This book will inspire you to always be in the moment, leave your comfort zone, and live your best life!"

Mercedes Martinez, Radio/TV host

"Cameron Hughes is one of the most passionate, energetic people I've ever met. His story is remarkable... a life of getting people to stand up and cheer. That's worth... well... standing up and cheering for."

James Duthie, Sports Broadcaster

"Cameron is a gift. Frankly, it all looks so easy. It's not. I've been in the entertainment industry for 20+ years, and I've never seen anyone successfully replicate what Cam does. Cameron's book will help people gain the courage to become unabashed cheerleaders for their families, friends, and co-workers. But I suggest you leave your shirt on!"

Bart Given, TORQUE Strategies

"When I was playing in the NHL, there's one super fan that stood out to me. The fans loved him, and so did we. Fast forward 20+ years and there he was again in Vegas. A highlight to Vegas Golden Knights' home games. I love Cameron Hughes. He has a great spirit, passion, and he knows how to have fun. What a guy!"

Brad May NHL Hockey Legend, AKA, Mayday!

"The best value of any act in sports. This book will shake people up and get stadiums cheering like never before!"

Jon Cudo, Founder Gameops.com, Director of Animal Control, Cleveland Cavaliers

"Just stand up! It's so simple, Cameron, not just in your story but everyone who has success. You've done an incredible job of combining the sports and entertainment elements of the business over your career. This book will inspire so many people to just stand up in their own lives. And yes, I would have brought you in for a few games!"

Oren Koules, Film and Television Producer, former NHL Owner, Tampa Bay Lightning

"Cameron-kudos to you. You were a pioneer in this space and cultivated many fans and copycats. I dare say, you might even have been ahead of your time! Sports and marketing executives will gain valuable insights from your journey."

Kristy Fletcher, former Toronto Maple Leafs Executive

"They hung on every dance move and t-shirt that was pulled off and thrown into the crowd. In that moment, he broke down every barrier that might hold a fan back from having a good time at a sporting event. It instantly put everyone in a good mood and set the tone for the rest of the evening. Overnight, the video received over a million impressions on Facebook. Then two million. Then three million. We officially had a viral video on our hands. His act was bringing joy to people all over again. His book will do the same for fans around the world!"

Lindsey Gullett, Director of Entertainment Edmonton Oilers, Manitoba Moose

"He's the best dancer in New York. Keep doing what you're doing buddy!"

Novak Djokovic, World No. 1 tennis player, dance partner

Fangage Media
https://www.cameronhughes.tv/contact
bookcameronhughes@gmail.com
@cameroncheers

First Edition

Hughes, Cameron Wilson, 1971 -
ISBN: 978-0-578-59664-8

This work is a memoir that depicts events in the author's life as truthfully
as his recollection permits, can be verified by research, and input from the
other individuals present. Some quotes have been edited for brevity.
Thank you to all those who contributed anecdotes to this book.

To my mom, my little girl, and my love: I'm so lucky to have such beautiful and inspiring women in my life. You'll always be my fuel.

WARNING

What you're about to read is an inspirational memoir, an outrageous behind-the-scenes sports scrapbook, an improv guide to life, and a public-dance-instruction manual all in one.

Keep out of reach of uptight people who are allergic to fun. On second thought, please, please, please give it to them! This is for anyone who has ever been plagued with doubt or felt afraid to live their life to the fullest.

This is for everyone.

STORIES

CHEER

VERB
1. shout for joy or in praise or encouragement.
"she cheered from the sidelines" – encourage, rally, spur on.

NOUN
1. a shout of encouragement, praise, or joy.
"a tremendous cheer from the audience" hurrah, shout, hoot.

2. cheerfulness, optimism, or confidence.
"an attempt to inject a little cheer into this gloomy season."

HOW I MAKE A LIVING BY GOING TO SPORTING EVENTS AND CHEERING

"Your life will fly by, so make sure you're the pilot."
Rob Liano

Jumping out of bed, I had to grab hold of the curtains to catch my balance. Squinting at the early morning sunlight, I was dizzy, my ankles throbbing, and I had absolutely no idea what city I was in. Three flights in three days will do that to you. And maybe I went a little too crazy with 20,000 people last night. As my eyes adjusted, I caught a glimpse of the Strip, already bustling with movement and color – all palm trees, passersby, and drunk tourists tripping over themselves as they staggered from the slots out into the blinding glare of the morning sun.

VEGAS, BABY!

In true Vegas fashion, I felt like the fifth member of the *Hangover* gang. Not because I had been out clubbing with the boys and got chased by Mike Tyson's tiger last night, but because smack in the heart of the entertainment capital of the world, I had put everything I had into pumping up the crowd for Game 2 of the 2018 NHL Finals – my 30th game for the Golden Knights that season.

I sat down on the bed and clung to the comforter to keep from tipping over. My legs burned from tearing up and down the stairs of T-Mobile Arena. Last night had been electric, firing up the already insane Golden Knights' fan base. I'd do almost anything to bring that extra spark of enthusiasm.

I packed up my golden shoes, lucky jeans, and trademark Superman belt. I had another plane to catch.

★★★

Curled up in my cozy-ish extra legroom window seat, I could barely keep my eyes open. My 6 foot 4, 230-something-pound frame was begging for a re-charge. I was about to drift off to dreams of Golden Knights and T-Mobile magic when a stern-looking guy wearing a Cleveland Cavaliers jersey stopped dead in his tracks and loomed over me.

"See you at the game tonight?" he asked, breaking into a broad grin and giving me a fist bump.

I smiled and nodded.

Yep. He would. I was heading to my third game in four days in two different cities. That night, the Cavs were hosting the defending NBA champion Golden State Warriors – my fourth run with LeBron and company in four years. I had to show up and give it my all. Cheer on the fans, help their experience be the best it can be, and get a big Cavs' "W." No excuses.

After all, this is how I make my living.

Seated in section 112 of the Q, I waited. Patience was key – like a crouching jungle cat stalking his unsuspecting prey. Early in my career, I'd often dance from random seats in the arena and hope my antics would naturally end up on the jumbotron; now, though, the fun was orchestrated with almost surgical precision. Who knew my ADHD would be so beneficial to my career? Everyone from the camera operators to the control room directors to the ushers and security guards must work together in unison to make the moment a success.

Out of the corner of my eye, I noticed the cameraman lumbering his way up the aisle. It was almost time. Tonight, I was doing the popcorn bit. My hands began to vibrate with excitement. A crowd of 20,562 was about to witness me go *off*. There was a stoppage in play, and then, a TV timeout. My time.

The camera panned over a few fans – eating hot dogs, chatting, laughing – then shifted to me.

This was it. The moment that would set the tone for the night.

Go.

I rose from my seat, a bag of popcorn in each hand and 40,000 eyes on me, waiting for my next move. The arena buzzed with anticipation. I could sense those who didn't know me scratching their heads, puzzled.

Who is this guy?

What's he doing?

Hold the phone… the dude's got two bags of popcorn? That ain't right. Something's…

BOOM!

I flung both bags sky high, popcorn raining down on unsuspecting bystanders. Then, for 75 seconds, I went *wild*. I slapped my hands together feverishly like I'd done hundreds of times before. Familiar to me, but unusual to the general population. It's not every day you see a grown man gyrate his hips and dance like a broken windmill. I never said my moves were good, but they were dance moves, nonetheless. And the joy was infectious.

As usual, the fans were shocked, pleased – and wildly confused. But I had their attention, and that was all I needed. They were along for the ride with me.

A feeling of euphoria washed over me as I realized that a chunk of the world was now watching me dance my silly dance. The feeling was always the same –

that of fear and adrenaline and ultimate joy all wrapped together. The fear said I could trip and fall down the stairs, ending my reign of cheer with a tumultuous faceplant. I could accidentally punch someone with my flailing arms. After all, who knows what could happen when a man is sparked with such unbounded cheer? *Anything* is the answer. But like I said before, everything had been calibrated. I had done this literally hundreds of times, and although I looked like a loon, I knew *exactly* what I was doing. No face plants or stray punches today (and hopefully not any day).

The adrenaline and the joy walked hand-in-hand like crazed lovers on a tropical beach somewhere, newly married and full of hope. They said, "Look at all these people. They're smiling. They're laughing. Their hearts are beating like crazy because they're witnessing someone break forth from their shell to become one hundred percent authentic. And in their own hearts, they're dancing. They're moving. They can feel it, too."

The popcorn soared. My legs kicked. I ripped my shirt open, revealing a Cavs t-shirt underneath, and screamed like a wild banshee. T-shirts soared into the crowd. The fans went insane, laughing, roaring, cheering. Smiles on the faces around me.

My work here was done. Well… kind of. All I had to do was twirl 264 more t-shirts over the next two hours, and keep the party rocking. *Then* it would be done.

After the game, I wobbled through the streets of downtown Cleveland, my body aching from the plyometric dance workout I had just been doing up and down the bleachers again and again. A husky, bearded fella walking towards me stopped and did a double take. I could see his gears turning.

"Hey, T-shirt Guy!"

Then a petite blonde woman.

"Superfan!"

Then a pair of excitable teenagers.

"Ginger-haired dude from the game!"

For a moment, regret settled in. I should've branded myself as *Superfan* 20 years ago when I had the chance. Now Cameron Hughes – or ginger-haired dude – would have to do.

The next morning, alone in the back of a black SUV en route to Hopkins International Airport, I gazed at the twinkling lights of the humble Cleveland skyline. Silence permeated the vehicle. I felt a pang of withdrawal as I started to wonder where my next crowd-induced high would come from.

Maybe the Cavs will bring me back for another one?
I wonder what's happening in Bakersfield?
How the heck am I going to top this?

The higher I went, the harder it always seemed to sting when I came down. This was how the players must feel – working their asses off, their bodies drenched in sweat as they played for the crowds night after night. Of course, they weren't just playing for the crowds. They were playing to prove something to themselves, to their families, to their old guidance counselors and parents and authority figures who told them, "Work hard, get an education. This basketball stuff is a pipe dream. More people win the lottery than become professional athletes. Get your head out of the clouds."

And they were playing because it's what they were born to do. It's as if the very moment they were born, everything was lining up to subtly point them in the direction of greatness. To a place where they could use their skills to inspire untold millions of people to hope and dream. To aspire to become like them, and to tell all those naysayers, "No, it's only a dream if you're asleep. And I'm wide awake."

Sitting back in my seat, drowning in the comfort of the cushions in spite of my aching body, I took a moment to reflect on the last 24 years of *my* life. I still couldn't believe this was my life. This was me. Cameron Hughes. That kid who didn't make the team. And now here I was, making a living doing what I loved: entertaining fans, twirling tees and spreading cheer at some of the biggest events around the world.

It was the stuff of dreams. But you know what? I felt wide awake.

You probably didn't know my name before you picked up this book, but if you're a sports fan, there's a good chance you've seen my "work." And maybe – just *maybe* – you've caught a stray t-shirt that has been flung at your face by yours truly. I've been hired by over 25 different professional sports leagues in 11 countries and have performed at two Olympic Games. I'm also going to go ahead and claim that I'm in the running for logging more face time on stadium jumbotrons than any non-athlete in history.

Some people call me a "sports crowd ignitor." Others have called me the "batshit crazy dude who tosses out sweaty t-shirts in Section 128." Still others have dubbed me a "Superfan," but that's not really accurate. What I do is travel from city to city, tapping into and unlocking the energy of *all* the great fans in different arenas. It's a fine line, but an important distinction.

When there's no previous category for your job, all sorts of made-up words and phrases get tossed into the mix. Despite whatever random thing they call me, one thing is certain: I love what I do, and can't imagine another career. Through a unique combination of stubbornness, foolishness, bravery, vulnerability, confidence, fear and *joie de vivre*, along with the crucial help of dozens, make that hundreds of smart, kind and experienced people along the way, I somehow figured out how to get paid to show up and get my crazy on. And I'm fortunate enough to travel the world doing it.

When people find out what I do for a living, usually they can't believe it at first. Then they have a whole lot of questions. I don't blame them. *I've* still got a lot of questions. In this book, we'll tackle some of the big ones, including:

How did taking a huge chance one night lead to a career performing for over 25 million people?

How did a guy who was in and out of university more than Frank the Tank, and who has no real skills, carve out a lucrative career in the sports entertainment business?

How does one go from being cut from their high school basketball squad to rocking the house with King James and making five consecutive trips to the NBA Finals?

What's it like doing the wave with Roger Federer at his charity event?

But without fail, the one question I get most often is:

How'd you DO IT?

Trust me. I get it. My career isn't exactly your typical nine-to-five. It didn't really exist before I made it happen. But it was a *calling*. I can wake up whenever I want, eat my lunches wherever I want, and am pretty much on an all-expenses-paid vacation at all times. I'm just a regular guy who figured out how to live his best, slightly irregular life. But it didn't happen overnight. It took years of struggling, trial and error, rejection and chaos, trying to prove to everyone around me that my crazy dream was one worth believing in. And, as you'll soon see, I almost gave up on it more times than I can count.

Whether you're working at a job you feel trapped in, feeling confused about the direction your life is heading, just graduated college or are even the CEO of a company looking to take things to the next level, I feel that what I've learned over the course of my journey could be the extra spark you're looking for – or at least inspire you in different ways. For me, everything seemed to click when I started to follow one simple philosophy, and that is:

Believe in the Power of Cheer

Which is what, exactly? I'm not just talking about dancing in the aisles at a sporting event like a possessed, t-shirt-slinging maniac. It's much bigger than that. When you put yourself out there and cheer yourself on, the crowd will support you. On a basic level, this same philosophy explains why certain smiles are contagious – because they come from cheer, and they are meant to be shared.

I'm not the guy who's got everything figured out, and I don't pretend to be. I've been struggling with ADHD for as long as I can remember, mostly without even knowing it. I wasn't diagnosed until my mid-40s. Why was I so afraid to admit I had a faster brain than normal and couldn't focus? You'll quickly see why working in an office wasn't my thing – nor was any "normal" career path.

I've also been struggling with my weight for many years, but you know what they say: "the t-shirts add 10 pounds." For many years, I was always running from serious relationships. I'd meet someone, get excited, then run or scare them. They say unexpected childhood trauma can do that to you. I didn't want to get hurt, so I'd run. We all have a story, a snag, a hurdle. And I'm proud to say I've figured out how to use some of the challenges I've encountered to hone my talents and turn my dreams into this wacky career.

As I got deeper into the writing process of this book, I started calling the people involved in some of the stories (team executives, athletes, colleagues, fans, friends, and my favorite mascot, Moondog, to name a few). And many of them have been gracious enough to provide a little extra color for your reading pleasure.

Thank you for coming along. And thank you for your passion and cheer. I feel it all. Not a moment goes by that I'm not grateful for the people who've believed in me and given me a shot, for the fans I've shared the magic with, and all the incredible people I've met along the way.

We all have a story of how we got to where we are; who inspired us; who believed in us. I hope my story will inspire you to cheer a little louder, smile a little wider, dance a little crazier, contribute to your team, be fearless, and most importantly, to GET UP and become your own biggest fan. I'm thrilled to take you on my journey and show you the true power of cheer.

LET'S GO!

As you dive into the book please note we've included videos and extra visuals to go with many of the stories and great moments! Please go to CameronHughes.TV for all.

Manitoba Moose mania! Photo courtesy of Jonathan Kozub of Point Shot Photography.

Lehigh Valley Phantoms t-shirt smiles! AHL hockey in Allentown. Photo courtesy of Jim Trocchio.

PART 1

Fettke family pretty in pink – Stockton Thunder Pink in the Rink Night. Always great to raise breast cancer awareness.

Lighting up Condorstown – Bakersfield Condors, ECHL & AHL. Photo courtesy Edward Medellin.

The gym where it all began and didn't! Go Lords!

Lisgar Collegiate High School, Ottawa, ON.

est. 1843

THE LIST

*"People will hate you, rate you, shake you, and break you.
But how strong you stand is what makes you."*

LeBron James

"**I**t's up!" I shrieked. My eyes bugged out of my skull with unrestrained excitement, as they often do. But this time they were zeroing in on, of all things, a high school gymnasium door. Never in my life had I considered that a *door* would be the harbinger of my life's path. But it was.

I was scared shitless to look at the list taped to the door. For the past three years, I'd been trying to secure a spot on the high school basketball team but had come up short. For as long as I could remember, I'd dreamt of becoming a professional athlete, racing out of the tunnel onto center court at Madison Square Garden, the mecca of all stadiums. Bright lights, and thousands of people cheering me on. That sound would be there – the same one you hear when you hold a seashell up to your ear – a quiet but discernible roar. Cameron trots out to the floor. Pristine jersey, comfy headband, a smile for the ages…

I'm getting ahead of myself. Three years, and I'd never even made the team. That's why that list was so intimidating, and I was shaking, scared just looking at it.

The first year wasn't exactly my fault. I didn't know how to run plays and focus on instructions the way I needed to. What can I say? I was a freshman. The following year, I'd learned more about the floor and plays, but I'd contracted the flu the week before tryouts and was still busy sipping herbal tea and popping Flintstones vitamins when Coach Fraser demanded we run suicides. As you can imagine, 'suicides' was an apt phrase for me that time around. And junior year – well – I'm not even sure what happened there. I was an undeniable freak in the paint, snatching up rebounds like Rodman and blocking shots like Mutombo. After learning I didn't make the team once again, I was in shock.

"Were you even *watching* me out there?" I protested, grilling Coach like one of my father's famous ribeyes. "What the heck was it this time?"

"Blocking shots during warm-up doesn't count," he'd said bluntly.

Okay, fine. I could accept that. Besides, I had one more year to try.

Easing the blow too was the fact that my buddy Jay couldn't crack the roster either. Three years, three tryouts, and three rejections, just like me. But we were both determined to make sure it didn't happen again. While Jay enrolled at a basketball camp to finesse his skills, I spent my whole summer vacation perfecting my jump shot, carefully shaving my legs to be more aerodynamic (naturally), and growing an extra inch to reach an even six feet.

We were shoo-ins this time around. And the tryout could not have gone better. I scrambled for every loose ball, fought for every rebound, and contested every shot attempt. I could tell Coach was impressed. After the whistle sounded, he gave me the "nod," which was akin to Johnny Carson waving a fresh-faced comedian to the couch after a set.

Now, Jay and I rushed to the gymnasium door to learn our fate, our hearts practically crawling out of our throats.

"Holy shit!" Jay exclaimed, flashing a jubilant grin. "I made it! Cam, I MADE IT."

Of course he did. Although he lacked height, Jay's ball-handling skills were suddenly off the charts. He'd developed a wicked crossover that was sure to wreak havoc on the opposition.

Cautiously, I inched my way closer to the all-powerful List, eyes wide open, palms so wet one might've thought I'd just tried out for the swim team. I scanned it up and down. Then I scanned it up again. Then down again. Then sideways and diagonally. I ripped the sheet from its place and flipped it over to see if maybe they'd started including names on the back of the page this year? They had not.

There it was. My answer. I had not made the team.

Four years, four tries, and still I was a failure. What would my friends think of me now? I had gone through high school without making a single team! I was crestfallen. Embarrassed. Why wasn't I good enough? God knows I tried. I practiced, practiced, practiced until my legs felt like they were sinking into the ground and becoming one with the court. I was even halfway decent!

Jay's smile quickly faded when he saw the expression on my face. I can only imagine it was apocalyptic. "Dude..." he said quietly, gently placing his hand on my shoulder. "I'm sorry."

Standing there by the gymnasium door, I felt my shoulders slump under the heavy weight of my shame. Not afraid to admit it – I felt like crying.

She's going to be so disappointed, I thought.

Through my misery, I shifted my attention to Jay for the first time.

"Sorry, dude," he repeated. "That's a huge drag. We could've used you."

"All good," I said, not meeting his eyes. "You should probably check in with Coach to see what the next steps are."

Taking the hint, Jay went into the gym to join the coveted ranks of the high school basketball elite. In the hall I lingered, left behind to reacquaint myself with my old enemy, rejection. I had hoped this was going to be 'THE' year. You know, the one where I made all my dreams come true… what little dreams they were. Namely, the joy of looking at my mom and saying, "Mom, guess what?"

"What?" she'd ask.

Then, smiling, because of course I wouldn't be able to contain it:

"I made the team."

She'd swoop in, squealing with delight, and give me the biggest hug in the world. She would be proud, and I'd be thrilled because I made her proud. It would be yet another memory in the photo album of our unbreakable bond. But it was not meant to be.

And I'd have to learn to be okay with it.

The Hughes Family. My mother-Deanna, sister-Andrea, father-David and myself. Our family log cabin summer days, winning best dressed year after year! :)

2

THE GREAT FUR FAKE-OUT

"This is part of what a family is about, not just love. It's knowing that your family will be there watching out for you. Nothing else will give you that. Not money. Not fame. Not work."

Mitch Albom, Tuesdays with Morrie

T he year was 1972. Montréal was hosting Game 1 of the infamous Canada-USSR Hockey Series. The game was sold out, but my father desperately wanted to attend. Naturally, he sourced an old-school fedora, donned the largest fur coat he could get his hands on, and marched right up to the Forum as though he were the mayor of Moscow. Miraculously, his ruse worked. Security thought he was part of Team USSR's entourage and let him in.

I'd never forget that story.

Though I wasn't always a performer, I always did know how to make a grand entrance, just like my father. I was born in the Civic Hospital in Ottawa, Canada, to David and Deanna Hughes, on one of the snowiest days on record. A true Canadian, you could say!

A nurse by trade, my mother loved nothing more than helping others and connecting with people. From as early as I can remember, she was always entertaining people at the house. My father certainly didn't mind. When he wasn't sneaking into sporting events, he was planning the next big backyard social. During Grey Cup season, he'd cover the entire yard with massive tarps and serve oversized bowls of chili and spiked punch. He and his friends would even go so far as to build makeshift bleachers so that the crowd of partygoers felt like they were on top of the action. People loved it.

Dad wasn't quite as passionate about his professional life as Mom was. He spent a few years bouncing around in various positions with the Government of Canada before finally securing a stable career in the Department of Public Works. Dad and I were close, but I was definitely a momma's boy.

From sneaking into her room every night to hold her hand while she slept until I was probably a bit too old, to quietly waiting by the window like an anxious puppy for her to return home, Mom and I were inseparable. While my older sister Andrea was the cool kid who had both parents wrapped around her finger, I was the young'un who'd run and hide in closets whenever my parents took out the camcorder and bawl my eyes out at every turn walking to school – shocking given my future career path, I know. Maybe it was an early sign of needing attention.

I attended Rockcliffe Park Public School with the children of preeminent politicians and ambassadors – among my classmates was future Prime Minister of Canada, Justin Trudeau. Justin and I became good friends, along with a group of kids in our class. His father Pierre was Prime Minister at the time, so I often found myself playing tag in the hallways of 24 Sussex Drive; other times, our entire class would be invited to swim parties at the historic house. When he'd come over for a playdate, the Royal Canadian Mounted Police would do a sweep of our house before we could start our game of hide and seek. It didn't faze any of us boys, though. We were just kids being kids... with armed officers watching over us. It was a great time to be young and fearless in Canada's capital.

I spent many weekends skiing with my parents and friends and going on playdates – it seemed like we always had fun social events to attend. Being social at home and school helped me break out of my shell and gain more confidence as a kid. Life was grand. Full of limitless possibilities.

Then... I developed a speech impediment.

For a kid in grade three just trying to fit in, this was a living nightmare. My friends would endlessly mock me and my newfound interpretation of the English language.

"Hey guys, wanna play during re-re-re-recess? Bahahahaha!"

I thought my life was over.

Fortunately, my speech-language pathologist, Mrs. Lynch, came to the rescue. Every day after school, we'd sit together for an hour practicing troublesome words, over and over. Given my undiagnosed ADHD, this was not easy for me. I could barely sit still. I didn't want to miss recess or playtime. But after six months of consistent, painstaking sessions, I finally reverted to my usual self. Things certainly weren't as bad as I'd imagined.

Little did I know I was about to be dealt something much worse.

Mom and dad married in Niagara Falls, ON in1967.

My sister and I, waiting for Santa circa 1973-ish.

Rockcliffe Park Public School grade 3 and 4 class field trip to the home of the Prime Minister, The Right Honourable Pierre Elliott Trudeau at 24 Sussex. See if you can find the current Prime Minister, The Right Honourable Justin Trudeau!

Clockwise from top: Celebrating a birthday with my beautiful mother and childhood friend, Ian Toth.

On a trip to Vancouver, BC for Expo 86 with my sister and father. Showing off the big hair days!

Sporting my favorite player for the Ottawa Rough Riders, Tony Gabriel. My early modeling days!

Andrea and my father supporting me at my return to an Ottawa Senators game in 2012.

3

YOU CAN'T HURRY LOVE

"Take more chances. Dance more dances."

Unknown

While I could sense my parents' relationship was growing tense, I was devastated when they broke the news that they'd be getting a divorce. I was going to have two separate lives now. Two distinct realities. The whole thing felt surreal. As it got underway, I slowly grew used to it. But I'd never get used to coming home to a half-empty home. It always felt like there was something missing.

After the separation, my sister and I spent weekdays with our mother. It was at her dinner parties that I first discovered my knack for unpolished dancing. The moment we'd finish eating, I'd grab my boombox from my room and fire up some tunes. Not sure why but Phil Collins' rendition of "You Can't Hurry Love" was always the first track in the queue on my kickass cassette player. I danced around the table and living room until I couldn't breathe. I would high kick, low kick, do fades, shakes, rattles, and just keep moving it. It was an awful sight to behold, with a few moves likely banned by the Geneva Convention, but I just wanted to put a smile on my mother's face. Plus, for reasons unknown to me, everyone applauded and cheered! Their support was powerful. It was the first time my "talent" – or lack thereof – was celebrated. It gave me a much-needed confidence boost.

Weekends, on the other hand, were spent with my father. Die-hard Ottawa Rough Riders fans, we quickly established a tradition of going to games together. Week after week, we'd meet up with my grandmother – who, incredibly, attended almost every game (via a 45-minute bus ride or with friends) – and his buddies Bob & Doug, who tailgated for hours before the game even started. I remember feeling like I was a part of something special, something much bigger than me. The power of sports to bring together the community was incredible. During each game, I witnessed the perfect synergy of cheering crowds and was awed by it. There was an energy there – something unseen, yet tangible, that you could tap into and draw from. But at that age, I wasn't sure what it was about.

One afternoon, I was sitting at the stadium with my father watching the game, when something remarkable happened. One by one, the fans sitting in front of us began rotating their heads away from the field and towards the stands, until virtually nobody was watching the game anymore. Curious, and hoping to catch a couple rival fans throwing down, I excitedly snapped my head to the source of the commotion.

Instead of fists flying, I caught sight of something much more unexpected: a rogue fan in Section C cheering his heart out. I was mesmerized by how people were reacting to his antics. Leg kicks resulted in *Oohs*. Claps translated to *Aahs*. He had the crowd in the palm of his hands, his magnetic presence making everyone feel alive and utterly drawn to his exuberant performance. Even my grandmother had a thing for this one-man pep rally. "My, my," she said. "Would you look at him!"

"I could get the crowd going like that," I said with unwavering certainty. My father looked perplexed. But I was transfixed.

Our childhood was as normal as one could hope for after the separation – summer days spent causing mischief and playing at the lake with my cousins. Our parents brought us between aunts' and uncles' homes, it helped us develop close ties to both grandmothers, and orchestrated fun family vacations. As our social connections and lives continued to develop as young kids, I started to grow this sense of wanting to make sure everyone was having fun. Not just having fun but having fun *all the time*. I wanted everyone smiling, laughing and being together. Maybe it was my own therapy of sorts? Who knows, but I certainly learned from the best.

My parents always made it a priority to make sure people had a lot of fun at every social event and made us part of the planning when they could. They were creative and kind, always looking for ways to bring people together. I caught the bug and felt this in me at an impressionable stage.

When high school rolled around, I was itching to be a part of something. I'll never forget being in the auditorium on our first day with my pals, Bill, Marc, Ian, and Jay, wondering what the heck was going on. On stage, seniors were doing crazy, fun comedic bits and introducing us to school life. One in particular, Colin Gray, stood out. With zero inhibitions, Colin captured our attention and made us laugh. Made us feel welcome that first day of school. I wanted to be that guy. I wanted to do cool stuff for students. Wanted people to go home after school and wonder, "Who *was* that guy? Wow did he make me feel welcome. He was so funny!"

Marc and I wanted to try out for the varsity volleyball team – we were both half decent and thought we had a shot, plus we'd have five years to become studs on the court. But when I walked into the gym and caught sight of the six-foot-six seniors slamming the ball into the stands, I did the fastest 180-degree turn out of there you can imagine. That moment has become one of only four real regrets in my life. Marc didn't flinch, though. And guess what? He made the team.

After failing to make the basketball team the first time, I refocused my efforts on running for student government instead. I was voted grade nine rep. One early victory in the books.

Marc had major confidence since we were kids, which was always inspiring and somewhat intimidating to be around. You know those people who just know what they want, even when they're five years old? Marc was one of them. Maybe it was the adversity of coming from Québec, an all-French area, to our English school in grade three. That's how he got his nickname, French Toast, and me, English Muffin.

Later, Marc left Canada to be with his mom and brother in Boston, where she was appointed Counsel General (like an ambassador to a large city). This was a hard one for me. Marc and I had been inseparable growing up. We had our first beers together, first double dates, first skipped class, first near-arrests, first time at camp, and so on. Thankfully, Marc would visit during high school often, always with a 12-pack in tow. (Of course, only when it was legal.)

Again, things weren't so bad. I had rejection, but so did everyone else to some degree. Everything felt… normal. That is, until something happened that would change every aspect of my life and make me who I am today.

4

THE TALK

"She told me one day that I should teach my kids to be as independent as possible so that they can fend for themselves. This, of course, turned out to be prophetic."

Lourdes Kelly, friend of Deanna Hughes

One afternoon near the end of the school year, Andrea and I arrived home from school to find Mom sitting alone at the kitchen table, gazing into the distance like she was watching a film that no one else could see. I hadn't seen that strange look in my mom's eyes more than a handful of times over the years, so it instantly gave me pause. Startled out of her fog by our sudden presence, she quickly shifted her attention to us.

"You're home," she said quietly. Her eyes kept flitting away from mine. I was standing right there; why couldn't she look at me? "There's something I need to talk to you about."

Andrea looked at me, and suddenly I knew that she felt it too. Something was wrong.

"Mom, what is it?" I asked. But she shook her head and led us to the living room, where we sat on the sofa together.

A deep silence enveloped the room, my mother's joyfulness uncommonly absent. I hadn't seen her wearing this look since she shared news of the divorce a few years earlier. She breathed a heavy sigh, and with it her shoulders slumped, and she seemed to shrink into her small body – like a balloon deflating.

"Mom…" Andrea said. "Tell us what's going on."

"I just got home from the doctor," Mom said. "I've been diagnosed with breast cancer."

All of the sounds of the outside world seemed to clash with the silence of that room. We sat in shock, not knowing what to say. I was completely confused, not quite sure what to make of it. *Cancer*? Back in 1986, there were no pink runs, no pink parades, and certainly no charities spreading the word to get "checked." But cancer was cancer. And my best friend and biggest cheerleader was suddenly in the fight of her life.

"Don't worry, I'm going to beat it," Mom reassured us. "Everything will be okay."

I relaxed a little. If Mom said everything would be okay, then I was damn well going to believe that everything would be okay.

It had to be.

SOLDIERING ON

Mom is going to be so disappointed in me. She's fending off literal cancer, and I can't even fend off a few acne-ridden eleventh graders to make the hoops team! Those were my thoughts after being rejected yet again and denied a place on the basketball team. It also didn't help that I was failing math and science, and my English papers had more red ink on them than blue. The last thing I wanted to do was give her another reason to worry about my future.

As I stomped in through the front door, completely pissed off at the world, hairless legs and all, it hit me: the aroma of Mom's famous roast beef and potatoes. My comfort food. It's like she instinctively knew I was going through the wringer, and she was pulling out all the stops. Mom always knew how to turn a negative into a positive.

Even with a tough diagnosis on her hands, my mother was determined not to skip a beat. She enrolled in the psychology master's degree program at the University of Ottawa and kept living her life to the fullest, quietly going about her chemotherapy treatment all the while. Home life didn't change much. The revolving door of friends and family still poured in for weekly dinners, keeping spirits high.

I did whatever I could to help her, suddenly very aware of the little things that would make her life easier. I always made sure she had her tea in the morning, a warm bath running, and clean laundry. I took extra care to tidy up the house, maintain the yard, and always have fresh flowers ready by her bedside. My mom was a nurse, after all, so I had the instincts to look after her after years of watching her take care of people. But, always selfless, she encouraged us to stay active. To see our friends and be social. So, my sister and I joined the local tennis club, where some of our friends were members and we could get away for some fun. It proved to be exactly what I needed.

Shortly after, the club manager asked me for a big favor. She needed to leave early and asked me to close up the club for her. For some reason, I decided that I wouldn't just close it up – I'd also scrub down the place and fix up the grounds and courts. It just seemed like the right thing to do, and it was a good distraction from the struggles at home.

The next day, the manager was so impressed that she hired me part-time. My first job! Not only did I get to play a lot of tennis in my spare time, but I met so many different people from all walks of life. It was a great place for me to sharpen my social skills. I was the young gun with the big spirit, though the only thing I ever won was the Sportsmanship Award (and let's be honest, what teenager wants to win *that*?).

The roast beef and potatoes went down as quickly as one might expect. As did the second helping, and the third. But by the time dinner was over and I began to nurse a food baby, I realized the talk was inevitable. I'd gruffly informed her I had been cut yet again, but the whole night I'd been tight-lipped about the day's events. Mom eyed me knowingly, ever the mind reader.

"Are you passionate about the team?" she asked.

I mean, obviously. I have shaved legs to prove it. Look!

"No," I snapped. I probably sounded like a petulant third grader being denied his juice. All of the shame came flooding back. "Not anymore. Why would I be passionate about the team when they don't even want me on it?"

"Cameron." She smiled and grabbed my hand. "There are other ways you can contribute to the team."

Other ways?! Sure, I'd been making some good money working at the tennis club, but now didn't really feel like the appropriate time to be discussing donations. We sat in silence as I brooded over yet another obstacle in my life. I was officially looking for a new way to spend my energy. My mother kept positive and was never, not for one second, disappointed in me. That helped.

Still, I felt stuck on her words. Other ways to contribute to the team? What other ways were there? I wasn't even on the team!

Despite doing everything in her power to live a healthy lifestyle – meditating, listening to spiritual music, changing her diet, going for walks, you name it – Mom *still* ended up back in the hospital. Her condition was worsening by the second. No doctor could look me and my family in the face to tell us what was really going on. We were all unsure what the future held. I was confused and scared as hell. This couldn't be real life. It felt like a horrible nightmare, and I kept wishing I'd

Just.

Wake.

Up.

Not knowing what else to do, I kept looking for good news. Some little shred of hope to cling to. "Your mom finished her lunch today," a nurse said casually. "Does that mean she's gonna be alright!?" I demanded.

Anything, however small, could prove she was getting better and would soon be back home with us. Chatting with her friends at the reading group she'd helped found. Listening to us kids talk about our days at school.

After a particularly rough week for her, I needed a distraction. Leaving her hospital room that Friday night, I gave her a soft kiss on the forehead and headed back home, no idea where my sister was, to cook a frozen pizza for my dinner for one. I had never felt so alone.

So when I got home, I decided to have a few friends over for dinner instead. I just wanted an escape, and friends were the perfect answer. Sure, we were young, but a few beers to lighten the mood sounded like the perfect plan. For one night, I was just a normal, happy teenager. We snuck beers from our older siblings, felt like we owned the world, and I even worked up just enough courage to flirt with the girls. It was a magical night – I still had my mom and a place in the world that made sense to me, so I could be in the moment and goof off the way teenagers do.

The next morning, my uncle showed up on our doorstep. "It's your mother," he said. "She passed away in the middle of the night." No one can ever prepare you for that moment. That new reality. And so my new life began, the one on the other side of losing your mom, the one where things made a lot less sense.

5

BUT TODAY WELL LIVED

"Yesterday is already a dream and tomorrow is only a vision,
but today well lived makes every yesterday a dream of
happiness and every tomorrow a vision of hope."

Kalidasa, "Look To This Day"

The Kalidasa poem (excerpted above), which hung on our kitchen wall while I was growing up, has stuck with me. It's the poem I read at my mother's funeral – the first funeral I ever attended. The place was so jam-packed with guests, they needed an entire extra room to accommodate everyone. It was beautiful to see just how many people she'd touched. My mom's dear friend Claude ended the eulogy by saying, "If the flowers weren't yet blooming in heaven, they are today."

Just a couple of days earlier, I'd been holding her hand in the same hospital where I was born. Lost, and shifting from one stage of grief to another, I felt myself slowly detaching from reality. I was crushed. I had never felt more alone. The whole time I believed she'd be okay, but as time went on, it was clear things wouldn't change. My father came over to lend his support. It was time to figure out a way to deal. Nothing seemed to matter anymore.

Shortly after my mom passed, I went to therapy. My therapist and I talked about healing; what my mom wanted for me; how she knew I'd be okay. Every time we talked about Mom, my therapist referred to her in the past tense, but I kept talking about her in the present. I couldn't help it. I'd say, "Mom's always telling me…" and then I'd choke up and cry. *"Was…"* I'd correct myself through tears and gritted teeth. "Mom *was* always telling me to find ways to connect with people. To be part of something greater than myself. But with her gone, I don't know what that is anymore. I have no idea what anything means now. I just feel so lost…"

"Cameron," my therapist said softly as I bawled my eyes out. Tears obscured the world around me until it looked like I was staring through a windshield covered in rain. "It's okay to cry. The pain reminds us of the things we love."

"I hate it," I mumbled. *"I hate it!"*

Many of our sessions went like this. It got to the point where the tissues were always on my side of the couch before I'd even entered the room.

What was the point of it all, anyway? I asked myself this every day. When you could so easily lose one of the pillars of your life – one of the most beloved and precious people you'd ever know – in the blink of an eye, what the hell was the point? Where was the justice in losing a loving mother whose very purpose in life was to help people?

Life was short and fragile. It was unfair. Confusing. Nothing made sense anymore because the very fabric of my existence had been shredded. You're driving down the road one day, and after blinking for one second, the road is suddenly gone. Where are you then? Nowhere. The destination has disappeared, and you are lost.

Back in my guidance counselor's office one day, he said something to me that I would never forget: "You're going to grow more in the next six months than most will in ten years."

Looking back, he was absolutely right.

Later that year, at Mom's college's graduation, I attended and proudly handed out the Deanna Hughes Memorial Award to the top nursing student. My mom had always wanted to make a big difference in her life. Ever since she was student president at her high school in Niagara Falls, it had been her mission to bring people together, to see the best in them. Ultimately, she chose to go into nursing – to help people heal. She was connected to a local college across the river in Québec where she eventually founded a nursing program. Through this program, she made a difference in the lives of thousands of women.

I teared up as I gave the award to the nursing student. Mom would be proud that the work she had done for this program would make a difference in so many people's lives. I knew the nurses understood what this meant to the program and our family. Leaving a legacy like she did makes me proud each day.

"Your mother had a warm, supportive nature, always encouraging and positive. She believed in the goodness of people and was non-judgmental. She always had time to listen to our problems, both staff and students, whether they were personal or professional issues, often offering sage advice or just helping us problem-solve. She was charismatic, always cheerful and the life of any party. She was friends with everyone within our department and across all disciplines at the college."

Rose Mary, colleague and friend of Deanna Hughes

WHAT'S FOR DINNER, DAD?

With grade 12 now well underway, I was all over the place. I had trouble focusing on anything. My anxiety levels spiked, and I had no real idea what the future had in store for me. I was transitioning into a life without Mom, and it felt every bit as alien as it sounds. Andrea and I were still living at the house, but Dad got

The home we grew up in from grade 7 to post-university days. A lot of memories, fun and neighborhood parties!

My dad, sister, and I at the "new" home in Manor Park, Ottawa.

rid of his place and moved into Mom's room – which just felt so strange, but he had to take care of us. I'd still get home from school and subconsciously breathe through my nose in anticipation, expecting to smell the next savory scent from whatever dish Mom would be preparing at the time. But instead there'd be the stale smell of the dusty mudroom full of shoes and boots.

Some days, I would spend entire afternoons remembering my mother's voice. Her full laugh. The way she teased us. The look in her eyes when we would explain some setback, for which she always had an answer and a remedy ready to fix it. And sometimes I'd cry, because these memories were fading around the edges like an old Polaroid left out in the sun. I would debate with myself, "No, she didn't say that. She said *this*. No wait… Arghhhh!" Wracking my brain to recall every historic event of my childhood with meticulous detail, only to discover the sad but inevitable truth: I was growing up, and with age came new memories, and with that more clutter and less space.

"I won't forget you," I promised. "Never, ever, ever."

6

OUTNUMBERED

"Underestimate me. That'll be fun."

Unknown

A few weeks after my mom's funeral, our senior boys' basketball team had their first away game of the season. Even though it was tough to accept that I couldn't make the team, I decided to go out and support my pals, especially after all the support they'd given me.

I took my seat in the bleachers, the lone Lisgar supporter among a sea of Ridgemont fans. Watching the plays unfold, my mind began to wander. I couldn't help but think about her. The team before me on the court was supposed to be my way of making Mom proud. Instead, I'd let her down. I'd never be able to make it up to her now. It was my last chance, and I blew it.

Fighting the urge to get up and leave, I took a moment to collect myself.

What did she tell you that one time? "There are other ways to contribute to the team."

I stumbled upon a new thought.

I am my mother's son.

And she was a *fighter*. It wasn't in my DNA to give up, nor would it honor her. In spite of her diagnosis, every day, Deanna Hughes had made the choice to get out of bed and live her life as usual. She didn't complain, she didn't hold back, and she most certainly didn't give up without a fight, so why should I? My mother GOT UP. My mother taught me to GET UP. No matter what, you GET UP. And you KEEP GETTING UP.

Suddenly galvanized, I refocused on the action on the court. We were losing by a few points, and chants from the home team fans were ramping up. My eyes ran over the crowd. As I watched the fans taunt our squad, I could tell my buddies out there were feeling the heat. I needed to do something. *Something* was brewing inside me. What was it? What was this strange sensation? Goosebumps started climbing up my spine, tickling my neck and arms. My nostrils cleared and I was suddenly high on oxygen and a strange sense of knowing. It was that same feeling I felt at the Rough Riders game all those years ago. Then, as though we were sitting across from one another at the dinner table again, my mother's words suddenly made sense:

There are other ways you can contribute to the team.

I slowly rose from my seat in the bleachers.

Drew a deep breath.

And unleashed.

"LET'S GO, LIS-GAR," I shouted with a conviction and confidence unlike any I'd ever felt – one that seemed to have magically materialized in that moment with the fervor of ultimate knowing. Suddenly, the picture became clear. I knew who I was. I knew why I was here.

"LET'S GO, LIS-GAR." I started clapping. Stomping on the bleachers. What did I have to lose?

200 rival heads simultaneously snapped towards me, like magnets to a refrigerator. *Who the hell is that kid?!* If anything, I might be able to boost my abysmal physics average, because I finally understood the universal law of cause and effect.

Silence.

Expressions of shock and awe passed over the faces of the opposing players and fans, not to mention the faces of my pals on the team. *Cameron's really lost it now.* Jay was looking at me, mouth agape, before realizing there was still a game to be played. He dribbled the ball up the court.

"LET'S GO, LISGAR! *Clap-clap-clap. BOM-BOM-BOM.*

This time so loudly and decisively that the guy next to me was visibly startled. Like, he literally jumped. Now the crowd was no longer in shock. They were pissed. Boos started to rain in. But that didn't stop me; if anything, it fueled my conviction. Made my voice louder and more powerful. Lisgar stole an inbound pass, and scored a quick bucket. You could feel the momentum shift. I kept going, my thunderous claps ringing out. What were the opposing fans really going to do to me? Maybe duct tape my mouth shut, at most. With a minute left, we took the lead.

"LET'S GO, LISGAR!" *Clap-clap-clap. BOM-BOM-BOM.*

When the buzzer sounded, our team managed to escape with the win – and I with my life. As I left the court, huddled with the team, I could feel unfriendly glares on my back. But I knew something special had just happened. Something remarkable.

Something life changing.

"Dude, what was that all about?" Jay asked, astonished. "You were out of your mind tonight!"

"I… don't know." It was as though some greater force had washed away my fears and anxieties and propelled me to stand up and be a living, breathing, screaming, *supporter* of my team. Whatever it was, it felt damn good.

Looking at Jay, I asked, "When's the next game?"

If I'd just gotten up that one time, it would have made a great story for the rest of my life. *That Time Cameron Went Insane at a High School Basketball Game and Almost Got Killed*, they'd call the unabridged version, and that would be the end of it. But I really had nothing to lose, I realized after that night. The worst thing I could imagine had already happened, so what else was there for me to be afraid of? The opinion of a crowd of rival basketball fans? I decided then and there that just getting up – like my mother did, time and time again – would become my way of moving on and honoring her. It would become my life mantra. *Just get up.*

Over the course of the next few games, dozens of students and faculty members alike poured into the gymnasium to witness and be a part of the new school spirit. Before I knew it, I was running up and down the sidelines in a painter's suit making crowds of hundreds go nuts. I was having a blast. Not making the team didn't seem so bad anymore. Suddenly, that shy kid who could barely pose for a family photo was now on a mission to take school spirit to new levels. I'd finally found my way of contributing to the team.

High School retreat with
Barrie Laughton (student
advisor) Jay Shore, Greg Fraser.

Lisgar assembly working
the mic, Student Council
co-president 1990.

The slickest tuxedo in the history
of high school proms courtesy of
Classy Formal Wear!

7

VOTE BIG RED

"Vote for Pedro. Vote for me and all of your
wildest dreams will come true."

Pedro, from Napoleon Dynamite

My newfound enthusiasm spilled over into every aspect of my life. I was taking more chances, putting myself out there and taking school spirit to new levels. I was in a rhythm, finally enjoying coming to school and having great friends to celebrate with. When I was in the moment with smiling people around me, I felt less sad. I felt like I had the night before my mom passed again, like a normal teenager. So much so that I decided to step up and run for student body president. Mom had been president at her school in Niagara Falls. It was always something in the back of my head that I felt I could do to make her proud. I wanted to inspire people like that outgoing senior Colin had done for me years earlier.

My slogan was worthy of Madison Avenue: "Vote Big Red." I mean, I wasn't a total ginger, but close enough. I littered the school with large black posters smothered in red paint. I handed out Big Red chewing gum to my peers and they ate it up, literally and figuratively. It stuck. My pal Dan Ages helped me write one of the greatest high school election speeches of all time. But being well-known wasn't going to cut it – I needed that extra punch.

And I think what took me over the finish line was Neil Diamond – who hasn't said that before?! My walk-on song before my speech was "Red Red Wine," by UB40 (did you know "Red Red Wine" was originally written and recorded by Neil Diamond?!). Red balloons flew from the rafters – and the spectacle all paid off.

I was elected co-president along with a young gentleman by the name of Leonard Tse. We were all-in on student experience, pushing our administration to let us create epic moments through dances, assemblies, theme weeks, pep rallies, and a sense of cohesion among fellow leaders at the school. We didn't see bullying like kids do now, because students wanted to come to school. They wanted to be part of something bigger than themselves. I did everything I could to make sure people had the right school spirit. It was mostly a healthy addiction.

Our staff advisor to council was my former geography teacher and guidance counselor, Barrie Laughton. He knew my story well, and he knew that it was best to let me off the typical high school leash. He supported me, encouraged me, let me try new things, let me fail, and most importantly, he let me be myself. There were no limits to what he would champion.

It's amazing how people respond when you let go of what others think of you. My final year of high school ended up being one of the best years of my young life. I believe the push of many people and the confidence I gained after my mom's passing lit a spark in that community.

And I wasn't about to lose that momentum. I'll never forget being on stage for my final speech as student president, thanking students, administrators and Barrie Laughton. It was the first time I'd cry openly on a stage, and it wouldn't be my last.

"In my capacity as a counsellor and advisor, I often met with Cameron to discuss current and future plans. Of course, I was aware that at an early and important stage in his personal life, he was devastated by the untimely passing of his mother due to cancer. But Cameron also displayed an ability to deal with any challenging situations with strength, determination and grace. We discussed at length what he would do after his high school years. A career in communication was a definite possibility – perhaps teaching, law, public relations or social work... However, never did I anticipate his present calling as the SUPER FAN!"

Barrie Laughton, Student Advisor, Guidance Counselor, Rock Star Human

---

Co-President Cameron Hughes

Hullaballoo, Hullaballoo, Rah, Rah, Rah! Yes, Lisgar we've just come off the most successful school year of the decade. (Perhaps of the century -- now, now Cam) It wouldn't have been possible without the support and enthusiasm of all the staff. We had a tremendous council, many great clubs and organizations in the school. The year was rather busy, from Grade Nine Week to the Carnival, to the Senior Girls' basketball finals, to the Semi-Formal, to the coffee house, to the Casino Night. But we all came together and proved we were number UNO in Ottawa with our spirit and drive to have fun. I just hope we all got our work done! AAH -- Test NEXT period, got to go. Thanks guys, -- Mr. Laughton, Mr. Buchanan, Mr. Grant, Luwella (our Head Thing) and Mr. MacDonald. Let's keep it up Lisgar – can't wait for the 150th. Till we meet again. Never let go of your dreams. Thank you all. I'll miss you Lisgar.

Excerpt from the yearbook in my final year of high school. A huge thrill to be student president at Lisgar Collegiate!

Pictured with Barrie Laughton 2011 in Ottawa holding our high school yearbook. No one in high school gave me permission to be me like he did. Every student needs a teacher like Barrie to believe in them.

Melonhead Mania at Bishop's University. Thank you to the local grocery store for having huge watermelons every fall, to the buildings and grounds folks who helped me make the signs, and to the students for their amazing spirit! GAITER PRIDE!

8

RAISE A TOAST

"Raise a toast to Bishop's University on the Mighty Massawippi Shore! We're conditioned to our fate, we will never graduate, we'll stay here forever more!"

Bishop's University fight song

When it came to deciding where I'd attend university, student life was at the top of my list. I wanted to go somewhere that had a close-knit community so I could get involved and carry on the same spirit I helped instill in my high school. Bishop's University fit the bill perfectly.

A liberal arts college just outside of Sherbrooke, Québec, Bishop's allowed me to continue discovering myself. The university was historic, had many great programs (including athletics) and world-renowned student spirit. To this day, I'm not sure how I got accepted. Maybe Barrie Laughton made some calls.

I packed everything into my trusty VW Golf and hit the road. My father came along for the ride. When we arrived, he gave me my first college-approved 12-pack and a big hug.

"Good luck, son," he said, shedding a tear or two. "I'm proud of you."

And he left. Freedom! I felt intoxicated by the thrill of new opportunity. Here, I could be anyone I wanted to be.

I was in my dorm room unpacking my crap, cranking Pearl Jam on my boombox, when I heard a loud bang on the door. I thought the administration had realized the mistake they'd made in admitting someone who couldn't tell you the difference between isosceles and scalene triangles.

Instead I was greeted by several enthusiastic students selling Bishop's University t-shirts with fun expressions on them. They quickly persuaded me to give them 20 dollars for one. I was wowed by their enthusiasm, but even more intrigued by the effect a simple shirt had on me. It instantly made me feel like I was part of the school. I watched with admiration as they got every parent and student on our floor to fork over 20 bucks without batting an eye.

It stuck with me.

Academically, I'd started out studying economics, but there were far too many numbers involved. Grades of 58 and 34 weren't going to hold up. I was a rudderless ship without a major: "socializing" too much (12-pack was a number I could handle); studying too little; and feeling a bit lost. I was disinterested, and also embarrassed. What would I tell my dad?

My social life was thriving, on the other hand, and I was having a *ton* of fun. My reputation was growing so quickly that I'd be called into the residence leader's office to be reprimanded for things I wasn't even involved in. (Like the time someone pulled the fire alarm and everyone had to hang outside in minus -30-degree weather in their pajamas and I *wasn't even in town!*)

The momentum of my student government success at Lisgar was something I wanted to build on. Neither the shaky grades nor the blossoming social life stopped me from winning the student council election and becoming the representative for our year. A fire was burning inside me to become even more involved.

In my second year, I lived off-campus with four good pals in a house dubbed the "Pink House." Picture *Animal House* meets *Old School*, but with pink trim. On football game days, we hosted everyone who walked onto campus. They had no choice – not only was the Pink House on the way to the field, but the oversized speakers blasting the band KLF at 9 a.m. demanded that everyone party with us.

Mark Hatfield, one of my roommates, played for the varsity football team, the Bishop's Gaiters. (He later went on to the CFL and NFL.)

"We need more fun at the games," Mark said. "You should do something to fire up the fans and get some energy in there."

Mark knew I was fearless, but he had no idea what was in store.

I decided to go for it and paint every square inch of my skin purple, wear a purple cape, and equip myself with a wooden letter *D* and a 3x4 white picket "fence." But something was still missing. *What was it?*

Early on the morning of the big game, it dawned on me. I darted across campus, burst through the doors of the local grocery store, and found the nearest available employee.

"Hi, excuse me," I said, panting profusely. My eyes bulged out of my skull as they usually do when I'm excited. The guy was positively terrified.

"Uh… what can I do for you?" he asked in horror.

"Where are your watermelons? I need a *massive* watermelon."

With the largest watermelon in the province, I hurried home and carefully carved it out, just enough that I could secure it atop my head like some kind of vegan football helmet. It had to be just right. If only I had this kind of focus when it came to my studies.

TIMEOUT

HOW TO MAKE A WATERMELON HELMET

- Trace a helmet design on the watermelon
- Cut along the lines with a sharp knife
- Hollow out the pink fruit using a spoon (scrape down to the white part of the rind)
- Smooth Vaseline over the edges and the inside to help preserve it
- Decorate (optional)

Stu Cowan, "Why the watermelons?," Montréal Gazette, 28 Nov. 2009

I gathered my props, painted my body, and pocketed a couple of cold beers. As I made my way towards the stadium, the looks on the faces of my fellow students ranged from confusion to excitement. This did not slow me down. Quite the opposite.

Mark and the rest of the team were on the sidelines looking as if they'd just laid eyes on... *someone wearing a watermelon on his head*? It was time to shine.

The crowd was ready to party. I mean, it was 1 p.m. on a Saturday – what else do you do? You get purple and you get funky. The Gaiters won. At the post-game party at the campus bar, Mark and the rest of the team bought me a few rounds to celebrate.

"I remember hearing this roaring laughter. I turned from the sidelines and saw this guy with a picket fence and a cut out watermelon on his head. My first reaction was "who's the idiot". Needless to say this kick started a crazy, wild and wonderful career for Cam. He put his heart and soul into each game, and campus life. But he's still such a bad dancer!"

Tom Allen, head football coach, Bishop's University

I quickly became the school's fearless purple leader, leading crazy cheers, firing up the crowd with my makeshift signs, and bringing people together. I think my purple cape gave me extra superpowers. Fans were all in. When the time was right, the DJ would hit the button and we'd all break into a dance party. Game after game, I'd show up with a fresh melon on my melon until I became known across campus as Melonhead. I was truly out of my mind.

After the school year ended, it was time to get working. I had no plan, but I knew I'd figure something out.

I always did.

THE HUSTLE IS REAL

Through networking with other students, I started to meet a bunch of entrepreneurs, including a guy from Montréal named Andre. He and his wife Kelly ran a clothing company called Bragwear, and we instantly hit it off. He was impressed by the small summer business I'd been quietly building, which I dubbed "Cam Can Do." I was like TaskRabbit 25 years before it existed, doing everything from landscaping and deliveries to house sitting and dog walking. I even had a few friends working with me by the end of the summer.

Selling tees seemed like the natural evolution of "Cam Can Do," and a fun way to spend time, so we went to work. Andre would supply the garments and I'd design and sell with my pal Roger for all the special events, like homecoming and carnival week. The university officials were confused by my all-cash tuition payments – especially when I tried to sell them t-shirts as well! I kept growing the business after Roger graduated and within a year or so I had reps across Canada selling to their schools, local clubs and teams. It was intoxicating to make money while spreading school cheer!

"We came up with original slogans, threw them on t-shirts and hustled our asses off to sell them to everyone on campus. Cameron was the master at building rapport. No one wants to buy something from someone they don't like. Within seconds, we had people feeling the pride of a school shirt and handing over 20 dollars. These life lessons served us both well in our future endeavors."

Roger Hardy, fellow Gaiter, Entrepreneur

I knew I needed to work hard at fixing my grades, but I was also very committed to spreading Melonhead-mania across campus. I kept getting up at games and had a ton of support from everyone around me, so I decided to up the ante and run for student council president.

"The school needs a leader, *not* a cheerleader," proclaimed opposing candidate Chad Schella, to mixed reviews from the audience. The school's administration also wasn't thrilled I was in the running, either. It's not that they didn't like me – they just didn't want someone who wore a melon on his head to be the face of their institution. But they knew I'd do anything for the students. All I cared about was everyone on campus feeling part of something special. This meant more people involved in clubs, supporting teams, playing intramurals and having amazing school spirit. At the end of the day, that's what won me the election.

I couldn't wait to get started. But my excitement quickly faded when I was called into a meeting with the Dean of Student Affairs a few weeks later. I already knew I was in for a whipping, but when I saw the look on his face, my heart sank.

"Cameron, let's get right to it," he said. "Your grades are abysmal. You have one summer semester to boost your average or your position as student president will be rescinded and you'll be expelled from the school."

Holy shit.

I had no choice but to buckle down. I enrolled in summer school and studied my ass off. I *did* raise my average in all four courses, and to be quite honest, I never thought they'd *really* kick me out. I was class president, after all! But when I got the grades back in the mail... numbers don't lie. I came up short.

I was out.

For a guy known for strutting around with a melon on his head, getting kicked out of school was an embarrassment of epic proportions. The class president had been impeached, and everyone on campus was talking about it. Feeling numb, I mumbled goodbye to Roger, packed up my new sexy four-colored-panel Ford Escort and drove back home to Ottawa to regroup. It was the worst road trip of my life.

Halfway through the journey, I stopped on the side of the road, got out of the car, and sat in the dirt, my back leaning against the car. Traffic whizzed past me, people going home, going to school, going to their jobs. And there I sat with my head in my hands – alone and without direction, going nowhere. I sat there for what felt like a very long time.

When I finally got home, I sat in the car for a solid ten minutes. I didn't want to face my dad with all of the shame that was weighing me down. What was I going to say? "'*Sup, Dad? Thanks for taking me in after I failed out. Is McDonald's hiring, or what?*"

I wanted to make light of it – that's what I always did; I joked and made people smile. But now I was wondering: had that always just been a form of escapism? Of ignoring the severity of the present moment; a way to create an identity for myself where there wasn't one? How could I escape *this*?

Dark thoughts, Cameron. Chill. Just chill. It'll all work out.

Or so I tried to believe, gathering the strength to go in and see my dad. When I finally did, he just smiled sympathetically and hugged me.

"It's good to see you, son."

He was loving and supportive. It meant the world.

SAY HELLO TO MY FURRY FRIENDS

"The most essential factor is persistence – the determination never to allow your energy or enthusiasm to be dampened by the discouragement that must inevitably come."

James Whitcomb Riley

S oon enough, I got a job at a local restaurant doing whatever they needed, eventually working my way up to bartender. I weeded lawns and sold tees to local schools. I did what college dropouts do, essentially – which is to say I fell into the trap of believing that if one didn't finish college, one did not make something of their lives.

Was this going to be my new life?

LYNX ON THE LOOSE

During the summer of '93, the Ottawa Lynx, a now defunct AAA minor league baseball team, were looking to introduce a new official team mascot, Lenny, the first in the franchise's history. Jay was working as communications manager for the team and was able to get me an audition for the role. What you've heard is true – it's not what you know, it's who you know!

I didn't have a résumé, so I brought along what I thought would be the next best thing: a photograph of me as Melonhead, a baseball glove, and some thoughts on what I felt it would take to be a good mascot.

"Yeah? And what's that, Mr. Hughes?"

"Well," I said, "a lot of folks think it's all about having passion for the game…"

The interviewer raised an eyebrow, not sure where I was going with this.

"But that's not enough. You have to have a passion for the fans. For the audience. They're there to see a game, sure. But they also want to feel like they're part of it all. And that's what I do. I'm not just a crazy mascot doing skits – I'm there to lead the fans and get them cheering."

I wasn't sure whether this struck a chord, because the executives just smiled and nodded.

Next, they handed me a bucket of baseballs and sat back to watch as I showed them my best stuff. I strutted atop the dugout and swung my arms around like I was the backpack kid, throwing a few souvenirs into the empty stands along the way. It all felt very natural to me, and I think they could see that.

I got the gig.

My first paying job igniting crowds. Sixty bucks a game. Plus, I wouldn't have to swing by the produce section on the way to the field. Who would've thought? On my first day they gave me my costume: a giant Lynx head, a baseball uniform, furry arms, a glove, and a foam bat. I would now introduce the world to Lenny the Lynx. *Take that, Dean Pritchard!*

Lenny's big reveal would happen in front of an audience of more than 10,000, my biggest crowd yet. The instructions were simple: jump over the center-field wall onto a crash pad, hop onto an ATV and drive into the infield, waving to fans and high-fiving players. Simple, right?

"Give it up for Lenny the Lynx!" the PA announcer boomed over the speakers.

That was my cue. Excitement rushed through me. I leaned over the wall, ready to get the party going – but as I was about to jump, I caught sight of a dozen or so players charging out to the mat.

This definitely wasn't in the script.

As I landed, top prospects and soon-to-be major leaguers – including Rondell White, Curtis Pride, Kirk Rueter, and Cliff Floyd – dog-piled on top of me. They just couldn't resist taking the piss out of poor old Lenny. With my fake head broken but spirits still intact, I slithered my way out of the pile and beelined it to the ATV.

The crowd went wild. That's when it hit me: the crowd never knows what the performer is going to do, so *the performer can do anything*. You just gotta roll with it – and roll with it I did, tattered mask and all!

I did 35 games my first season, and it was an incredible learning experience. (I even had to join a mascot union for $50 annual dues. What a privilege!)

"The Lynx sold out dozens of games that season. And with players bouncing back and forth between the minors and the majors, the most consistent presence and one of the biggest stars of the show was Lenny. He was edgy. He took risks. He bent the rules. He tested the limits. He was fearless and funny. And he endeared himself to the fans."

Mark Sutcliffe, local media personality

I had a good run as Lenny the Lynx, but one season was enough. I didn't want to get arrested for assaulting fans with my foam baseball bat. Seriously. It's insane how often they'd come after me in playful but aggressive ways. Fans felt this crazy sense of connection because I represented them, but they'd often take it too far – from slapping my furry head when I wasn't looking to trying to trip me in the stands.

My biggest takeaway from that gig was that I knew I loved making people laugh and smile. So, when my friend Marc approached me that winter with a new business opportunity about entertaining kids, I was all ears. Marc was friends with the general manager of a local ski resort that was kicking off a big kids' ski program. They wanted to have the kids interact every weekend with a new mascot, "Rocky the Raccoon," and I was the obvious choice.

"I assume you can ski?" the general manager asked.

Uh…

I was an intermediate skier at best, but with the costume on, I'd be a hazard to everyone. But sometimes you just have to say yes, even if it involves hurtling downhill in a massive, 8-foot-tall furry suit.

So, I went from being a lynx to a raccoon. Picture a giant furry black and white onesie with a massive raccoon head. (That's going to be stuck in your head for a while, eh?)

I was nervous about the skiing part of the gig, but excited about bringing joy to kids. I was set to kick the "Kids' Ski Day" off with my inaugural trip down the hill. Before a crowd of about 500, off Rocky went down the course! I felt unstoppable, as though I were in a race in the Alps. Two gates to go! I could feel the finish line, the fans cheering, the bells ringing. I was about to be the world champion of… skiing racoons.

And then my left ski caught the edge of a gate, and I lost my head.

Literally.

One hand over my face, I crawled a few feet and grabbed the head before any kids had a panic attack. *Who was that un-masked man?!* Then I ran back to the warm ski chalet and had a good laugh. Fortunately, I wasn't hospitalized. This time.

Lenny the Lynx scaring the kids and eventually being hired by them... see Senators Full Circle story.

I think everyone should be a mascot for an hour – maybe just not on a ski hill. There's something powerful about entertaining people anonymously. You can become someone else. But I missed the face-to-face interactions with the fans that I felt in my Melonhead days.

Next, I took a less glamorous job at the local hockey rink making $7.50 an hour cleaning the ice and managing the shed. I was also still doing clothing sales with my friends Andre and Roger at music festivals and F1 races, finding my entrepreneurial spirit, but I wasn't sure if I really wanted to make a career of selling t-shirts. Nothing against people who do, but I had other ambitions. I could hear my calling and I knew it involved bringing smiles to crowds of humans, I just had no idea what that meant. Plus, I was living in my dad's basement, which wasn't exactly ideal.

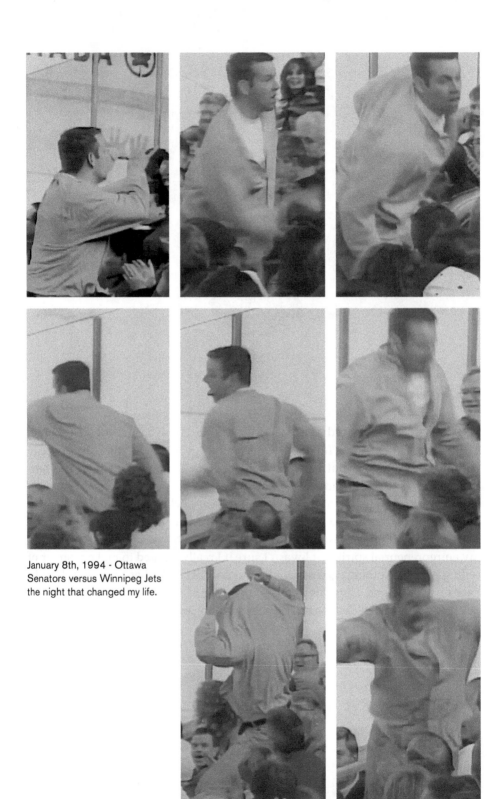

January 8th, 1994 - Ottawa
Senators versus Winnipeg Jets
the night that changed my life.

10

WE ARE FAMILY

"Everything you want is on the other side of fear."

Jack Canfield

As 1994 began and I was still finding my way, I was offered a good distraction: tickets to see the worst team in the NHL, a new franchise known as the Ottawa Senators.

It was a super-cold night in early January. A few feet of fresh snow had just settled – but not enough to stop any good Canadian from attending the game. My friend Elliott had season tickets on the lower deck of the ten-thousand-seat stadium. Great seats. Not-so-great team. The Ottawa Senators started in 1992 and introduced at a small junior-level arena, while the 18,000-seat arena was being built on a farm field. Ottawa loved hockey, and it was fun to be part of the big leagues now.

But this particular game was as dull as watching paint dry. In the third period, I found myself not only bored to tears but agitated. The energy in the arena was nonexistent. The crowds in the 200-seat gymnasium at Lisgar put them to shame. Something was brewing inside me. Something I'd felt before. I knew something had to change. This isn't why you go to a sporting event.

With eight minutes to go, this team needed something. This *crowd* needed something.

"Okay, next song I'm getting up," I nodded. "Next song I'm getting up."

"What?" Elliott laughed.

And then it happened: perfect seat, perfect timing, and the perfect song. "We Are Family," by Sister Sledge.

Elliott might never take me to a game again, I considered. *But oh well.*

I sprung from my seat, suddenly possessed with superfan fervor. I started to flail my arms and dance – horribly, but I didn't care. I kept going. Bringing me back to my childhood living room. I didn't stop until the song ended. People were shocked.

As I took my seat, I looked around. The previously dumbfounded faces now wore huge smiles. Fans were into it.

"What did you think?" I asked Elliott.

"You are freaking crazy, Cam."

There was a new buzz in the arena. You could feel it. Fans wanted to party. Fans wanted *something*.

Adrenaline continued to surge through me. Something bigger had called me out to own the moment. I didn't look to my left or right for permission, I just went for it. All heart. No mask, no melon. Just me. And the story could have ended there, but the reason I ended up with this accidental career is because of what happened next.

On the next stoppage in play, "Everybody Dance Now" echoed through the arena. Ten thousand fans turned to look at me, expecting me to do something. They demanded it.

I zipped past Elliott and sprung into the aisle, rocking up and down the stairs, flailing my arms and losing my shit. I was smiling, I was laughing, I was so in the moment it was insane. I only cared about one thing: *the crowd coming with me and getting into the game.* They were cheering with my every move, dancing to every beat, and by the end of the timeout, they gave me roaring acknowledgement for taking the chance and going for it. Out of the blue, we had just made magic together. The crowd wanted me to succeed – and thanks to them, I did.

"As the song's beat got into your bloodstream and you looked out upon the moderately energized crowd... you kept saying to me, 'Okay, next song I'm getting up, next song I'm getting up.' You fluttered your arms and legs like a bird taking first flight, and as your hands began to clap to the beat and you drew the attention of the fans within the adjacent sections, your training wheels fell off and the Dancing Guy was born."

Elliott Little, brave friend, Senators season-ticket holder

When I returned to my seat, I was surprised to find a member of the Senators' staff waiting there. I thought he was there to tase me; instead, he wanted my contact information. I couldn't believe it. I gave him my phone number, thinking that would be the end of that. I was still in shock. But wow, did I have an extra kick in my step.

I'd cheered at many venues, but always with a mask or melon on. Never had I been totally myself – a random dude in denim jeans and a large tee with energy that could fill a stadium. I felt like I'd stepped through a door – make that danced through a door – and even though it was new territory, and kind of overwhelming, it just felt... right.

The next morning, my father was reading the local newspaper and saw a line that caught his attention: "A red-haired guy in section 18 even had the normally sleepy crowd rockin'" Let's just say I had a few things to explain to him. .

"I don't know if I was surprised. Impressed is probably a better word. He was fearless… willing to put himself out there and motivate the crowd to be loud in a uniquely entertaining way. I thought, 'Wow… this guy is something special.'"

Randy Burgess, Former Director of Events, Ottawa Senators

DANCE, DANCE, DANCE!

A few days later, I got the call. It was Randy Burgess, Director of Events, Ottawa Senators. I went in and met with him and discussed the crazy night. We had a good laugh – and he offered me a chance to come back.

"To do what, exactly?" I asked.

"We'll give you tickets to six more games, and some team paraphernalia," he said. "Just do what you did a few nights ago."

I wasn't sure what that meant, but I was excited. I wouldn't be paid, but that was okay with me. In my mind, I had to earn it.

I went back. And wow, was I scared. One of the execs even said, "Have a few beers if it helps." So, before the game began I went to a local bar with my pal Brian for some liquid courage. I thought it would help. But once I got up, the fans were ready to come along with me. I had to dig deep. And boy, did I. And it turns out, never again did I indulge before a game. This was serious business to me! I quickly became known around Ottawa as the "Dancing Guy" from the Senators games. It wasn't quite a "job," but it was a start. I was thrilled. I wasn't exactly sure what my act was or how to monetize this calling of mine. Was dancing with no inhibitions enough to sustain a career? Seemed unlikely.

I started to let loose a little more. I'd dance in the crowd, then at the end when I had their complete attention, I'd lead more cheers to get the fans involved in the action. The team was still having a hard time on the ice, so the license to be creative in the crowd was wide open. The organization was open-minded and wanted the extra fun.

My friends back at university were pretty sure I'd never be back at this point. I wasn't sure myself – but for the first time in a while, I was actually excited to find out what happened next.

★★★

The NHL was going through a tense lockout, with the suspended season putting the Dancing Guy's new career in jeopardy. Once play resumed, though, I got a call from the team. They wanted me to do 14 games and would offer me

$250 per game! Real money. My dad was even more shocked than me. We didn't negotiate.

Resuming my university career seemed more doubtful than ever. I signed an exclusivity agreement with the team stating something to the effect that "[I was] strictly prohibited from performing with any other team in the National Hockey League during the regular season." (Guess how many I've signed since? Nada. But that's another story).

The season started in January, and I was busy trying to figure out how to leverage my visibility. What else could I do to connect with fans?

I raced back to Bragwear HQ to discuss how we could integrate t-shirts into my shtick. After some discussion, Andre and I came up with the idea to throw out shirts at the game that would read "The Dancing Guy" on the front, and "Powered by Bragwear" on the back. For reasons I don't totally comprehend, (or maybe I knew!) I had the thought that I'd *wear* them, *then* toss them out. Like a PG-rated strip-tease. This is something no one in the world was doing at the time. We had some leftover inventory and thought it would be a great way to promote our brand while exciting fans.

I had no idea this would work, but once it did, we needed more Dancing Guy tees! This became my signature move, and fortunately the Senators were totally cool with it. Not only did my clothing line sales spike, but so did my confidence. There's something about a lunatic giving you a t-shirt off his back that makes people go wild. And I felt the same sense of appreciation toward my hometown team for giving me this golden opportunity to spread my wings.

As the end of the 1994-95 NHL season neared, the Senators were eliminated from playoff contention, meaning my exclusivity deal with them was up. There was only one way to find out if what I was doing would have the same effect in other stadiums. After all, it wasn't about which team's logo I had on my chest – it was about entertaining a crowd.

That time I shared a t-shirt twirl in front of 18,500 people with the Right Honorable Jean Chrétien, Prime Minister of Canada in 1996.

Working the crowd at Civic Center in the early Ottawa Senators days. No clue what I was doing!

Toronto Maple Leafs Legend, Daryl Sittler, giving me a pep-talk before the big game.

Let's Dance and Original "Dancing Guy" T-shirts.

Let's Dance!

The Dancing Guy!!!
POWERED BY...
BRAGWEAR
INTERNATIONAL

11

DOUBLE DARE

"Hell, there are no rules here – we're trying
to accomplish something."

Thomas Edison

I had two options: Stay in Ottawa and keep up the momentum by trying to book gigs with minor league teams and sell more shirts, or take my friend Chris Klotz up on his ambitious dare – drive from Ottawa to Toronto to fire up the crowd at a Toronto Maple Leafs playoff game, to see if they'd hire me. He was always pushing me to do more with this.

The Leafs were going up against the Chicago Blackhawks in the first round, and the whole country would be watching. This was the very definition of a "dare to be great" situation. *I mean, my routine had worked in Ottawa – why should Toronto be any different?* I had to give it a shot.

Chris wouldn't be coming with me – I was on a road trip for one. After five hours and a few dozen delicious, doughy Timbits, I arrived.

Toronto was buzzing with excitement. Fans filed into the historic Maple Leaf Gardens in droves. The game was sold out. Fortunately, I had an in.

Larry Kelly, a family friend, was a prominent hockey agent. He represented Hall of Famers like Steve Yzerman and Leaf legend Doug Gilmour. He was kind enough to call up the general manager and president, Cliff Fletcher, and put in a good word about me. (I wish I heard what he said!) Fortunately, Cliff had an open mind. He was willing to give me a shot. No paycheck. Just a shot.

Sometimes that's all it takes.

Larry called me a few days later. "Cameron, your instructions are to show up at the Garden and ask for Bob."

Ask for Bob. Okay. Easy enough.

I pulled into a parking lot by the Gardens and quickly changed out of my t-shirt and jeans into something classier – a jean shirt with a tie and khakis. This was a new business opportunity, after all. I swear I thought this was a good look.

My hands trembled with a mix of excitement and anxiety as I got out of the car and approached an attendant working at the front desk. "Hi, I'm looking for Bob."

"One moment," he said, and picked up the phone.

Before I knew it, a security guard was chaperoning me up to the management office. I was in awe and feeling quite out of my depth. On our way, we passed

Darryl Sittler's office – the Maple Leafs legend. *Holy shit.* My eyes bugged out and the security guard eyed me up and down, probably thinking, "Is this dude going to be a problem?" I regained my composure and played it cool, acting every bit like I knew *exactly* what I was doing. If only they knew…

Finally, we reached the office of Bob Stellick, the director of business operations and communications for the Toronto Maple Leafs. This guy had some serious pull. He stared at me, seemingly perplexed. I had to act like a big boy and own the moment. He didn't seem sure what to make of me.

"Here's your seat," he said, pulling out a glossy ducat and placing it ceremoniously in my hand. "This is a huge game, good luck!"

I went to my locker room (the stairwell) to change. To make the most of the moment, I'd created 12 t-shirts (all I could afford): standard white XL tees featuring my face atop a simple phrase: "The Dancing Guy." I slipped all 12 of them on and made my way into a room of 15,726 strangers.

I was ready – definitely nervous, but in a good way. I couldn't believe I was in Maple Leaf Gardens about to go nuts.

From my seat in the reds (the rinkside section), I just watched the game, and the crowd, for a good long while. Trying to absorb it all and read the vibes, I guess. Finally, I "hit it" when I felt it. I was so nervous, but I knew this was a pivotal moment. My schtick wasn't refined, but I stuck to the bad dancing, tossed a few tees, and rolled with it. The big-city Toronto crowd ate it up! After that, I toured the arena, hitting every section.

I went absolutely berserk. Off the charts. And the cherry on top: the Leafs won!

"As the first game went on – perhaps more than halfway through the first period – we thought that he wasn't going to do anything but watch the game. In hindsight, he was picking his spot."

Bob Stellick, former Director of Business Operations and Communications, Toronto Maple Leafs

---

"You were great," Bob said after the game. "We'd love to have you back on Saturday. We'll give you $300 and put you up in a hotel."

$300?!

H-E-double-hockey-sticks, I couldn't believe what I was hearing. Not only had the crowd at the Gardens supported me, but one of the biggest organizations in professional sports was willing to get behind me, too, and even raised my rate! To top it all off, they wanted me on Saturday night.

S-A-T-U-R-D-A-Y.

For those of you not from the Great White North, our Saturdays are pretty much a religious holiday known as *Hockey Night in Canada*. Millions of Canadians from coast to coast gather around their television sets to soak up the action. And I was about to be right in the thick of it. A shiver of excitement ran down my spine.

"Only on one condition," Bob continued. "You'll have to wear Leafs shirts instead."

Wouldn't be as pretty as my face on the shirt, but I guess it would have to do! I floated across the street to Gardoonie's, the local sports bar, for a celebratory drink. As soon as I entered, the place went *wild*. People high-fived me, hugged me, and offered to buy me drinks. What a rush. But then the mood quickly soured.

"They tore you a new one!" yelled a patron, almost giddy.

Huh?

That's when I discovered that, during my performance, the commentators had mocked me for all of Canada to hear.

"This guy's going to have a swollen head in the morning. I hope he's got someone taking him home." (Author's Note: "Swollen head" means hungover in Canadian, not a big ego.)

I was immediately hurt and embarrassed – I hadn't even been drinking, I was just spreading some cheer! *Was that it, then?* Was my dream now over before it had even begun? For a moment, I felt like a bit of a laughingstock and didn't know what to do. But the fans at Gardoonie's had my back, and I shrugged it off. I had faith I was on the right path.

BRIGHT LIGHTS

Saturday night and the city was electric. Despite the minor mental setback, I was ready to take the Gardens to a new level of hysteria. I don't know if I swung my arms higher or kicked my legs harder that night, but I scored rave reviews. Pre-game, I even met with Leafs DJ and piano man Jimmy Holmstrom, a certified Toronto institution, to get on the same page. Millions watched as legendary commentator Harry Neale gave his take on my performance:

"Look at that guy go – he's unbelievable! He's got the crowd on its feet. He's Cameron Hughes, a 24-year-old motivational consultant. The crowd just loves him – and look at those moves."

I'd been determined to win them over, and I did.

I thought of Mom on the drive home, remembering her words, which now seemed oddly prophetic: *There are other ways you can contribute to the team.*

I now felt like that proclamation meant something much more profound, and it had taken all of these years and experiences for me to realize it. My mom was acknowledging that I was different but had just as much chance of making a name for myself as everybody else.

Between more Timbits and laughs, I just knew I had to do this for a living. The *how* didn't matter. I'd figure it out.

So how did my on-air reviews turn around so fast? Turns out my dear childhood friend Michael had watched the broadcast of my first performance in Toronto and taken the commentators' jabs at me a little too personally. Furious, he'd sent a note to the president of CBC Sports and Ron MacLean, the host of *Hockey Night in Canada*.

"They've got no right to talk about Cameron Hughes," it read. "He's just a young kid from Ottawa trying to make a difference by getting people to have fun. Harry Neale should be ashamed of his actions."

"Well lo and behold, on the next Saturday night broadcast of HNIC, during the first intermission, Ron mentioned Cameron and said he and Harry loved what he was doing for the crowd that night. It went to show what a classy person Ron MacLean really is, but more importantly was possibly one small step in Cameron's success in the ensuing years. A gratifying moment!"

Michael Bridal, family friend, mentor (I used to babysit his kids!)

Coming back to Ottawa with some extra swagger and recognition, I was up for new challenges. I didn't know what, but I was open to exploring all opportunities. Then I got a call from a representative of the new roller-hockey team, the Ottawa Loggers.

"We'd love to hire you to do some games for us," he said. "What's your rate?"

My rate?

He had me on the hot seat. What was my rate?!

I was making $250 per game at this point, $300 from the Leafs, but I felt I was worth more. I had to see if my value was worth what I felt the reactions from fans were.

"I'll do it for $1,000 per game," I said confidently.

To this day, I don't think I've ever heard someone laugh so hard. "You'll never make $1,000 per game doing this in your life," he said.

Gut punch.

Maybe he's right, I thought. After all, I'd only been doing this for a few months – what did I know about how much I could or couldn't make? I patiently waited for his laughter to subside.

"We'll give you $300," he continued.

I took a few deep breaths, then proceeded to do my worst negotiating of all time.

"Okay," I said. I needed the work, and it seemed like fun. But his words lit a fire in me. How much *could* I make doing this? What was my worth? And would I be able to get other teams to buy into it? This was about more than the money: it was about whether I believed in myself and this crazy dream. Was I onto something, or was I in over my head?

TIMEOUT

18 years later I was having lunch with my pal Jeff Jackson, then Assistant GM of the Leafs, when we saw Bob ("Ask for Bob" Bob!) across the restaurant. I wrote a note on a napkin and had it sent to his table. After reading the message, he looked around, confused, before finally catching my eye. We shared a hearty laugh. The message? "Willing to dance for $300 and a hotel."

12

SHOW UP

"Some people want it to happen, some wish
it would happen, others make it happen."

Michael Jordan

While I wasn't exactly making a steady living off my performances, the community was starting to express interest in my story. Calls came in from various high school administrations asking if I would come in and inspire their students with tales from my non-traditional path. Not quite Chris Farley's "I live in a van, down by the river" kind of speeches, but definitely something different and relatable for the students. Of course, I accepted! I had absolutely zero idea where to start, so I partnered with "an older fart" (his terminology) and former pro football player named Tom Pullen, who I'd met at some community events. We thought it would be fun to have the crazy young firecracker and the "grey hair" inspire students together, so we started booking gigs.

At schools across Ottawa, I found myself telling kids to "get involved," to "build their foundation," and to "stay in school," the latter of which I hadn't even done myself. *Who was I to tell them to do what I hadn't?*

I started feeling like a fraud. I needed to practice what I preached.

So, at age 24, I reapplied to Bishop's to finish what I'd started – to finally get my degree.

A few weeks later, I was accepted. And this time around, I wasn't going to fail.

During the coming weeks, I attended my sociology classes at BU, and on the weekends I fired up crowds in Ottawa, Montréal, and wherever else I got the call. My social life was non-existent, but I was okay with that. This was important to finish. And yes, that fall, I even carved a few more watermelons for the football games.

Then one day after class I got a call from the newest NBA team in the league. The Toronto Raptors.

The seven-hour drive from Québec to Toronto made me laugh, think, and realize that maybe – just *maybe* – this was all meant to be. Maybe not making the high school basketball team was a sign that there are other ways to be part of something special. I mean, I was about to do an NBA game in Toronto for the Raptors' inaugural season.

Team officials had already seen me perform for the Leafs, so they knew what I could do. On a call with Brian Cooper, Director of Marketing, he explained that the team was looking for new ways to engage with their fans, as they felt the SkyDome was just too big. They wanted me to be the wild man, dressed like "one of the fans" – ripped jeans, a Raps jersey, and a hat – but with extra attitude. There was only one catch.

"We want you to stay in the upper deck," Brian instructed plainly. The focus was to be on the fans far from the action and make them feel engaged.

"Sure thing," I said. Easy enough.

During the game, I had the upper levels in hysterics. My legs were kicking higher than a Radio City Rockette; my arms were flowing like two strands of cooked spaghetti. But I just couldn't help myself from eyeing the fans down below. I wanted to do more for them. If, hypothetically, I were to situate myself in the lower bowl, folks in the upper bowl would still be able to see me and get a feel for what I was doing. Plus, I had a few friends at the game sitting closer to the court who I wanted to say hello to.

My adrenaline was through the roof; sometimes that's what gets me into trouble. At the start of the fourth quarter, I decided to spread the cheer and make the trip down.

There must have been 15,000 fans down there. Nevertheless, I got the entire stadium popping. Pure pandemonium. That is, until I saw a representative from the team approaching.

Gulp.

"We asked you to stay in the upper deck," he said. "What are you doing down here?"

This was a very important early lesson for me. While the crowd was loving it, they weren't the ones *paying me*. While the fans are always my ultimate measuring stick on whether a game goes well, I needed to keep my employers happy and not go rogue.

I made my way back to the upper level for the remainder of the game. Although the Raptors brought me back a few more times that season, they made sure to keep me in check. Eventually, "the crazy guy in the upper level" was replaced by a spirit team.

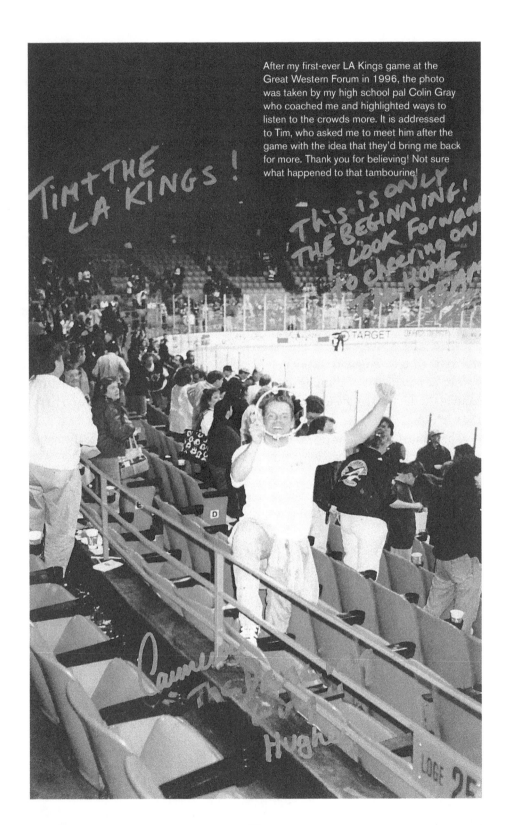

After my first-ever LA Kings game at the
Great Western Forum in 1996, the photo
was taken by my high school pal Colin Gray
who coached me and highlighted ways to
listen to the crowds more. It is addressed
to Tim, who asked me to meet him after the
game with the idea that they'd bring me back
for more. Thank you for believing! Not sure
what happened to that tambourine!

TIM+THE
LA KINGS!

This is only
THE BEGINNING!
I LOOK FORWARD
to CHEERING ON
THE HOME
TEAM

13

SPRING BREAK DREAMS

"First, think. Second, dream. Third, believe. And finally, dare."

Walt Disney

Some kernels of ideas were starting to pop. It was Spring Break of '96 and two new friends of mine at Bishop's, Tom and Peter Godber, took a special interest in my career. They knew I'd had a bit of success. While most of my fellow students were hitting Fort Lauderdale, I was ready to see if my gig could really become something real. By this time, I was finally close to finishing my university career. But I needed a plan.

I had told the Godber brothers that I'd always wanted to go to Hollywood to see what it was all about. I had this vision that I should go straight to Cali and create new opportunities for myself in the sports entertainment industry. I knew a few people from my hometown who were living in Hollywood, and I had a good feeling about the idea.

Impressed by my passion, Tom and Peter *bought me a round-trip ticket* with a "get us back when you can" coupon. I mean, who does that?! This was proof that there was a special connection among our alumni – and that belief in someone is powerful. Buoyed by the Godbers' show of faith, I even made "Dancing Guy Tour" t-shirts. (It wasn't a tour, but it felt like one to me!) I figured I'd just show up at a game and show what I could offer.

These days, I probably would have just sent a video link and hoped they'd call me back. Boring, right? But in 1996, I had to hop on a plane to LaLa Land and bring my résumé, LinkedIn profile, and website all rolled into one – ME. Then I'd "deliver" it in real time. I had only one weekend – I needed to make the most of it.

I'd hit three games in three days.

GAME ONE – BULLETS VS. LAKERS

The grand "LA Experiment" would kick off at the fabulous Forum in Inglewood, home of the Los Angeles Lakers. I changed into my trademark tees from the comfort of my personal locker room, this time the men's washroom at the nearby McDonald's. Fortunately, I was able to score a cheap seat off a local ticket seller.

Walking into the arena, I could feel fear and fearlessness coursing through my body, all in the same breath. Nicholson. Denzel. Magic. Vlade. And some crazy Canadian who couldn't dance to save his life. *What the heck am I doing here?* I nervously asked myself for the first time. If there was such a thing as hitting the Big Time for the career I was trying to create out of thin air, this was it. And I could not fail.

I took my seat *way* up in the 300s. Nosebleeds. As I studied the location, I frowned and shook my head. This wouldn't do. I was starting to learn the importance of placement: I had to be in precisely the right area of the arena to increase my visibility. It wasn't enough to show up – I needed to be *seen*. Eyeballs equal energy.

So, I started to inch my way down the aisles and closer to the court. Then closer.

A timeout halfway through the third quarter. My moment?

YES.

The California cool crowd got warmed up fast by a big red blast of Canadian sunshine! As my tees started flying, the fans began to play along. At one point, I even threw Goldie Hawn a t-shirt!

The first time "Mony Mony" (the Billy Idol version) and I would gel was at this game.

The arena was old, so the noise I made jumping around on the floorboards behind the hoop was percussive and beautiful. I commanded the attention of the Hollywood crowd the entire timeout – and wow, was it fun!

I was hoping to get "discovered," half-waiting for Magic to swing a spotlight my way and tell Jerry Buss to hire me… but no such luck. Still, if I could fly in from north of the border and get the Lakers fans going wild, maybe I could make this dream come true!

Great start. Off to game two.

GAME TWO – KINGS VS. CANADIENS

This time around, I brought my friend Colin as backup – someone who could provide both guidance and moral support. He was the same Lisgar senior I saw on my first day of high school; the one who amped me up. Fast forward a decade, and now I was the one doing the amping up while sleeping on his couch in LA, so the least I could do was bring him to a game.

Now an accomplished writer, director and former Broadway star, Colin was in Los Angeles pursuing his acting dreams. He'd just finished a stint as Frank Hardy in the TV adaptation of *The Hardy Boys*. Colin understood the art of entertaining and would be able to provide some pointers on my biggest performance yet. It's always great to have someone in your corner who just *gets it*.

Back in the Forum again for the Kings game. The hits were popping. The fans were rocking. During the first intermission Colin gave me strong feedback on the crowd's reactions, based on when I was getting up and the flow of the game.

"Okay, that was *good*, but you should wait for the crowd to be quiet before getting up next time," Colin suggested. "You can't go every whistle. As soon as the next whistle blows, go to a section where you'll be super visible, pop up and do your thing. Feel it out a bit more – don't rush it." The man is a talented director – so I did as directed.

Whenever the Kings made a big play, I got up; whenever there was a lull, I got up – but when the fans were going wild on their own, I sat back. Colin felt I shouldn't get up just because I could. He challenged me to read the action more and be the spark when it was needed. It was making more sense to me. And it seemed to be working.

"I don't remember who was playing, I don't remember the score, but I'll never forget Cam getting up during an interlude in the hockey action, music blaring in the arena, and he just starts dancing like a maniac while stripping off layers of Kings t-shirts he'd magically put on underneath his jacket. The place went absolutely bonkers. People leapt to their feet and started clapping along with him while cheering madly. Then he was off to another section. He jumped up again, dancing and throwing t-shirts. Then another section. And another. But this time there was a group of 10-15 kids following him into each section, dancing and cheering alongside him as the crowd went wild wherever he went. I was gobsmacked. I'd never seen anything like it. Who was this guy from high school? I knew he was onto something!"

Colin Gray, The guy from HS, Broadway Star, Writer-Director, Knighted in Hungary

---

After the game, a representative from the Kings approached me. "Would you be able to come back?" he asked.

Come back?

"Of course he can come back!" my "agent" Colin chimed in. Business cards were swapped. I could feel something in my gut telling me this Spring Break trip was going to pay off down the road. Not sunbathing at Señor Frog's Disco Bar in Cancun was definitely the right call.

GAME THREE – MIGHTY DUCKS VS. LIGHTNING

The ride down to Anaheim in my rental car through palm trees was beautiful. I had just enough t-shirts left and was riding some momentum.

The arena was packed with crazed Mighty Ducks fans (yes, the team was originally named after the Emilio Estevez movie, and their name didn't get shortened to just the "Ducks" until 2006). At the time, the team was still owned by the Walt Disney Company, so this felt like an especially big opportunity for me. This time, my goal was to make it onto the big screen in Hollywood: the jumbotron.

TIMEOUT

*Jumbotron technology made its debut at the 1980 Major League Baseball All-Star Game in LA's Dodger Stadium. The original technology was developed by Mitsubishi Electric and Sony, which coined **JumboTron** as a brand name in 1985.*

But when I went for it, the crowd totally wasn't having it. Five minutes later I was up again. Still nothing. The first period was a dud. I'd flown over 3,000 miles for this and had an 8 a.m. flight back to school the next day. Arrgh. Welcome to Yawn-aheim.

Taking a breath, I waited for the right moment, reading the crowd per Colin's advice. It was a close game in the second period. The fans were on the edge. This time, when I got up and jammed out, they were all in. Felt great! The next hour or so was a non-stop blur of exciting hockey and exhilarating crowd pumping.

With about six minutes to go in the third period, I was in the lower bowl taking a break from the crazy and felt a tap on my shoulder. A man in a nice suit greeted me. "Can you follow me, please? I'd like to have a word with you."

Disney wants to put me on their payroll! I thought. *I'm going to get my own doll! This is amazing! I just wish Mom were here to see this.*

As I turned to follow the man up the stairs, I glanced up and realized my every move, every bead of sweat on my face, was being broadcast on the jumbotron. And then came the moment where 18,000 total strangers clapped for me. I'm not exactly sure why, but my gut tells me they were supporting a kid who'd put himself out there and given it a shot. I felt like Rudy for a split second, minus the pads.

"So what's this all about?" the man asked as we walked.

"Just trying to get the crowd going!" I panted.

"A lot of people think what you're doing is great," he continued, "but the Disney corporation would like you to stop."

Record scratch.

Huh? That was not in the script! Rudy did not get penalized for jumping offsides! How could Disney, an organization whose mission was to entertain, not recognize the magic we were creating together?

"What, Mickey and Minnie were upset I was acting a little Goofy?" I quipped. I was escorted back to my seat by two other men, and that was it.

The fans in my section buzzed upon my return, but I felt defeated. I was certain of one thing: crowds everywhere were the same. They just wanted to get out of their seats, catch a t-shirt, and let loose. And I could be the spark that allowed them to do that. I'd already proven it.

As if I were being taunted by the cheer gods, the Mighty Ducks scored not even 45 seconds later. The place erupted. It took everything inside me to refrain from running up and down the aisles. But then the cheer gods threw me a curveball: everyone in my section turned to look at me. It was just like that night in Ottawa.

Well.

No one had said I couldn't dance from my seat...

I jumped up and twirled my last two tees with everything I had. I cheered. *Hard.* Soon after, I got another tap on my shoulder. I can still feel it today.

Not security. *Phew.*

His name was Chris Mulcahy, and he told me he'd seen me at the last three games. Chris was the director of entertainment for the Washington Capitals and Washington Bullets, and told me that what I did would be perfect for the fans in DC. I took his card and told him I'd love to chat. I think I skipped out of the arena.

When I got back to Colin's place that night, he was over-the-moon happy for me. Having a friend to celebrate with was the icing on the California cake. Before going to bed, I learned I'd made #3 on ESPN's "Plays of the Week." I was in shock. This was my calling – and it was happening.

I flew back to university with renewed confidence that this unusual calling, this uncharted path I was somehow compelled to follow, was *exactly* what I was meant to do.

"It was soon after your mother had passed and you said, 'I am never really going to work for a living.' We knew you were crazy... or thought we did. Now we're the crazy ones!"

Bill Knowlton, childhood friend

Clockwise from top: Mark Hatfield (Bishop's University roommate), Jim "Big Whiskey" Reid, and Mark "Sweet Step" Stepnoski at the 1996 Houston Oilers training camp. Surprise!

Chris Webber, Washington Bullets (now Wizards) 1996-97 season.

Eagle U 1996- Miss USA Ali Landry, Miss North Carolina, Miss South Carolina and Miss Texas.

Reggie Miller playing against Wizards at one of the games. (Sorry, no backstage photos allowed!)

14

I'LL BE THERE

"Give your dreams all you've got and you'll be amazed
at the energy that comes out of you."

William James

I was on a plane to DC to perform in the US officially for the first time. Like, with credentials and pay. I should have been at school, but hey, it was the weekend – and how often do the Bullets and Capitals call with back-to-back games?

At the Bullets game, my locker room (a real one this time!) was located right beside the Bulls'. Michael Jordan, Scottie Pippen, Dennis Rodman, good ol' Canadian boy Bill Wennington, and me. The atmosphere was dizzying! The Jordan aura was palpable. The fans were definitely into my performance, and the team was happy. You aren't going to beat the Bulls, but you do what you can do. After the game, as I walked past Washington star Chris Webber, C-Webb teased me good-naturedly about my dance moves.

The next night was hockey. Prior to the Capitals game, I learned that Vice President of the United States Al Gore would be in attendance. I was told in no uncertain terms not to interact with him or go close to his section – one of the first times I'd get such instructions before performing, but certainly not the last. *(But how perfect would it have been if I was dressed as a Secret Service agent stationed behind Al, and then popped out my earpiece, ripped off my jacket and started going bonkers?)*

Still, I had a blast with the DC crowd – monumental energy from a monumental town. Oh, and the Caps won.

AND WE'RE OFF

As I flew home, I knew one thing for certain: it was time to graduate and follow my passion, ASAP! It was pretty obvious that, given a taste of what I could bring to the party, top professional teams were willing to invest in my powers of cheer. I just didn't really know how to make it a steady career.

My friends back at Bishop's couldn't believe what I'd been up to on my weekends. But hey, to me, I bet it felt just like what a business major might experience when they get an internship on Wall Street. A taste of the big leagues. Of what could be. I had an extra kick in my step for the last few months and was ready to start a new chapter in my life.

"I always said that doing what you did, going back to Bishop's University and finishing your degree, took more balls and bravery than anything you've done in a sports facility, ever! You didn't have to go back. Your career was taking off and you weren't even sure they would take you back... but they did take you back and you finished what you started six years earlier. Most people we know would have taken the other door, the easier door. But you didn't."

Brian Murray, lifelong friend

TIMEOUT

I've barely won anything in my life, so when the graduation committee told me I'd be winning the Jeff Cannon Award for outstanding contribution to the life of the school, I was floored. When it was announced at the ceremony, I stood up and my fellow students cheered at the top of their lungs. Goosebumps. I turned around, faced the students, and started belting out the school song as I walked to the stage. The entire student section joined me, en masse, until I thought the gymnasium rafters might come tumbling down!

MMMBOP

Post-graduation, I went straight to Los Angeles, hoping to get some momentum going there. I managed to score a spare room in Studio City with Colin, and beyond that, I knew very little other than that I had a dream to perform. Not uncommon in LA, I realize. I just wanted more opportunities.

After picking up a few non-sports-related jobs here and there to keep myself going (including odds jobs for the manager of Hanson, Christopher Sabec), it seemed like my first big break arrived. Like, *7' 1" big*. The Lakers organization had seen me tossing shirts to Goldie Hawn a few months earlier, and they wanted me to be part of the party for Shaquille O'Neal's first game in purple and gold. But while they were still in the planning stages for that, I needed a cash injection. I decided to fly back to Canada for a weekend, set up shop at

Bishop's, and sell a boatload of t-shirts for some extra income. The plan started off without a hitch. After netting about $4,000, I made my way back to the airport in Montréal to fly back to Cali with a bankroll and boosted confidence. Time to make shit happen.

I handed my boarding pass and passport to the customs agent. That's when I hit a snag.

"What's the purpose of your trip?" the agent asked.

"Just visiting," I said. "And maybe doing some work for the Lakers if they decide to hire me."

He squinted at my passport. "Work? You don't have a visa for that. Do you have a letter from the Lakers?"

"No, but – "

"I'm sorry, sir. I can't let you in."

What a gut punch this was. Rejected by customs. I didn't have a plan B. I'd hinged everything on making a go of it in LA and now I wasn't allowed in the country. I'd screwed up royally.

There are about 29 lessons in this story, but the main takeaway? Always have your ducks in a row, and don't volunteer more information than asked after partying all weekend at Homecoming. I had to call Colin and tell him I wouldn't be renting his room, until I could come up with a plan to secure a work visa. I was in a jumbo-sized pickle. (And who was going to break it to Shaq?!)

Once again, I was left trying to figure out my next move. I had a lot of pride and felt that going back home would be another loss. So, I retreated to my friend Roger's place in Vancouver to get my plan in place and began a series called "Cam's Cozy Couches."

After considering my very limited options, I was left with no choice but to fly home and move back in with my father. Between weeding lawns, doing chores around the house, and trying to quietly bring dates home, I was suddenly back to square one. I had my diploma, but my career path was seemingly blocked. I was miserable.

SCREW IT

That's when I had my first "Screw It" moment.

For me, these are the moments when, in the face of a reality that doesn't align with your values and spirit, you say "SCREW IT. There's no way I'm doing this," and decide to pursue your *true* passion, no matter what the consequences are.

SCREW IT. I'm not living in my dad's basement and weeding lawns.

That was mine.

It was time to do what needed to be done: go back to Toronto and give this thing a fair shot. I packed my bags again, only this time, with everything I owned.

Toronto had way more opportunities in my "field." If I was going to build a career in Canada out of my crazy idea, this was where I needed to be. Ottawa, the nation's capital, had just two professional sports teams – the Senators and the Rough Riders. But Toronto, nearly three times larger, with a population of 2.5 million, had four (the Leafs, the Raptors, the Jays, and the Argonauts). It was a no-brainer.

There was a small, affordable room available in my friend Peter's house. He was a huge sports fan, so this was a win for both of us. With my launch pad secured, it was time for the next steps of my journey.

DID SOMEONE CALL SECURITY?

My past employers, the Maple Leafs and Raptors, were in the off-season, so I shifted my focus to baseball. And I was in luck. An old buddy from Bishop's, Charlie Wilson, was now the assistant to the general manager of the Toronto Blue Jays.

"Hey Cam, what about doing the Jays?" he suggested. "I think I can get you a meeting with Peter."

The following week, I was sitting in the Blue Jays' offices across from Peter Cosentino, the team's Director of Entertainment. He instantly took a liking to me and wanted to give me a shot! I was learning to develop rapport and common goals with every executive I was meeting.

It was a Friday night with a crowd of about 35,000, and I was incredibly nervous. The team's representatives were nervous too – this was the first time they'd allowed anything like this. With my t-shirts on, rocking a wacky pair of shorts and a loud shirt, I was ready to go. In the middle of the second inning, I ran down the stairs from my seat, leapt up onto the dugout, and went absolutely nuts, dancing with no inhibitions. It had been a while, so you could say I had some pent-up energy to burn. What happened next was both funny (kind of) and terrifying (mostly).

No one had mentioned anything to security.

When I'm hired to do a gig, all internal parties need to be made aware of it, because typically a big red-haired guy going bonkers on top of the dugout is considered a "major security threat." Next thing I knew, six husky security guards were barreling down on me.

Remember my "SCREW IT" moment? Well, this was my "HOLY SH*T I'M SCREWED!" moment. They were charging at me full speed, so I did what anyone in their right mind would've done in that situation: I kept dancing!

But not for much longer.

They grabbed hold of me and started dragging me up the stairs. I was frantic, yelling at them to let me go.

"I'm allowed to be here! I'm allowed to be here! Why else would I have all these shirts on?!"

But they weren't having it. Luckily, the crowd wasn't having *them*. A cacophony of boos erupted in protest of the security guards. When we were halfway up the stairs – and I was practically in handcuffs – security finally got word over their walkie-talkies that I was, in fact, authorized to be there. #FreeCam.

I sprinted back down to the dugout to reclaim my turf, all 35,000 fans going wild. They leapt to their feet as if they were doing the wave at the exact same time and went nuts. Who knows, maybe they believed their vocal support caused my release? Either way, my adrenaline was on overdrive. I was unleashed.

"We didn't want the idea [of bringing you in] to get shot down by our head of security, so we left it out of the notes. We got in shit for not bringing it up, but it was worth it. Begging for forgiveness was way easier than begging for permission. Trust me! [When] we started bringing you back regularly on Friday nights, we made sure you were prominently mentioned in the pregame meeting and notes!"

Peter Cosentino, former Director of Events, Toronto Blue Jays

---

It turns out my chaotic adventures paid off that Friday night. The fans loved it, inspiring team executives to bring me back almost every Friday that season. And yes, they'd pay me – and give me some serious jumbotron time! The exposure was huge. We started to conjure up different ways to reveal me to the crowd to make it more fun. One game, they had Tim Johnson, the Toronto manager, call the bullpen in a pre-recorded video and say, "Bring him in!" Then the camera cut to me coming down the aisle and jumping onto the dugout. Yes, security let me back on the dugout. Those Friday Night SkyDome sessions were out of control! I'm pretty sure on some of those nights, I lost more water weight than at any time in my career.

FAN FEEDBACK

"One Friday night game we had the wave going around the Dome 22 times... Krazy George would be proud."

FAJITAS ANYONE?

I was now starting to become known as "The Superfan." Someone in the media gave me that name, so I ran with it. The Jays were paying me decent money, but it was only a once-a-week gig. Cash was still tight, so I took my good friend Michael up on his offer to work at one of his restaurants as a server's assistant. Michael (who'd written that supportive letter to the CBC) was the president of the Lone Star Cafe, a chain specializing in Tex-Mex cuisine. The deal was pretty sweet; not only would I generate a stable – albeit small – income to cover my living expenses, but thanks to Michael's generosity, I'd also get a few comped meals for myself and some of my pals. No strings attached. He wanted to see me succeed. So I agreed to his thoughtful and generous offer, and would show up for training a week later.

On the face of it, it was exactly what I needed: a failsafe in case my new career went to shit. I was hustling hard, but my career wasn't what you'd call *steady*. It was freelance, and I was on a crazy path. But the more I thought about it, 25 hours a week at the restaurant meant 25 hours *less* a week to put towards realizing my dream. I could feel myself approaching a point of no return. "Just a couple more hours here and I'll make some more money... but wait, what about the next game?" A quasi-comfort zone was taking shape for me, and I didn't like it. I thrived on the freeform energy of the crowds, not the structure of a "regular" job. If I took this job, I realized, it would be hedging my bet on myself.

And so, the day before I was supposed to go in for training, I called Michael. "I quit! Well, I'm not starting."

Though he was a bit perplexed, Michael, being Michael, instantly threw his support behind me once I explained my reasoning. "Well alright, but you and your friends can still eat here for free whenever!"

Talk about a golden parachute! Thanks, Michael.

After that, I had to go all in and stay focused. Had to find a way to make it work, no matter what. Some would say it was brilliant; others, completely irresponsible. Personally? I have no clue what word I should use to define that decision, but had I not made it, I wouldn't be where I am today. So, I call it PROGRESS.

I started trying to do it all. No limits. Nothing was off the table. Between my Friday night stints with the Jays, I locked in a few more Leafs games to keep getting up and putting my name out there. I was also doing more speaking events at high schools across the country. But even so, it was scattershot. I reached a point where I felt like I was constantly waiting for the phone to ring, not sure of my next move.

I remember thinking, *That cushy restaurant gig and a regular paycheck sounds pretty nice right about... NO! Get your head in the game, Cam! You can do this. GET UP!*

I guess you could say I managed my expectations by constantly inflating them. Not only did I shoot for the moon without any astronaut training, but I constantly pushed beyond it. No limits. No boundaries. It had to happen. It *would* happen; all I had to do was be ready to get up when the moment struck.

And then one afternoon, it did.

"You have one new message."

I came home to find Peter with a smirk on his face.

"Hey Cam, you got a call."

"Oh yeah? From who?"

"Seymour Knox," he said. "From the Buffalo Sabres."

Seymour's family had owned the Sabres since the team's inception in 1970. This could be big – but I thought Peter was full of it, especially when he claimed that he ended up talking hockey with Mr. Knox.

"I told him how the Sabres should get rid of Pat LaFontaine and make some trades," Peter boasted. It reminded me of when girls would call my house and my sister would do her best to ruin it for me. Peter gave me the phone number. Amazed and in disbelief, I dialed.

"Seymour, it's Cameron Hughes returning your call."

"Ah, Cameron. My executive and I were recently at a game in Toronto. We loved what we saw. Can you come to Buffalo and help us out while the arena fixes the board?"

Let's rewind a bit.

Earlier that week, *this* happened:

"Nov 17th, 1996. The $4 million scoreboard at Buffalo's new Marine Midland Arena crashed onto the ice Saturday, just hours before the scheduled National Hockey League game between the Buffalo Sabres and Boston Bruins. The game was postponed."

Scoreboard Smashes Onto Ice at New Sabres Arena: None Hurt, Chicago Tribune, 17 Nov. 1996

Of course, I instantly accepted. Peter and I hopped into his car and set out on the short drive to Buffalo, picking up my cousin Taylor in Niagara Falls along the way. Next thing I knew, we were kicking back in the owner's suite.

This was clearly a code-red, "Ghostbusters" type of situation: cheer was desperately needed in Buffalo. The first game in a new city is always a blast, but the vibe here was completely dead. It took a bit longer to spread energy without the jumbotron to focus the attention of the crowd of 18,000. So I worked the room the old-fashioned way – I hoofed it to pretty much *every section* that night. This was in the pre-Fit Bit era, but I guarantee you if I had one that night, it would have shorted out. Taylor and Peter were eight beers deep in the suite, but I was on a mission to deliver cheer. The fans absolutely loved it.

After the game, Team President Larry Quinn invited me to perform at an NCAA tournament, so I stayed in Buffalo for the weekend. On Sunday night, they sent me home in a Town Car. I can remember riding back across the bridge to Canada with the biggest sense of joy and accomplishment. It was the momentum I needed, and dang, did they have good wings in Buffalo!

A few days later, the Sabres called again. The scoreboard repairs were going to take another few months, so they wanted to keep the party going. As my profile was increasing with the sports gigs, people started to see the value in having me do talks for their events, companies and schools. I'd been asked by Eagle University in Austin, Texas, to present motivational speeches and facilitate goal-setting workshops for their weeklong youth leadership retreat. They wanted to hear my story since I'd found (some) success pursuing a somewhat unconventional path. Of course, I accepted – guilt-free now that I actually had my diploma!

I didn't know it at the time, but that one simple "yes" would change my life forever. And – I can't make this up, folks – Miss USA, Miss Texas, and Misses North and South Carolina would all be there.

The event was eye-opening for me. From Miss USA Ali Landry to various business leaders, I met many interesting and successful people, but none would impact my life more than Dr. Terry Rigdon, a dentist from Tulsa, Oklahoma.

I know what you're thinking: a *dentist*? Really? How could he, a dentist, impact *you*, a rabid dancer? By removing teeth I broke from dancing too hard? Not quite.

Dr. Rigdon was intrigued by my story and keen to lend a helping hand.

"There's this guy in Tulsa who's a great act named Myron Noodleman. He's represented by a guy named Jon. You should meet Jon," he said with an air of certainty. "You two would hit it off."

I was taken aback. I had no idea there were dedicated agents out there representing "acts" like me – I'd never even considered myself an "act." I was just a kid from Ottawa who wanted to put smiles on peoples' faces, wherever the road took me. And now a dentist from Tulsa (hey, another smile guy!) was suddenly opening my mind to a whole new world of business and branding opportunities that I needed to explore.

"That would be incredible," I said. "I appreciate you thinking of me."

He scribbled something onto a piece of paper and handed it to me. Alongside a phone number, he'd written: "*Jon Terry, SRO Agency.*"

"Give him a call sometime." And just as quickly as he entered my life, the dentist of destiny was gone.

I glanced down at the paper.

What the heck is "SRO Agency"?

When I meet people, I like to help them if I can. Some would say "Why bother? You don't need to do that!" But think about all the benefits, all the enjoyment we get, out of connecting with other people. Whether it's doing the wave with 50,000 other like-minded souls, or lending a helping hand to a stranger in need, it just makes us feel *good*. If Terry didn't take the time or have that thought, who knows what would have happened to me? You might just think of a fleeting kindness as "no big deal," but you *never know* the lasting impact it might have.

Clockwise from top: George, myself, Myron, and Jon Terry of SRO Agency at the Baseball Winter meetings in 1998 in New Orleans.

Myron Noodleman, one of the clown princes of baseball- and how I met my first agent
– Jon Terry!

Krazy George – the World's Sexiest Cheerleader.

15

STANDING ROOM ONLY

*"I've never protected my voice from
sssscccreeeeaaammming in 30 years!"*

Krazy George

F ounded in 1979 by Jon Terry, The Standing Room Only (SRO) Agency began
as a concert promotion and production company, eventually evolving into a
multipurpose entertainment company. From corporate events to galas to fashion
shows, they did it all. Where I would supposedly fit in was the company's Sports
& Variety division. SRO represented a variety of "novelty" acts that, like mine,
provided in-game entertainment for major and minor league sports teams.
These artists, past and present, are folks like me, who live to fire up stadiums
and arenas. Among Jon's clients have been such trailblazers and innovators as:

Krazy George Henderson – The legend who wore tiny jean shorts, banged
a drum, and yelled like a madman at sporting events. He's credited with being
the first person to get the wave going. I love Krazy! His act was big in the
NFL, college football, and minor league hockey. The NFL even came up with a
short-lived penalty for home teams who made too much noise during George's
thunderous stint with the NFL Houston Oilers. Terry Bradshaw of Pittsburgh
became visibly rattled during a game at the Astrodome, sparking that ill-fated
decision.

Morganna the Kissing Bandit – The Dolly Parton of trespassers would run
onto the field at big sporting events and kiss the star players. She's well-known
for interrupting some big games with her big heart – and got paid big bucks to
do it! She smooched lots of baseball stars in the 1970s and '80s, among them Pete
Rose, George Brett, Cal Ripken, Jr. and Nolan Ryan, and even gave pecks to the
likes of Kareem Abdul Jabbar, the San Diego Chicken (!), and of course Jon Terry.

Myron Noodleman – He was described as the Jerry-Lewis-meets-Pee-Wee-
Herman of in-game entertainment. Myron made a great living on the minor
league baseball circuit and became known as the Fifth Clown Prince of Baseball

Mad Chad – The madman who juggled running chainsaws and other wild
stuff; the Evel Knievel of juggling.

There were clearly some colorful characters in this mix. I wasn't sure if I
should be flattered or offended that Dr. Rigdon thought I'd fit in with them! I
didn't call Jon right away. I was feeling nervous about putting myself out there,

and I wanted to gain some more momentum to lead me into the call and make it impossible for him to say no.

FREE BOOS IN NEW YORK

After my stint at Eagle U. wrapped up, I flew out to New York City for a guys' weekend with some of my old pals from Ottawa. New York, as it happened, held a special place in my heart. Whenever I began plotting the future of my career, I would make lists of my "dream scenarios." One that topped the list every time was performing at the world's most famous arena, Madison Square Garden.

The boys wanted to hit a Rangers' game, which doubled as my opportunity to make a dream come true – and see if NYC could handle The Dancing Guy. I bought a few random tees from a local souvenir shop and was ready to make my "unofficial" official debut at the Garden.

I waited for a good time in the second period to go for it. Like a good surfer, you need to *sense* that wave swelling before you can even see it. I got up at just the right moment, shredded the song in full-on "madman mode," and the New York crowd quickly came with me. I had them. The video board was on me, and the place got even louder. The roof flew off when I tossed those tees.

I sat back down, and my pals and I had a good laugh.

"Okay," my good friend Karim said, "just chill the rest of the game! Enjoy it!"

No such promises were made.

During the last timeout in an exciting game, they played a big dance song – "Strike It Up" by Black Box. I couldn't resist. I got up again, and the camera came to me. The crowd exploded.

And then they cut to a bald guy up in the 300 section.

Wait, whaaa?

Little did I know, but Rangers season-ticket holder Larry Goodman was a regular on "Garden Vision," getting jiggy in the aisles in the third period. "Strike It Up" was his cue to go nuts. Dancing Larry started going off, and his loyal following of 18,000 strong went *wild*.

Then the jumbotron cut back to me.

BOOOOOOOOOOOOOOOOOOOOOOOOOOOOOOOOOO!

Startled, I glanced around. Yep, officially my first time being booed. Not exactly the momentum I was looking for, but we had a good laugh. At the time, I couldn't understand why they'd boo me. Who was this other guy? Why didn't they like me? But after I learned about Dancing Larry, I understood. I was in Larry's house now. Know your audience.

The following week, I returned to Buffalo, and the team caught fire. During our 10-game run together, the Sabres *won all 10*, providing a much-needed boost for a crowd recovering from the jumbotron nightmare.

Mission "Restore Morale" complete, I started my trip back to Toronto with no real idea of what was coming next. I knew I needed help, that much was evident.

I pulled over to the side of the New York interstate and got out my brick-sized cell phone. I made the call.

"Hi, Jon? It's Cameron Hughes," I said. "Terry Rigdon referred me to you."

"Cameron! I've been waiting for your call!" he said with his wicked Oklahoma accent. "Caught you on ESPN the other night doing your schtick for the Sabres. Great stuff."

For a half hour, we had a fascinating and in-depth conversation about the business. I had no idea it really *was* a business! Until recently, I hadn't even known all these acts existed, nor could I believe what they were making per event. Jon felt there was a void in the "superfan" space. A lot of teams liked hiring the legend Krazy George, but more and more they wanted someone like him, but different. And let's face it, there were a lot of teams that needed some extra fun.

"I'd like to meet with you in Tulsa," he said. "If it all goes well, I want to represent you."

I had no idea what being represented meant, but for a guy just trying to figure out the wild, wild world of arena entertainment on his own, this seemed like a wise step.

"Okay," I told him. "Let's do it."

"Having been someone that had worked with Krazy George, I was, at that time, unaware that there were any other professional cheerleaders in existence. I saw that Cameron Hughes brought his own unique ways to get the audience's attention and that he had concocted a way that would work every time. I was in from the start."

Jon Terry, President, SRO Productions

I flew out to Tulsa and spotted Jon from afar. Yeah, that was my guy for sure. Jon had a big beard and an even bigger heart. He also had the gift of gab and a cool business that was going to help this naïve Canadian kid make a go of it. We instantly hit it off, and I knew it was the right move for me. Even though I'd be giving up 20 percent of my fees, I felt it would be well worth it in the long run.

He would get me gigs I wouldn't have gotten on my own. He would negotiate my rates, freeing me to just perform, and keep my relationship with the teams more pure. I had to let go and trust someone who had a vision for me.

This was the start of my life on the road. A life filled with long flights and hotels and motels in the middle of nowhere. Of tracking time in miles, not hours. Tracking benchmarks by team, not by date.

Jon booked me in Washington State, North Carolina, Florida, Colorado, and everywhere in between. He even took me to the baseball winter meetings in New Orleans to meet different buyers and had me do some games to see if teams were keen to hire me. Suddenly, that "$1,000 per game" request I had made to the Ottawa rollerblade hockey team wasn't such a laughable idea. I was now making $1,250 minimum per event, plus travel. I couldn't believe it.

I still remember the first check I got, realizing with that check alone I could pay for rent and food over the next few months. Steady income was not something I had ever been accustomed to. Not that I was suddenly rich – but this shift from part-time daydreamer to full-time, bookable "client" was truly life changing. I could do what I loved – connecting with people – and *make an honest living doing it*? It was a big, joyful, grown-up step forward for me.

SERIOUS PRIDE

I was in Virginia to perform for the Richmond Braves, the Atlanta Braves' Triple-A team. Between innings, a runner from the team found me and handed me a note. *Hmm, had yet another cutie noticed me?*

Nope, it was from one of the players.

"It's Curtis Pride. Come see me after the game and we'll get dinner."

I couldn't believe it! Curtis, who I'd met way back in my Lenny the Lynx days in Ottawa, was a great guy and one of the most celebrated deaf athletes in history. I didn't know he was on the team, so it was such a pleasant surprise. A few hours later, I was sitting across from him, reminiscing about old times in Canada's capital. Curtis was born deaf from rubella, but he didn't let that stop him. He was an outfielder who played parts of 11 seasons in the major leagues, socking 20 home runs. He never heard the fans cheer for his heroics, but as he famously put it: "I could feel them."

I remember being blown away by him back when we first met in my Ottawa days. Over dinner, he gave me some keen insights into ways to get the crowd going more. I had so much respect for him and listened intently.

His advice? "Cam, look at the fans more when you want them to get up – and once you have their attention, take your time."

Wise words from a wise man.

The thoughtfulness in his ideas was powerful, opening up my mind to a whole new approach on ways to interact with fans. What was most exciting to me, though, was this insane new energy I felt. The energy came from the unknown of meeting random people, from airplane passengers to hospitality people to fans – it was like winning the lottery for me. *I loved people!* They were the source of my momentum. I was suddenly creating sacred connections with people from all over the world, and it was addictive. I realized that this was meant to be my life. It was a high worth chasing, no matter where. Not a job, it was a purpose with a capital P. Purpose. Because doing what I loved equated to putting smiles on peoples' faces and making them feel a sense of community and belonging.

There was nothing in my life more important than that. It's what I was born to do.

YOU HAVE A COLLECT CALL FROM CAMERON

My life on the road was the start of a meaningful new tradition with my father. On my way to performing in a new city, I'd call Dad for a life update, sharing where I was, how I was, and what game I was off to.

"Hey Dad, I'm on my way to Red Deer, Alberta, for a Rebels game," I said. "Never been out there before. Should be fun."

The next day, he'd call to tell me the score of the game, ask how it was, and follow up with a tidbit about the city I was in.

"Four to one – you must've been their good luck charm!" he said. "The Sutter Brothers started their careers in Red Deer, you know. All six brothers played in the NHL at one point. Remarkable, Cam."

They started off as collect calls from payphones, eventually evolving into more regular contact as communication became more reliable. The catch-up would sometimes last two minutes, and other times 20. It became our special ritual. I felt recharged after each call, comforted by the structure it added to my often unpredictable life. While Dad may not have always been as vocal about me chasing my unusual career, our chats made me feel like he finally understood me. After all, wasn't I living out his fantasy in the Russian fur coat? Except instead of a fur coat, I wore a dozen sweaty t-shirts.

"My favorite element by far was watching you quietly sit down in the crowd and wait for the right time to stand up and turn on the entire section you were sitting in, and then move to another unsuspecting section. Fans were mesmerized by where you'd be next!"

Thom Hager, Team President, Lake Charles Ice Pirates

16

A WHOLE LOT CAN HAPPEN OUT OF THE BLUE

"The key to spontaneous wit is an unburdened mind."

Darwin Ortiz

Between gigs, I was always itching to do more. Back at my home base in Toronto, I wanted to work the room a bit harder and see if I could get some other media opportunities. I didn't have a full plan, I just wanted to entertain *more* people and make *more* people laugh.

One night, at a cocktail event featuring some of the top media professionals in the city, I sparked up a conversation with an art director from Ammirati Puris Lintas, one of the hottest ad agencies in Toronto. Her name was Elspeth Lynn, and she was dating a friend of mine at the time, so we already had a connection. Fascinated by the line of work I was in, she gave me her card and told me to get in touch.

Over the next few weeks, I called Elspeth several times to see if she'd be open to grabbing a coffee, but she'd never answer. For fun, I left a couple of absurd voicemails on her machine in hopes that she'd get a kick out of them.

"Hey, Elspeth, I'm on your porch with a huge box of popsicles and they're melting! I need to get in fast!"

"Elspeth! What do I and the door leading into my backyard have in common? They've both been screened!"

A few weeks later, I was surprised to discover a voicemail of my own: It was from none other than Elspeth and her creative partner, Lorraine. They thought I'd be perfect to audition for a radio campaign they were working on, sponsored by Labatt Blue. They were looking for someone to prank call random people and try to elicit hilarious, spontaneous interactions. I can't make this up! I guess my off-the-cuff calls to Elspeth had left quite an impression. When I told my dad about the opportunity, he was convinced I'd get the gig based on my childhood experience prank-calling people with my pals Chris and Ian.

My "audition" was set for Monday. *Just be yourself, be yourself, be yourself.* That's what they want.

When I arrived at the studio, I was greeted by the director of the spots, Terry O'Reilly. He handed me a phone book and asked me to ad-lib and have a good time. After a few calls – and more than a few laughs – we called it a day.

"Cam called a duct-cleaning service to ask what they charged while ducks quacked noisily in the background. Cam called a lawyer to say he slipped on his own stairs and wanted to know if he could sue himself. Cam called a pharmacy in a panic to say the Viagra he'd taken hadn't worn off after four hours and he had to go to work. Cam called a locksmith to say he was chained to his bed and couldn't reach the key. Cam called a comedy club to audition as the "Knock Knock King" – and proceeded to tell them the worst knock-knock jokes known to man. You get the idea. Fearless."

Terry O'Reilly, Under the Influence Podcast Host, Author, Speaker

---

Before I knew it, they hired me to do more. Then a few more, which eventually became three years of having the time of my life – and for the first time, I had my own office! They were winning international awards, and it was starting to lead to other events and a bigger profile – all from a crank call.

"The 'Out of the Blue' campaign eventually became one of the most popular and awarded radio campaigns in the country. We did dozens of commercials in the campaign, and Cam made it all work. A herculean effort. But Cam was built for it. Even though I directed over 500 commercials a year, that campaign remains one of the most memorable experiences I ever had."

Terry O'Reilly

I now had multiple revenue streams for the first time in my life. But I needed to keep working my connections in the sports world. Jon felt it would be smart if I flew to Nashville to attend another round of baseball winter meetings and see what we could make stick. This is when you sit at a booth and sell your dance moves. Since no brochure could possibly convey the magic of my spontaneous choreography, I had to do a few live demonstrations. Needless to say, I worked that room like I would a stadium. Build rapport, listen, ask what your audience wants, and then share your mission and always get the business cards.

YOU BROKE MY HEART

As I made my way through the airport terminal – trusty Stetson and all – a well-dressed gentleman in his 40s moved toward me.

"Excuse me, but can I tell you a story?" he said.

"Uh." Strange as this was, I was intrigued. "Sure?"

The man breathed a deep sigh. "You broke my heart."

Now I was *really* intrigued.

I frowned. "Did I?"

The man in question was Bruce C. Phillips. Bruce went on to tell me how he was a Toronto Maple Leafs' season-ticket holder and that he'd loved seeing me perform at the games.

"No one other than Doug Gilmour himself could rally a crowd like you," Bruce said with a smile. "My family and I *loved* being at the games you performed at. Then one night it all changed."

A few months earlier, Bruce took a trip down to Montréal to see the archrival Canadiens play his beloved Maple Leafs, and who do you think he saw there?

Me.

Decked out in full Canadiens gear, cheering on the enemy.

Awkward.

Bruce grew visibly upset. "I was in *disbelief*. I thought you were an actual Maple Leafs superfan. You broke my heart."

Breaking the heart of a 44-year-old man was never something I thought I'd do in life.

"Sorry," I said. "Cheering for more than one team was the only way I could make a living out of this."

Bruce waved off my apology with a smile. "Oh, I figured," he said good-naturedly. I asked where he was heading. He said he was taking his daughter on a trip to New York City to celebrate her 13th birthday.

This interaction struck a chord with me. Fans are passionate about their teams, and I had to respect that. I couldn't be performing for one NHL team one night and another the next night against the same team, could I? How to find that balance? It was a strange new tightrope I was walking, and the rules were hard to understand because it was brand new and there was no rulebook.

When I arrived at my gate later, I saw Bruce sitting with his wife, Sandy, and daughter. *What can I do to make his daughter's birthday feel special?* Suddenly inspired, I trotted over to the gift shop and bought 13 boxes of Smarties and a *Seventeen* magazine, on which I scribbled "Happy B-day!" I threw everything in

The Phillips Family- Bruce, Brigitte, Ally, Baby Willa, Sandy, Hayden and Urs – missing Adam- find him in another pic soon! Bruce has told me his heart has been repaired. Grateful they told me that story.

Terry O'Reilly, the Adman – Host of "Under the Influence" author, speaker, and friend!

a plastic bag and walked up to the birthday girl with a big smile and handed it to her.

I thought that would be the end of that, but guess who my seat neighbors on the plane were? We had such a good time chatting that we didn't want to get off the plane. We exchanged phone numbers and hugs as we exited the airport, and I had a feeling this wouldn't be the last time I'd see them.

A few months later, the entire family came to watch me perform at a game. Next thing I know, the Phillips kids are on my shoulders. A close friendship was forming. We started to hang a lot more often at events, summering at their cottage, and shared many special moments. Ally was set to attend university when I suggested she try out my alma mater, Bishop's University. She got in. On her first day there, I gave a guest lecture to first-year students, with Bruce and Sandy in the front row. Ally's brothers, Adam and Hayden, would soon join in on the Purple Spirit, too.

In her second year, Ally met her boyfriend, and in 2011, I am happy to report I was the MC at their wedding in Toronto. And yes, you can bet that when Ally turned 30, she got 30 boxes of Smarties! I don't think Bruce's heart is broken anymore. You never know what a simple hello can lead to.

Steve Nash rolls into town and thinks he owns the place

SHINAN GOVANI'S

THE DAILY DISH

So why exactly was **Steve Nash** (right) banned from a slew of Toronto bars and restaurants last week? 'Cause the guy was on Rollerblades, that's why. And rules are rules, even if you're a basketball virtuoso and a made-to-order Canadian Olympic hero. The Dallas Mavericks star spent much of Thursday on his set of wee wheels, hanging around SkyDome. He was with his pal **Cameron Hughs**, a.k.a. Super Fan, that tornado-like rooter spotted at various sports events who even has his very own show on the Comedy Network starting next month. So, anyways, when Steve and Cam attempted to graze at various eateries in the area,

they were sent packing. Fortunately, I hear, **Wayne Gretzky** came to the rescue. Well, at least his restaurant did. The eatery owned by the Great One allowed the two blade runners in. P.S. Although there's much talk about Steve's very special relationship with beautiful **Elizabeth Hurley**, the Victoria-bred hoopster insists they're just friends. His agent, though, is clearly more optimistic. He had this to say to *Sports Illustrated* about Nash's recent adventures with Hurley in Dallas: "They ended up hanging out, and there was some chemistry. The relationship is authentic." Might this be what they call playing one-on-one? ▪ Bits and

Bites: *Survivor's* **Michael Skupin** is eyeing a run for the U.S. Senate. "I'm giving it a lot of thought," confirmed the pig killer at a Republican fundraiser in Michigan last week ... *Fortune* magazine reveals that **Bill Gates** just got his first pair of bifocals ... **Dolly Parton** says she wakes at 3 a.m. most mornings. "I was born at three in the morning," she tells Britain's *Sunday Times*, "so my mother says she thinks that's why." *Continued on next page.*

National Post – Sarcasm alert. You never know what will happen when Steve rolls through town!

Flapjack and myself on the set of Game Face.

Ticket from For the Love of Breasts events.

Andrew Bottecchia, "The Designer Guys" Steven Sabados and Chris Hyndman celebrating at a For the Love of Breasts event.

for the love of breasts

94

17

PUT YOUR GAME FACE ON

"Cameron was a great host because he wasn't trying to be slick.
We just hung out like two Canucks would!"

Steve Nash, NBA All-Star, first guest on Game Face

During the "Out of the Blue" campaign, I brought in a friend from Ottawa, Matt Hopkins, to help punch up the creative. After I saw the killer flair this sketch-comedy actor and writer added to the Labatt campaign, along with how well we clicked in the writers' room, we decided to create and pitch our own project.

Co-starring myself and Matt, a.k.a. Flapjack, *Game Face* would be a sports comedy television show featuring off-the-cuff interviews with famous sports personalities, as well as sports-inspired sketches. I knew the producer of the new hit series *The Tom Green Show*, so I thought I'd get in touch. *Why not?* But why do it the "normal" way?

I sent a pizza to her hotel room door, replacing two of the slices with a VHS copy of my demo reel and my phone number. She called me the next morning, eager to hear our pitch. She was in (and I nailed the pizza choice). With her help, we shot a pilot for the show and shopped it around to a few networks in Toronto.

Within weeks, we got the news: *Game Face* had sold to The Comedy Network for a 13-episode order. I suddenly had my own national television show! We had a lot to figure out in a short period of time.

Bring it on.

Our first guest on the show was future NBA Hall of Famer Steve Nash, a fellow Canadian. At the time, he was a fast-rising star with the Dallas Mavericks. My friend Chris from university had grown up with Steve and was kind enough to ask if he'd do an interview with us.

Flapjack and I flew out to Dallas for the interview, along with the sound guy. Unfortunately, our director never made it – he missed his flight. It was up to the three of us to get this interview shot. Very first show, and we're playing musical chairs! Flapjack became the boom operator, our sound guy was now the director, and Steve Nash was now confused as to why he'd said yes.

During the interview, I presented Steve with a Canadian care package, which included maple syrup, a Canadian flag, and a six-pack of Kokanee beer. Just as we were cracking one of the cans open, Mavericks owner Mark Cuban wandered into the room.

"What is going on here?" he inquired, eyebrows raised.

"Just shooting a Canadian TV show with the one and only Canuck," I replied.

After a moment of understandable confusion, Mark laughed. "I love Canada! Steve's our guy, and clearly has the best bedhead of any NBA player!"

And then it got even better – we decided to take the conversation and camera to the courts where I found myself shooting hoops with Steve Nash and Mark Cuban. Maybe not making the basketball team wasn't so bad after all.

Game Face was off and running! Flapjack and I toured across North America, interviewing the likes of Michael Andretti, Bret "The Hitman" Hart, Jennifer Botterill (on a fake *Blind Date*), squash genius Jonathon Power and Vince Carter, among others. We also "interviewed" Mark Stepnoski and Daryl "Moose" Johnston from the Dallas Cowboys, "Cribs"-style – a.k.a. we drank dozens of beers together.

Once, in my "regular" job, I was hired by the Calgary Flames to get the crowd going – so I brought Flapjack along to join in on the fun and get some juicy footage for the show. The fans knew who I was but had no idea who Flapjack was. We were sitting next to each other in the stands when the "Kiss Cam" cut to us on the jumbotron. Flapjack and I stared deeply into each other's eyes, which really got the crowd roaring. Then we fake kissed and rolled into the aisles.

A few months after we taped *Game Face* together, Steve Nash came to Toronto. We ended up going rollerblading (it was very cool back then!) down by the SkyDome and stopped for cold beers on any patio we could find. Unfortunately, not all the bar owners were as receptive to us wearing rollerblades indoors as we'd hoped, kicking us out at pretty much every spot we hit, except Wayne Gretzky's restaurant! The next day, our shenanigans were even written up in the *National Post*. By the way, it's a lot of fun to bar-hop on blades!

Any press is good press, right?

FOR THE LOVE OF BREASTS

After we hung up our rollerblades, I had a committee meeting to attend for my breast cancer charity in honor of my mother – "For the Love of Breasts." Steve was kind enough to run in and say hi to the gang, then we got down to business. I was living my mom's life's mission by connecting, bringing people together and celebrating life, for a great cause. I knew I had to do something that would represent my mom and her legacy.

Two months later, I woke up in a fog, threw on some old sneakers, and slowly made my way to the theatre where the inaugural fundraising event had been held the night before. Pink balloons littered the floor, the marquee was emblazoned with "FTLOB", and through the cracked side door smells of alcohol poured out – it had been one hell of a night.

As I sat there with my friend Michael Lende, the theatre manager, reminiscing about the past evening, I knew my mom would be proud. That first event sold out and was a huge hit, bringing together a community of like-minded people for a worthy cause. We would go on to do the event for eight years in both Toronto and Ottawa. And, yes, you had to wear pink to get in! Special thanks to my long time friend Michael Landsberg for the push and support!

DESIGNER GUYS

Around this time, my new girlfriend, a fashion publicist, was keen on making sure I was even sexier – was that even *possible*? Okay, let's face it, I needed some help, and not just in the style game. She was a great influence in me getting my home and life more organized. I needed a push. *Guys? Anyone?*

I was finally making enough money to move out of the apartment I shared with Peter and into a place of my own. I found this insane 1,800-square-foot loft – the ultimate bachelor pad – just outside of downtown Toronto. It could double as a production space for the show.

You've heard of the "Designer Guys," a.k.a., Steven and Chris, right? These handsome studs had a design show where they made over living spaces that needed a sexy splash. My girlfriend suggested I meet with them to get my place a much-needed makeover. We immediately hit it off; I was so different from their usual guests – I was male, in my 30s, deeply into sports, and in need of help!

I'll never forget walking into my revamped place for the "big reveal": the guys were watching sports highlights shows, drinking beers, and wearing my sports jerseys! And the place? It now had a mini hoops court that they'd perfected after a visit to the Raptors' practice court, a small pool table, a spiral staircase, and a bunch of cool add-ons. I'm positive more people saw that episode than all of *Game Face*, combined.

(Author's note: The world sadly lost Chris in 2015. What a life force.)

18

FASTER, HIGHER, STRONGER CHEERS

"The most important thing in the Olympic Games
is not winning but taking part; the essential thing in
life is not conquering but fighting well."

Pierre de Coubertin, father of the modern Olympic Games

While I was doing *Game Face* and developing other TV ideas, Jon kept pushing me to focus on landing more sports gigs. Looking for some more excitement, I decided to set my sights on something with a bigger stage than a lot of the fun minor league games I was doing. I was targeting the 2002 Winter Olympic Games in Salt Lake City!

My friend Peter was involved with producing the in-game entertainment for the Olympics. He'd been a major supporter since the early days of my career when he brought me in to do Calgary Flames games. (Did I mention how much I love "Harvey the Hound," the Flames' mascot!) Peter took a chance on me back when not many would. He knew what I was capable of bringing to the games, so we had a great chat about coming to Salt Lake and what it would look like.

"If you show up, I can get you a pass," Peter said. "We can't pay you, though."

So, what did I do?

I showed up! It was the Olympics!

My relationship with Labatt was strong, so I approached them about sponsoring some fun segments for their new website, Beer.com, which could also air on season two of *Game Face*. In return, we'd shoot some videos for them, get a fee and a couple cases of Blue.

I reached out to my pal Brian, a downhill ski champion for Canada, and he agreed to be my co-host.

My pals and I flew into Las Vegas, rented an RV, and made a road trip to Salt Lake City. A word of advice: never start a road trip in Vegas. Chevy Chase meets Johnny Knoxville, anyone? We decked the RV out in Team Canada flags and set ourselves up at a local RV park. It was so glam!

I had a pass to nearly all the big hockey games and did what I was meant to do – get the fans fired up. The international flare of the Olympic Games was intoxicating. I was meeting fans from around the world, Roots Clothing gave me free merchandise to throw out and wear, and I ended up doing fun interviews with media outlets from around the globe. I even skied (okay, snow-plowed) with Brian, one of the best in the world, and Canadian golfer Mike Weir; two months later he won the Masters – you tell me if that's a coincidence! We shot a lot of fun segments with fans and athletes in the amazing social scene. I mean, it's not often you're at a small club with an Olympic athlete you've just met on your shoulders (can't remember her name!) watching an impromptu Barenaked Ladies performance.

After performing at half a dozen games, shooting a whack of videos, and being Mr. Spirit wherever I could, I was spent. (Yes, I do get tired sometimes.) But I had a huge weekend ahead: on Saturday night, a Tragically Hip concert, and on Sunday, a performance at the Canada-USA hockey game for all the golden glory. This would be a pinnacle for my early career of cheer.

My excitement overshadowed my exhaustion.

And then I got a call from Peter.

"Hey, dude…" he said tentatively. "Sorry to be the bearer of bad news…"

"Out with it, Peter! You're killin' me here!"

These days, I was talking a mile a minute. My thoughts were an unending freight train of enthusiasm.

"I just wanted to let you know that the Salt Lake Organizing Committee doesn't… well, doesn't want me to give you a pass to the Finals."

"Oh," I said, slumping in my chair. "Why?"

"They think you're too pro-Canada."

They *what?!* Why didn't people understand? I wasn't all in for one team or one country; I was there to elevate the fan experience, no matter which side their team played on.

Luckily, the Olympic spirit helped soften the blow. Some friends working with Games sponsor Coca-Cola kindly asked if Flapjack and I would be interested in spending the final weekend at the hotel. Clearly, they felt sorry for us for the way we looked after spending 14 days in an RV. They had an extra room available, so we could just park our RV and chill for the weekend. A hot shower and two orders of room service later, things were starting to look up again.

The next morning, I was in the hotel lobby and noticed a striking blonde leaving the spa. After a double take, I realized it was Janet Gretzky, the actress otherwise known as the Great One's beautiful wife. Wayne was the GM of Team Canada, trying to lead the team to its first gold in 50 years.

Janet recognized *me*. I was in shock.

"I'll see you at the game tomorrow!" she enthused.

My face dropped. "Actually, I just got a call from the organizing committee. Turns out I'm not allowed to be there. They felt I was too pro-Canada."

"That's bullshit!" she said, echoing my sentiments. "I'll talk to Wayne about it. Meet us in the lobby at 10:30 tomorrow and we'll look after you. We need you there!"

How could I refuse? 24 hours later, I rolled into the lobby, my Team Canada gear in tow – mini-Canadian flags, maple leaf temporary tattoos, and Roots tees. Janet, her children, and a group of her friends filed through the lobby and into a 20-seat Sprinter van parked outside the hotel. Janet gestured at me.

"Get in!" she motioned. Next thing I knew, I was on the way to the game, sticking tattoos onto the Gretzky kids, singing Hip songs, and belting "O Canada" at the top of my lungs. When we arrived at the arena, Janet handed me a ticket – for a platinum seat. "Have a blast, and go Canada!" she said, sporting a huge smile.

Team Canada went on to win the game 5–2 and take home the gold. I was able to fire up the fans and cheer on the team – all thanks to having a few friends, both new and old, in high places who believed in me.

I sent Janet a thank you note to show her my deep appreciation. What a rockstar move, by such a wonderful human. Years later, I shared the story with her son, Ty. He loved it.

TIMEOUT

The first time I met Janet was after the 1997 NHL All-Star Game in San Jose. She saw me sitting in the lobby of my hotel looking pretty rough, and called over the hotel manager, then later 911. The diagnosis? Dehydrated from my performance! Thanks, Janet!

The Gold Medal ticket – Canada vs USA – Thanks 99 and Janet!

Aaron Evans from the RV in Salt Lake – You never know who may need a ride in your camper to a hockey game with a bottle of Pucker!

Brian Stemmle, World Champion Skier, Roger Hardy Bishop's University, and lifelong pal.

19

SHOULD I STAY OR SHOULD I GO?

*"Take a chance. It's the best way to test yourself.
Have fun and push boundaries."*

Sir Richard Branson, my favorite entrepreneur, future
Necker Island tennis partner… hello? Richard?

When the insanity of the Olympics was over, I was faced with whether or not to keep *Game Face* going. It was exactly the platform I needed to get more experience hosting on-camera, make new contacts in the sports industry, and build connections with top athletes. But after two seasons, 26 episodes, a lot of chaos, and some great fun, I felt in my gut it was time to move on, but I still wanted to stay focused on my TV and media career. As a result, Jon and I felt it was a good idea to mutually part ways but keep in touch as our careers moved on. Life in Toronto was great – I had a cool loft apartment, an amazing and supportive girlfriend, awesome friends, and was considered by some to be an E or even D-level celebrity. But I could hear that voice inside again, that calling, that there was more I needed to do with my work. I could feel myself wanting to give it another go across the border, where there were more opportunities and more people to connect with. That chapter was unfinished. I couldn't live with the "what if." Something was telling me to "Get Up and Show Up." Move. Make something happen. So, I made one of the most difficult decisions I'd ever had to make on April 9th, 2003.

It was time to go.

THE DAY MIKE KENSIT BELIEVED IN ME IN NEW WAYS

I had met Mike Kensit when I was paired up with him at a charity golf tournament. Mike ran a GM dealership in Newmarket, Ontario, a small town just north of Toronto. A beauty of a human being, he loved connecting with and helping others. Over the years, he evolved into my own personal cheerleader. One of the loudest.

Back when Flapjack and I were making *Game Face*, we needed a way to get around town for our shoots. Mike and his dealership looked after us for both seasons, with a souped-up minivan to cruise around in, for free! That is, until I had to pay off $1,238 in parking tickets to be registered!

When I decided to hit Los Angeles again, I called Mike to fill him in on my plans. "I'm going to give it another shot," I said, bursting with excitement. "I'm going to LA. This time, I have a plan. I'm prepared."

Or so I kept telling myself. Silence stretched over the phone line. "Get here as soon as possible," Mike finally said. "And have someone drop you off. I've got something for you." I arrived at the dealership later that day to find Mike with a wicked grin on his face. "Catch!" he said, hurling something in my direction. It was a set of keys to a Chevy minivan. "All yours. We'll look after the details later." He reached into his pocket, pulled out a wad of cash, and stuffed it into my jacket. One thousand dollars Canadian, to be exact. "Best of luck, Cam." *Tears. Unbelievable!* With an extra grand in my pocket and a brand-new minivan, I set out for the next chapter of my life.

"It's rare to meet someone who mirrors oneself in the relentless pursuit of their dreams – when I met Cameron Hughes I fell in love with his heart, his dreams, and his passion. He was the first person who I felt required a soundtrack for his day-to-day activities!"

Mike Kensit

I was ready to roll, Bono and friends cranked to the max. I'd been toying with the idea of moving to Hollywood for a while, and now it was a reality. It would be one of the greatest road trips of my life. It was a new chapter, setting out in search of the ultimate freedom. For all I knew, it was the greatest mistake I'd ever make: leaving behind my first true love, all my friends and family, and what little success I'd achieved and the name I'd made for myself in Canada. As one friend aptly put it: "Dude, you aren't even famous here, why go to LA now?"

But I had a vision, and nothing could stand in the way of it. To maintain my enthusiasm, I screamed to my favorite tunes in the car most of the way there. Got out at truck stops and danced. High-fived random strangers who stared at me in bewilderment. *Who is this crazy motherf–*

Heading west on this epic adventure was about letting go and moving forward with no regrets. As difficult as it was to say goodbye to Canada and my life there, I knew if I didn't make the leap, then I'd *never* know.

Welcome to Hollywood! What's your dream?

When someone believes in you. Thank you for the wheels and extra cash to head to Hollywood, Mike Kensit.

TIMEOUT

My absolute favorite road trip song of all time is "Hard Road" by the Sam Roberts Band. I start every road trip with this song to get me going. Give it a listen – you'll see why!

20

EVERYONE HAS A DREAM

"The future belongs to those who believe in
the beauty of their dreams."

Eleanor Roosevelt

When I made it to Los Angeles, the first thing I did was hike up to the Hollywood sign. To me, it symbolized that I'd arrived. I hadn't "made it" yet – but I had definitely arrived.

As I stood alone at the top of the Hills overlooking Tinseltown, my new home, I couldn't help but grow teary-eyed by what it took to get there. By what I'd left behind. And by what the future had in store; however uncertain it may be.

I thought of my mom. What would she say to her son now, having taken her advice from all those years ago and *somehow turned it into a profession*? I'm not sure she would say anything, really, but she would shake her head and smile. Reflected in her smile would be a boundless reservoir of love and pride and belief, as I'd seen so many times in my life when she was still here to share it with me.

YOU KNEW, MOM. YOU ALWAYS DID.

The faces of old friends began to fly through my mind's eye. Faces of lost loves and near misses. Lessons learned and unrealized. Failure, and the pain of not knowing who I was or why I was here. All of that flew by and merged with the LA haze, as I realized that this was the end of something. But as with all endings, it signified the beginning of something else.

I was growing up.

You know that saying, 'Witness to history'? We're all witnesses to history – our *own* history. Most times, we're not even aware that it's in the making. Let's just hypothetically say, you meet the love of your life after spraining your wrist at center court of the NBA Finals, and during the meal while you're icing your wrist, she's cracking up at how silly you are; how crazy your job is. By the end of the meal, *she's* holding the ice pack herself, smiling.

And in that smile, you've just discovered the future of your life. One of the most remarkable and meaningful journeys you'll ever embark upon just began with a single smile. From a lovely woman holding an ice pack just like a nurse – your mother's calling. You didn't know it then and you probably won't know it for quite some time, because that's the way this all works. We are witnesses to our own history. It's a beautiful thing.

But sometimes, we *know* it. Can feel it in our bones. That tiny voice in the back of your head? It's not that you're crazy, although if you're anything like me you're crazy passionate about things, but that's different. Sometimes we recognize the moment – it's rare, but it does happen. We're at a crossroads and we make a decision. We pack the car and head west. We say yes to that new opportunity and no to the old situation that was holding us back or even dragging us down. And for a short glimmer of time, we're elevated to a point of quiet euphoria, where we say, "*This* is it. I'm doing it. This is the beginning of the rest of my life."

Sitting there on that mountain and gazing down at the city before me, I knew I was living in one of those remarkable moments. I bore witness to it. Lived it.

Thank you, I said to no one in particular. *I'm ready.*

After some self-reflection, I made the drive to settle into my new place and greet my roommate.

When my pal Marc moved to Boston back in high school, he became good buddies with a whip-smart kid in his grade named Bill Callahan. I'd often run into Bill over the years when I'd visit Marc, but we eventually lost touch when our lives took different directions. After college, Bill moved to LA to pursue his dream of becoming a comedy writer, landing gigs writing and producing on hit series like *Spin City, 8 Simple Rules,* and *Scrubs*. When I made the call to hit LA, I reached out to see if he wanted to catch up over a drink sometime. The timing couldn't have been better. Bill offered me his spare bedroom while I got my feet wet. I mean, it was a futon, but luxury for a guy chasing a dream with a minivan. My swanky *Designer Guys*-ified pad was well in the rearview now.

They say who you surround yourself with is who you become. To me, Bill was an inspiration. A guy living out his dream. Exactly the kind of person I needed to be around. I instantly got a taste of his relentless work ethic and knew there was no time to waste in my own life. My plan was to get hustling right away, focusing on four main things:

- Landing an agent/manager
- Creating, pitching and selling new television shows
- Performing at sporting events whenever possible
- Establishing myself as a TV host

I took a deep breath and dialed the number.

"This is Cameron Hughes calling to set up a meeting with Mr. Lyle," I said to the receptionist on the other end of the line. "I was asked to get in touch with him when I got to LA."

Traveling back and forth from Canada to Los Angeles over the years, I'd met a lot of people in the entertainment industry. My friend Rob said he'd set up a few meetings for me to get my ass out there a bit faster and with more confidence, this being one of them.

David Lyle was the president of entertainment at Fremantle Media, one of the world's largest international TV production companies and distributors. Fremantle was riding high with the success of a little show called *American Idol* but was looking for its next big hit. The plan was to pitch him a reality show idea I'd been developing with my pal Colin and his filmmaker sister, Megan. *Now or Never* was based on the idea that we all have something we've always *really* wanted to do in life. We would find unsuspecting guests and challenge them to do something out of the ordinary, "now or never." For example, you'd be on your way to your anniversary dinner, but Troy Aikman would call you and invite you to a Cowboys game in Dallas and you'd have to decide if you'd do it or not.

After listening to a symphony of keyboard clatters, the verdict was in. "It'll be about six weeks or so before Mr. Lyle can meet with you," she said. I paused, unsure of how to proceed. On the one hand, I didn't want to develop a reputation for being "difficult." But I knew in my gut that I needed to ride my momentum and capitalize on the creative energy Los Angeles sparked within me.

It was now or never.

"I drove 3,128 miles to see him," I said. "Is there anything you can do, please?"

Another long stretch of silence, I thought because she'd finally decided to hang up. Then, more keyboard clicking.

"How's next Thursday at 11?"

Colin, Megan and I strode into David's sprawling office in sunny Santa Monica, our pitch memorized down to a T. He was Australian. Personable. Kind. After exchanging pleasantries, it was time to get down to business. We had 15 minutes to sell this thing.

We took turns sharing the idea. We asked him, "What's something you've always wanted to experience?"

He said, "Skydiving."

"And what if it was on the same day as your wedding anniversary or your kid's graduation? What would you do?"

And so on. As the meeting progressed, I found myself feeling slightly embarrassed. I was a total newbie, and yet here I was pitching one of the biggest guys in the business on an idea. Was it good enough? Would he bite?

"Great that you came in," Mr. Lyle said at the end of it. "We'll be in touch!"

After the meeting, I leaned back against the minivan in the parking lot. Pressing the back of my head to the cool metal, I looked up at the sky and sighed. What was I doing here?

"How do you think it went?" Megan asked, wringing her hands.

"I don't think we got it," I said, defeated. "He thought it was lame."

"Regardless, "Colin said, "let's celebrate that victory."

I turned to him, perplexed. "What victory?"

"Take a minute to acknowledge that you were in the room, that you had the moment, that you made a new contact, and that you got to this point, "Colin said. "Most people don't ever get into that room, Cam. We did. So whether we got the gig or not is insignificant. What matters is we were there."

He was right. A lot of people would have killed to be in that room. Although we later found out we didn't get the show, it certainly was a victory. You don't always get those, so appreciate them when they come.

ENTOURAGE

Okay, so I wasn't going to take over Hollywood without some help. I decided to focus on getting an agent. My "Jon Terry of the entertainment world," so to speak. I spent the afternoon printing out dozens of headshots and submitting them to every agency in town, confident that it was just a matter of time before I'd be working in television. I was a pretty big deal in Canada, after all. (*Sniff sniff, sarcasm...*) One by one, though, the rejection letters started to come in.

"Thank you for your submission, but we've decided to pass at this time."

"Call us in a couple years when you have more experience."

"No."

Why did I leave Toronto again?

Just when defeat was starting to set in, the phone rang. It was from the office of talent manager Michael Sugar.

Before Michael took home the Academy Award for Best Picture for producing the 2015 film *Spotlight*, he was, like me, out there trying to prove himself. I'd been referred to Michael through a mutual friend from Canada, and he happened to be looking for new clients. We met for lunch in Beverly Hills and, after some brief banter, got down to business.

"What is your goal?" Michael asked, eager to learn if a partnership between us would prove fruitful. A lull gripped the conversation as I deliberated. What *was* my goal? From sports to doing commercials to creating shows, I wanted to do it all. But it would all have to take a backseat to my goal *right now* – my big-time Hollywood ambition.

"I really want to host a TV show," I replied, practically salivating at the thought of reliving the glory of my *Game Face* days. But it was tough to read Michael. He had an air of quiet confidence and decisiveness to him that was difficult to decipher. Like he'd already made up his mind before we even sat down to chat. Plus, I knew I sounded like every other Joe Schmoe out there in Hollywood – he'd probably heard the same *spiel* from 10 others just like me that day alone.

But I had a dream. And I was going to keep putting myself out there until I made it happen.

"Okay then," Michael said, my future resting on his next few words. "I'd like to represent you."

With an up-and-coming manager in my corner, I felt like it was my time to shine. I adopted an "everyone needs to meet with me" mentality. I was hot – the next big thing! The crazy Canadian willing to drive across North America in a goddamn minivan! Michael set me up with agency meetings to land a hosting agent.

I got one.

Then more meetings to land a commercial agent.

I got one of those, too.

Could this be real? Things were coming together too well. My goal was to reach more people and I knew this was where that could happen. Like so many "artists," you want to be where you can grow a bigger audience.

Michael then sent me to auditions for hosting roles and also "generals" – casual meetings with executives and producers so they could get a sense of what you could bring to the party. *Um, hello?!* People were looking for a fresh face and being from Canada helped a lot. Michael was opening doors for me all over the city. I was great in the room but having a hard time closing. Like, zero luck. I was close a few times, but everyone was looking for the next Ryan Seacrest. My teeth weren't as white, and my abs were slightly less solid. Or maybe I just wasn't ready for this town.

I was working all my creative juices and contacts, usually over long lunches at the 101 Coffee Shop. I was close on selling two shows I'd created for MTV and BET. I was close on hosting a game show.

They told me I had it. I was that close. *So* close.

But what did that look like?

In the blink of an eye, eight months had gone by – and with it, my savings.

Career-wise, I was at a standstill. None of the auditions and pitch meetings I'd taken were materializing into paid work. Even if they did, my work visa hadn't come through yet, so it was doubtful I'd even be eligible for any given gig.

I had no choice but to ask for help. After explaining my situation to my roomie Bill, he agreed to let me stay a bit longer. A godsend. To give him space, I picked up the occasional house-sitting gig, and would even pet-sit for friends who went out of town. Whatever I could do to get by, I did. I was hustling at a whole new level just to survive. It was "Cam Can Do, Part 2: Hollywood Boogaloo." But the loneliness that comes with being new in a big city was starting to seep in.

IT'S JUST LUNCH

A friend from back home suggested I meet his pal Mike over lunch. Given that the only human interaction I'd had that week involved eight people saying "no" to me, I was eager for some social time. I'd been on plenty of blind dates before, but never a blind "friend" date!

Mike, a professional music supervisor, showed up wearing a wacky outfit complete with a John Deere trucker hat and some silver high-top kicks. I took one look and grinned – we'd get along just fine.

Mike and I decided we'd meet more regularly and play some tennis to keep sane. Noticing I had some half decent racket skills, he invited me to a ping pong tournament the following weekend. Fear gripped me – it felt as if I were being invited to rush a fraternity. But while my pong game was rusty, I couldn't turn down the idea of some fun and community on a Saturday in LA

YOU'RE DOING WHAT TODAY?

Decked out in tearaway pants, a hockey jersey and some outrageous bandanas, I arrived at a bar in Hollywood, closed to the general public for the morning, and forked over the "$20 & case of beer" entry fee. I could tell the guys thought I was slightly unhinged because of my outfit, and I confirmed their suspicions by doing jumping jacks and skipping rope in the corner to get myself warmed up.

Although I finished 15th of 16 in the tourney, I met a ton of interesting guys who invited me back to play in the next one – called "Wimbledon," in honor of one player being from England. We wore all-white and had strawberries and cream with our beers!

The funny thing about these guys was they rarely if ever talked about business. We probably had a rough idea of each other's careers, but it was all just solid pong fun. One day, I hit up a Dodgers game with three of the guys and they asked me what I did for a living.

"Want me to show you?" I said, smiling widely.

Looks of confusion covered their faces.

"Yeah, show us," someone said. It was the only impetus I needed.

I stood up, took a deep breath, and tore my shirt off. Then I proceeded to scream, *"Go Dodgers Go!"*, soon 45,000 fans joined in.

TIMEOUT

My pal Colin and I eventually hosted the Canadian version of the tournament, the Canuck Classic. It had it all. A DJ playing great Canadian tracks from Rush & The Hip, a giant trough of Labatt Blue beer, and a Canadian flag that had once flown high on Ottawa's Parliament Hill. Alanis Morissette – full-on motorcycle outfit and all – presented prizes to the winners, including autographed hockey jerseys, sticks, and pucks.

"Cameron and I played against each other in many backyard Ping Pong tournaments. After his inevitable early exit from competition, he'd always stay around to cheer. At the time, I found it distracting, but now I see that it was a prelude to an incredible career."

Jay Chandrasekhar, Director of Super Troopers

Keeping the sports-socializing trend going, I also started playing beach volleyball in Manhattan Beach. Don't be shocked, I have the perfect beach volleyball body, am I right? Katie, who I grew up with in Ottawa, had married NHL star Glen Murray, who, like many NHLers, made Manhattan Beach his home in the off-season. At their Nova Scotia wedding I was prompted to say a few words to get the party going.

I told the crowd of 250 that "I met Katie in high school." (Pause) "For those of you who play hockey, that's what you do after grade 8!" 238 people roared with laughter – while a table of 12 NHL players stood up and booed me, looking ready to rumble – all in good fun! The Murrays kindly invited me out to play with the gang. They didn't need to ask twice.

A former Los Angeles King, Glen was tight with many current and past players, including Hall of Fame defenseman Rob Blake. Rob hosted a volleyball event at his place on "the Strand" in Manhattan Beach, and I managed to score an invite after showcasing my passable athletic skills at one of Glen's games. I couldn't jump, but I could move fast – I even earned the nickname "Twinkle Toes." Probably had something to do with the fact I couldn't get more than two centimeters off the sand. This just in – I've got no ups!

I was then invited to join the NHL guys at the annual six-man volleyball event in Manhattan Beach. Just your classic Cali beach party! More than 10,000 people hit the sand during that hot, sunny weekend.

The team consisted of me and six NHL players – Blake, Murray, Marty McSorley, Sean O'Donnell, George Parros and Nelson Emerson – all super humble guys I admired. You'll never guess who was the most vocal on the team?! ROB BLAKE! J.K. – it was me. What I lacked in talent, I made up for with spirit. It was epic fun, and a great way to meet a ton of interesting people in the sports and media worlds. I also got to work on my tan and of course take my "Flip Cup" game to new levels.

I mean, c'mon, what else do you do between games?! If there was a "Flip Cup" pro tour, there'd be no stopping me.

CATCH ME IF YOU CAM

Remember that van I drove down to LA in? Well, a few months after I arrived, General Motors dispatched a county sheriff to retrieve it. Apparently, the car was in the country illegally.

I was out of town at the time when they initiated their investigation, so I called Colin and had him hide it for me. A week later, I loaded it onto a truck and shipped it back to Toronto. (Apparently, my great champion Mike, like me, was a bit of a rule-breaker, too! Thanks, Ace!)

Even though my community was starting to grow with the Venice crew of great friends, and high school friends, my financial situation was becoming dire. My main source of sustenance became Dodger Dogs, Kraft Dinner, and whatever leftovers I could scavenge from my host-of-the-week's refrigerator. I was struggling like I never had before.

"I'm done, man," I said to Bill one night over dinner that I was secretly hoping he'd pick up the check for. The strain of Los Angeles was weighing on me like it never had before. "I can't live like this anymore."

I had given LA a fair shot, but it was time to throw in the towel and try to rebuild my career back home. Bill eyed me, probably knowing that what he was about to say could alter the course of my life.

"See that plane?" he said, pointing to an airplane high in the sky flying away from LAX. "I wonder how many people on there are going home because they just couldn't handle it anymore?"

With my first Hollywood manager – Michael Sugar, and agent, Lance Klein, thanks for taking the shot!

Working the room off-court with my volleyball teammates LA Kings General Manager and Hockey Hall of Fame member-Rob Blake and All-Star and Kings Director of Player Development-Glen Murray in Los Angeles.

A few "headshots" from the day-put yourself out there they say!

That hit me hard.

There was no way in hell I was going to be the guy who flew back home only to tell people I couldn't do it – that I just couldn't make it work. There's always a way to make it work. I wanted to make my dad, sister, and friends proud. And Mom. I had to get up every day and cheer myself on with the same enthusiasm she did, no matter how bad shit was.

After that night, I just decided to trust that things would one day be okay again. I stopped worrying about where my next meal would come from, my next set of accommodations, and if and when my visa would be approved. It didn't hurt that Bill said I could stay with him for another month, rent-free, on the condition I walk his dog, Fenway (go Red Sox!). I was lucky to have good friends in my corner in one of the toughest rings in the world.

And then one day, it came in the mail.

My US visa. And with it, a renewed sense of purpose.

Clockwise from top: Megan Raney-Aarons, Nicole Renna, Colin Gray and " MacGyver" on our Daytona 500 shoot- we pitched, we shot, we hustled and always celebrated the wins!

Rooftop action on the set of Planet Fandamonium at the Daytona 500.

Matthew Riley and Justin Fahsbender from the mighty Bakersfield Condors- Team A-List! (File under people who believe in you.)

Jonny and Amanda Greco from Gwinnett, Cleveland & Vegas fun!

21

KNOCK, KNOCK, KNOCK

"When it comes to networking, farmers will always beat hunters."

Ivan Misner

I needed to go back to my bread and butter – working sports gigs to sustain my dream-chasing in Hollywood. I had to push myself to find some income and stop pretending the big deal was always coming. My connections in LA were ready to be hatched. But selling "a guy who dances badly and tosses tees while screaming like a nut" can be a challenge. I needed cash, bad. Maybe I shouldn't have blown it all on a posh loft apartment back in Canada? Or maybe it was the ADHD performer mindset – that I always just assumed there would be another gig.

Over the course of several hours, I pulled up every team website in California to see who I may know. To my surprise, I discovered that a guy I knew from Canada, Greg May, was the Assistant General Manager of the Bakersfield Condors, a minor league hockey team based in the ECHL. We had worked together years earlier when Canadian icon Don Cherry owned the Mississauga Ice Dogs.

Boom. I had my in.

Bakersfield, California, is a town known for oil, natural gas, country music and agriculture – not hockey. But the team's president, a former minor league baseball promoter, knew he had to spend money to market the team. After reaching out to Greg and pitching my idea, the team decided to give me a shot. Being in a rink totally re-energized me. The Bakersfield fans were a battery, and it hotwired my heart.

"We had you in, loved it, and haven't missed a season since. Don't think we'd be nervous. If you were horrible and got booed out of the arena, that would have been entertaining as well!"

Matt Riley, Bakersfield Condors Team President

I started doing more and more games for the Condors. It became a second home of sorts. It helped set me up financially and gave me the confidence I needed to move my career forward. Plus, I was able to leverage a lot from my appearances. I did some ads for the team, which featured me pulling up in a limo and pretending to be an "A-list" personality in Bakersfield. I even had a feature in *Los Angeles Magazine* that shared the Bakersfield story.

Showing up was everything. This fresh exposure was generating buzz and interest in my shtick all over the sports scene. The opportunities started to flow, with minor league teams keen for some crowd-pumping crazy. And the realization hit me: In Hollywood, I was a little fish in a ginormous pond. But in a minor league arena – heck, any arena – I was a killer shark! No, make that a dolphin! You know what I mean. ;)

I would end up performing more for the Condors over the course of my career than any other team (60 games so far!). That's a lot of tees and smiles. It's kind of funny that the Condors were named after a California bird that nearly went extinct in the 1980s before fighting back to flourish. Without the welcoming nest of the Bakersfield Condors, at the Rabobank Arena, I just might have gotten on that next plane, despite Bill's encouragement.

TRUST IT

"Hey Dad, I'm on my way to Gwinnett, Georgia, from Charlotte," went my voicemail.

A few hours later: "That's great, Son. Did you know Charlotte's the largest city in North Carolina? For the longest time I thought it was Raleigh. Have a wonderful time at the game. Be safe. Call you tomorrow."

There's a deep, almost mystical connection between the city and teams of minor league markets, and Gwinnett was no exception. The stands aren't always full in minor league arenas, so I can really get into the fans' space, and the rules and restrictions are far less of a challenge. That night in Georgia, the connection was palpable. I was on fire. Flying over seats, dancing like Travolta, feeding off the love of the crowd.

After the game, as I made my way to the locker room, a small group approached me and asked more about what I did. I had no clue who they were, but that's never mattered. Sure enough, in this group was Head of Entertainment for the NBA's Cleveland Cavaliers, Amanda Smith! Plus her husband, Jonny Greco, who ran the production for QTV, the in-arena entertainment with the Cavs. They were in town to visit family and, being dedicated professionals, decided to check out a game.

"Cameron, we are amazed at what you can do with a crowd," Amanda said.

"We'd love to talk to you about doing a Cavs game in the near future."

I acted cool – *yeah, this happens all the time* – and we exchanged contact info. But the truth? This kind of connection is what keeps me going – reinforces my belief in *always* being open and maintaining a strong work ethic. You never know who's paying attention to what you do, so *always* do it with pride and dedication.

"We didn't know what you were, who you were or how drunk you must've been, but we had to meet you and say thank you for the smiles. It was original, real and fun. When we met you and you were totally sober (and drenched from dancing), we knew we'd love to try this in our world."

Jonny Greco, former Director, QTV, Cleveland Cavaliers

As soon as I got back to my hotel room, I sent an email to Amanda, thanking her for saying hi and expressing my interest in visiting Cleveland. A couple days later, I received this:

Hey Cameron!

Thanks so much for emailing me! We really were impressed with how you worked the crowd. It seemed like the second you lifted a finger to start clapping, they were right there with you. Kinda eerie. . . but kinda cool too!

What month would work best for you to come up? How far out would we need to book you?

How much do you charge? I would love to have you come up for a couple games that are close together. Would you be available December 13th and 15th? No problem if you aren't – I know it's way short notice.

Thanks again and I'll talk to you soon,

Amanda

And just like that, I had landed another sweet gig.

While I'd done a few NBA games in the past, something about Cleveland felt *different*. Amanda and her team worked with me to make the fan experience as memorable as possible, and I felt they wanted me there. The games were a blast. I was making connections with fans in ways I hadn't experienced before. My performances at minor league games had involved more intimate connections, since I had more time to sit in the stands with the fans. The NBA was a completely different beast – the big leagues – and it started bringing me more and more exposure.

I was never looking to belong to just one league – I was a free agent – but it certainly didn't hurt to get a few ins with representatives across the NBA. A tight-knit crew, they shared ideas and promoted top acts amongst themselves, creating a kind of circuit... I mean, have you seen the Dancing Grannies, the FAT GUYS or the Kid Acrobats? Ask your sports fan friends across the country. Bet they have, too. From Cleveland, I got calls to fly to Denver to perform for the Nuggets, the Thunder in OKC, in New Orleans, and the Atlanta Hawks. I was piling up the air miles and feeling it again. This crazy roller-coaster ride was starting to go the right way.

OUR NEXT GUEST IS...

I certainly wasn't expecting to hear from the producers of *The Tonight Show*.

Earlier that month, my friend Ryan O'Dowd was working for the show and passed my information along to the talent bookers without my knowledge; now they were considering having me on as a guest.

The producers and I went back and forth, trying to figure out what my angle would be. Actually, it was more like back and forth and back and forth – we once had eight calls *in one day.*

"Cam, we want you on the show. Can you do a Friday slot sometime soon?"

Scheduled to appear on Jay Leno's couch Friday, April 27, 2007 alongside guests Conan O'Brien and Kings of Leon, the thinking was I'd be a guest they'd have on every once in a while: "The guy with the wacky career; can't believe you do this for a living" guest.

It was official: Cameron Hughes was going to be on *The Tonight Show*. I couldn't wait to call the dean who had me booted from University! Unable to contain my excitement, I told everyone with a pulse about it. I even did an interview on a local NBC affiliate in Bakersfield to promote my upcoming appearance.

And then, over the weekend, Miss America 1944 blasted my late-night dreams to pieces. True story. Venus Ramey, 82 years old, had made headlines by confronting thieves on her farm, then *shooting out the tires* on their vehicle so police could apprehend them. Fierce! So yeah, I got bumped for the vigilante octogenarian beauty queen. "Sorry," I was told. "We'll have to schedule you for another time." Which never happened... yet.

It was frustrating, but hey, this was showbiz, and even *I* had to admit Venus's story was something worth cheering for.

ACTION!

With this newfound momentum (and money!) I was able to move off Bill's couch and into a new apartment in Venice. I finally had the mental space to resume my dreams of selling a TV show. I shot a pilot for a Travel Channel show called *Quit Your Job and Move*, which aired all of one time. The show challenged people to get up from their homes and leave it all behind for their dream job and location. *Sound familiar?* Then I shot another pilot for the Travel Channel called *Borderline Rivals*, pitting neighboring cities against each other in everything from sports, culture, history and pride. I even shot a pilot called *Arenaman*, where I would go to arenas and be challenged to accomplish weird things. We thought we were close on this too, but nope. Then MTV and BET almost bought shows I created. But nope. Nope. Nope.

Still, the inspired ideas kept flowing. They would come to me in the middle of the night, waking me from a dead sleep. Or while singing in the shower, or hyping myself up in the car before a big game – my eyes wide with the fervor of a newfound idea. I'd scribble notes down in an illegible scrawl: *REmeMber NeW pilOT IDEA!!* Then I'd scamper off to the field or the rink or the court, putting a mental post-it note in my mind to return to later and flesh out.

At the top of my list was *Planet Fandemonium*, which had been percolating for quite some time. In it, I would explore the world's greatest sporting events and give viewers a wild glimpse of what went on behind the scenes. I thought shooting a trailer for it was the best way of selling it. Tired of waiting for permission from the TV world, I talked to my car dealer pal Mike Kensit back in Canada. Mike wanted to support me and be part of the TV world.

He was in. Next thing I knew, we were in Fort Lauderdale in an RV in the middle of the infield of the Daytona 500. We partied with fans, worked our way into the pits, and discovered what makes the Daytona 500 such a special event. At one point I was even on a school bus with 20 strangers sampling moonshine!

We turned it into an eight-minute promo reel and got ourselves a great agent through my manager. Our goal was to get the buyers excited and create a bigger version of the show together. Our agent would work the phones and we'd bring the magic – kind of like the Hollywood version of "Show and Tell." *How could it miss?*

It didn't sell.

In retrospect, we should have just thrown it on this new website called YouTube.

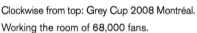

Clockwise from top: Grey Cup 2008 Montréal.

Working the room of 68,000 fans.

In a sexy pair of jeans!

My trusted dear friend, Palmer West- thank you for the email and believing.

Martin Brodeur 2010 Vancouver Olympic golden moments.

New Jersey Devils, 2009 fan fun.

22

EYE ON THE PRIZE

"Starve your distractions. Feed your focus."

Anonymous

F-O-C-U-S

L iving with ADHD is tough, especially when pursuing a career where there are virtually no rules or structure. Without an agency like SRO behind me, I was constantly disorganized, with no cohesive playbook to manage my life. And keep in mind, this was long before virtual assistants or management software. I didn't know what payments were coming in or when; what invoices I did or didn't send. It was all a hodge-podge of frenetic activity. Wake up in Dallas, go to sleep in the Big Apple. Write down this note – *Cam, call about Cavaliers gig!* – and then forget it at the hotel. But then there's the flip side: when you have ADHD, you have zero patience. You also have zero ability to slow down, which is partly what helped my career.

Over the years, family members, teachers, friends and pretty much anyone who's ever met me imparted the same advice to me: *Focus.*

Should I go to more auditions?

Should I get up at games again?

Should I get a real j-o-b?

Focus, Cam. FOCUS.

MASTER OF ONE

I was determined to break through as a TV host, preferably with my own show. All I could do was keep putting myself out there. The competition was intense. I had to find an angle. How was I new and different and unique? Was I marketable? Promotable? Did I have a platform? Did my intonation work well on camera? Was it an intonation?! There were a million people out there trying to make it, just like me. Would I ever get a TV show? What was my angle?

One of the guys I met in the pong club, Palmer West, became a great pal and cheerleader. Palmer took a special interest in my career, admiring my determination and entrepreneurial spirit. He was an entrepreneur in his own right, having produced a ton of cool independent films, including *Requiem for A Dream*. We often had long lunches discussing all aspects of life, including the unpredictable entertainment industry. It was helpful for me to talk to someone regularly who I could share it all with and who supported me.

Eventually, Palmer would send an email that would change everything for me:

"Here's something I want you to do for yourself. Ask yourself this question: 'What do I do best?' Not a list of things you're really fucking good at, but one thing that you do best. Don't do this at the same time you're thinking about a career. Fuck that. That comes second, and frankly quite naturally if you figure out the first part.

What are you best at? Obvious things come to mind, but I am not going to lead you here. You have a shitload of ideas, a shitload of irons in the fire. Be a master of one, rather than a professional at many. Make sense? Step back, deep breath, ask yourself this question and see where you end up. Again, this is not the time to think about money, family, security or occupation. Give it a rest for a second and just think about Cameron, just Cameron.

What are you best at? One thing, one trait, or one gift that comes to you naturally. You will know the right answer when you come across it, and the answer could be a paragraph. It doesn't have to be one adjective. It's your answer. There is no blank that needs to be filled. The answer could be huge or small. The smaller the better for this first step.

Give it a shot, and buddy, regardless, you are loved by many, my friend. That in itself is a hurdle not enough people can say they have cleared these days. Give it time, give it time."

Palmer West, dear friend, solid pong player

Palmer was right. I was all over the map. I kept fooling myself into thinking I could do it all, but I couldn't. I needed to focus. My ADHD had me chasing one TV pilot after another – usually in between gigs or while I was working on perfecting another skit for the fans.

BOOM!

Idea. Idea. Idea.

Attention – gone, gone, gone.

Well.

That's how my mind felt at all times; firing on all cylinders 24/7. I was constantly being bombarded by new ideas before I even had time to fully execute the old ones. How could I make a dream happen if I was asleep to the reality that

I had *far too many dreams*?

I got up that night in 1994 – the high school game in Ottawa – for a reason. I got up after high school for a reason. I got up, and I got up, and I got up, time and time again, for a reason.

I was meant to spread cheer.

Boom. Done. Fact.

So, why was I moving all over the place and not focusing all of my energy on cheer? The TV path kept leading me down dead ends – but the cheer path kept leading me to new opportunities! From Bakersfield to Gwinnett to Cleveland to the rest of the NBA!

My mom inspired me to connect with people in person, to connect with the human spirit. All I had to do to make her proud, to fulfill my destiny, was focus on that. Palmer did me a huge service with that email.

It was time to put myself out there and FOCUS solely on bringing the CHEER to live events in sports, and special events. It's the road where I truly belong.

OUI, OUI, OUI, BONJOUR!

Perhaps in return for putting my powers of cheer out into the universe, I got a phone call from the organizers of the PR company promoting the 96th Grey Cup, Canada's version of the Super Bowl. Not only did they want me to perform at the event, to be held in Montréal, they also wanted me to *host the halftime show*. That's right, HOST! YES! This was HUGE! Unfortunately, their request got even bigger.

"Are you bilingual?" they asked. "You'll have to deliver your lines in both English and French."

Mm, yeah. About that… remember my skiing skills?

While I'd studied French in school, I'd managed to retain only enough to order a crepe, and even that was an embarrassment. But I wanted this gig. *Needed* this gig. And I would have it.

"*Oui, oui!!*" I quickly replied.

"Great! Our publicist will be in touch with all the details, including a French proficiency test."

Crap. (Whoop – Merde.)

A few sleepless nights later, I got the call.

"Bonjour, Cameron, je m'appelle Sylvie."

Walking down the street, caught completely off guard, I channeled my grade six French immersion persona and worked the phone with as much flair as I could. My high school French teacher would have been proud.

Sometimes in life there are moments on which you look back and wonder, "How the heck did I manage to get through that?" Like this moment. Because guess what? I passed! Just barely, but I passed! *Incroyable!*

I showed up in Montréal later that week to begin my French assimilation. The Grey Cup was upon us. I had some brief media training in French (where I was basically told I wasn't bilingual – *How dare they?*), a few days of fun events *en Français*, and then it was game on – 66,000 people strong, my biggest crowd to date!

I had about a minute on the big screen. I danced, threw some t-shirts, went NUTS – and the crowd was in. It was electric. The camera would pan to me going nuts, then go back to the fans losing it in response, and then back to me. It was perfectly orchestrated, with the fans totally locked in and participating.

But that was the easy part.

Then I had to prep for the halftime show. I was fired up and letting all my Facebook friends know it. I'd been updating them with post after post, writing things like, *"GREY CUP FEVER! A few more rehearsals to go . . ."* and *"GREY CUP GAME DAY READY! TSN 6 p.m. EST . . . performing and hosting halftime! A dream come true..."*

Here's one post I found especially interesting in hindsight.

Yes, I said "hindsight" – that's kind of a clue. There were 4.5 million fans watching at home and 66,000 watching live. The moment had arrived. Sporting freshly styled hair, a crisp pair of jeans, and a beautiful Grey Cup jersey, I was ready.

45 seconds to go now.

My heart was beating the steady rhythmic beat of war drums. My spine was covered with goosebumps. Mad butterflies raged in my stomach.

30 seconds.

All that was left to do was take a sip of water to get rid of my dry mouth. I had 35 seconds... now 34... 33. Plenty of time.

Bending down to retrieve my water bottle, I heard the most god-awful sound ever to ring through my eardrums.

Rrrip.

No, no... NO!

Surely, it was a bad dream. It had to be. But no: my jeans had split.

And I mean *split*. Ass to air. We had contact.

With mere seconds until showtime, I had a ten-inch hole running from my crotch to my inseam. Panicked, I whipped around to face the floor director, my eyes ablaze, hoping he could save me from this Larry David-esque predicament. Instead, he grinned widely. "You have to go on, kid!"

No, no, no...

10, 9, 8...

With no other choice, I pulled my jersey down as far as I possibly could. Suddenly those last-minute line revisions didn't seem like such a big deal anymore. They were, in fact, the perfect distraction. I went on to introduce the sponsor, Diet Pepsi, and the halftime entertainment, Theory of a Deadman. And no one noticed my pants – as far as I knew. Or, did they? (So yeah, now I can honestly say I got "drafted" in the CFL *and* have something in common with Janet Jackson, besides killer dance moves... yeah yeah!)

Oh, and I nailed the French part. *Bien sur.*

"As the newly crowned 26-year-old Director of Game Operations, I wanted to ensure that our expected capacity crowd for the Charlotte Checkers would be lively. I contacted a friend and colleague who worked for the Idaho Steelheads and inquired about a performer I'd seen at a game there earlier in the season. The entertainer, an older gentleman, led fans throughout the game with various coordinated clapping routines. His schtick was tame, family-friendly fun that would meet the desires of our conservative ownership group and add a little life to the party. My contact provided me with a name and phone number, and a few short hours after leaving a voice message, I received a call back. The ball of fire on the other end of the line seemed a bit more lively than the performer I'd seen in Boise, but I figured he was fired up to be performing at an All-Star game in front of a national audience. When my staff member picked up the performer from the airport, she failed to mention that he was 25-30 years younger than the guy I'd described. It was not until later that afternoon that I met Cameron Hughes for the first time. I tried not to panic (or mention the case of mistaken identity) in front of the young man who seemed to have been shot out of a cannon preparing to perform at that evening's game. I nervously decided to roll with it and see what came of the surprise. Cameron absolutely brought the house down – he shook, he danced, he stripped shirts off his back and threw them to an overzealous crowd who for some reason was eating this all up. It was the first of nearly 40 times that Cameron performed for teams that I worked for – in San Diego, in Charlotte, and in New Jersey for the NHL's Devils."

From the desk of Jeff Longo, Sports Executive

Through a serendipitous case of mistaken identity, I eventually found myself working the crowds in New Jersey. Jeff Longo convinced Lou Lamoriello, the CEO, and one of the most non-marketing hockey guys ever, to give me a shot for one game. The Devils relied on their hockey to market to fans, but with the new arena, they needed to change gears. Jeff and the execs warned me the crowd may not react well. The first time I got up, I got nothing from fans. And I mean nothing. Okaaaay.

Second time, crickets.

My heart started to sink. It wasn't working at all. I always felt I could win over a crowd. Crowds want the spark. They're craving it. But when it busts and you get nothing, it's crushing. What was I doing wrong? I had to regroup and figure out another way. Switch gears. Read the crowd. Understand them. Assimilate. Then launch at precisely the right moment, so they can't help but feel the undeniable energy that's right there, just waiting to be unleashed..

Then I waited and waited for the perfect time to get up, and BAM, I had them! I didn't stop until I had the entire arena with me. The team won that first game, and I was summoned to their offices the next day. I had a new gig! 16 games later, it was a party in NJ! No one in hockey could believe the Devils were marketing a fun time.

TIMEOUT

Occasionally, after games, I run into the players in the hallways by the locker rooms. One night in Jersey, I was dripping buckets of sweat, trying to catch my breath, when legendary goaltender Martin Brodeur walked by me and said, "You should have been third star, at least!" (Note to non-hockey fans: A. Why are you reading this book?! and B. After every NHL game, they announce the top three players of the game, and they skate out onto the ice...)

MIME TIME

The only time I lost my voice in my career, I was scheduled to do a Devils game. At first, I thought I should cancel, or at least tell the team. But then I realized I'd done enough games at this point that it would be a good challenge, and may be a fun way to mix it up. Who needed a voice when you had hands, arms, legs, a killer smile and a will to cheer? My friend Curtis Pride has given me great advice on smaller ways to connect.

I showed up and mimed my cheers and craziness, and I owned it. The reaction was actually louder than most games. I guess having rapport with your fans comes in handy.

It was going so well with the Devils that the *New York Post* ran a Page 3 article sharing my story and mentioned my performance. I went home feeling good. Until I checked my email.

You are a d-bag. stay out of jersey. if you are at the devs games next year i promise you will be booed out of every section. last year only the hardcore fans in 216 knew that you were a "professional fan". now everybody knows and nobody likes you. go work for the rangers or something. you're not wanted in jersey.

Shortly after that, a loud "fan" did in fact try to mess with me at a Devils' game, and the organization had to send security guards to intervene. Ugh. The idea of security following me wasn't great for the cheering soul. How many times had I encountered this by now? Many. I'd been called names like "sellout" many times, but those people were simply missing the point. The point was to get up, spread cheer, and make the fans feel alive. People like my friend Bruce Phillips "got it," even if they had an initial sense of confusion or betrayal. I eventually learned to stop caring what anyone thought of me doing different teams or their games. Unless there was a threat!

"That he's rooting for one team on Tuesday and another on Saturday isn't the point. What's more important... is that he's rooting for you. To be inspired. To cut loose. To dance in the aisles. That's the spark he wants to ignite in the crowd."

Greg Wyshynski, ESPN

Clockwise from top: On the set of the Today Show at the Vancouver Olympics - Natalie Morales, Meredith Viera, Al Roker, and Ann Curry.

Team Canada Women's hockey stars – Jennifer Botterill, Tessa Bonhomme along with media maestro- George Stroumboulopulos.

With Willie Geist – the interview that launched his career before hosting the Today Show :)

Flying at the Games, Dahron Rahlves, US SKi team legend.

Olympic crowd cheers!

Hayley Wickenheiser Team Canada Hall of Famer.

23

RINGS OF CHEER

"Without hustle, talent will only carry you so far."

Gary Vaynerchuk

When it was announced that the 2010 Winter Olympics were being held in Vancouver, Canada, I knew I had to be there. You never know what the pinnacle of your career is going to be, but as a Canadian, I felt this would rank pretty high.

My friend Scott Henderson, who'd been my publicist for *Game Face*, suggested I reach out to Christy Nicolay, the head of sports production for the Vancouver Olympic Committee (VANOC). If anyone was going to hire me, it would be her.

I scoured the Internet for her contact information but could find only her Facebook profile page. I had no other choice but to – as the kids would say – slip into her DMs. Wow, did I take that FB message seriously! After undergoing several rounds of revisions, my carefully constructed message explaining who I was, what I did, and why she needed me was launched into cyberspace.

A couple of days later, she replied with enthusiasm. Just like that, I was off to the Olympic Games!

Nope. In my dreams, it really was that easy.

After not hearing back from her or her team for a while, I decided some respectful persistence was in order. I sent her one more email. It had to be clever, concise – and yes, focused. I'm not sure I've ever worked so hard on an email in my life. I wanted this gig. I just knew I would bring extra spirit to the Games. With the clock ticking on my dream, less than three months before the Eternal Flame rolled into town, I hit "send" again. Nothing to lose.

A few days later, I was back in Canada, sitting in the Vancouver Olympic Committee's offices talking to the manager of entertainment about what I could bring to the Games. I couldn't believe it! Ask and you shall receive. But I still had to seal the deal.

"I think we'd like to have you do our curling matches and some hockey, maybe even ski jumping," he said. Curling? I can confidently say that he'd never seen my promo reel before.

I hesitated. "Why don't we stick with hockey?"

They told me they'd get back to me. Uh-oh.

Two days later, back in LA, my phone rang. I'll never forget pulling over at the corner of Santa Monica and Doheny to take the call.

"Hi Cameron, it's David," he said. "Pack your bags. We want you for 34 games."

YES!!! To top it off, they'd also agreed to pay my fee.

As soon as I hung up, tears of joy streamed down my face. A dream come true. And unlike my stint at the 2002 Games in Salt Lake City, this time it was official. I called everyone I knew. The pride I felt was immeasurable. For all intents and purposes, I was an Olympic performer! From last place in my grade eight cross country race to this!

Then reality sunk in.

Wait... did he say 34 GAMES?! That was more than I'd performed in the entire first two years of my career. I'd been hired to do 34 games in 16 days, which averaged out to 2.125 games per day, at six hours per day. In the shape I was in, those numbers basically added up to "Hold me over that flame now because I'm toast." But I'd made the Olympic Committee believe that I could do it. So somehow, I had to do it. This was a once-in-a-lifetime opportunity.

I called up my friend Margaret, a health coach, who helped me set up a fitness and nutrition plan that was so intense an outsider might have wondered if I'd be *playing* in 34 games rather than cheering at them. (Honestly, though, some games I probably burn as many calories as a player does during the course of a game... of course, I don't get cross-checked into the boards.) I cut out most sugars, took every vitamin on the market, followed a strict diet and got into the best shape of my life.

Without any prompting from me, the Olympic Committee had come to the sudden realization that the physical exertion necessary to ignite a crowd for 34 games would probably result in my being hauled out of the arena in a body bag. They told me I could bring on a helper to haul around T-shirts, and help produce my "hits." So I asked my friend Scott Modrzynski, who'd assisted me back when I was cheering on the New Jersey Devils. He was a great young guy who was always smiling and willing to do whatever we needed. Once I got Scott home from the bars at a reasonable hour after the first few nights, we had a rhythm. We were all in.

This was the Olympics, so I turned my patience button on and did my best to find some sweet spots to get the arena rocking. What a wonderful experience meeting fans from Belarus, Finland, Sweden, the US, and across Canada. I even had Vice President Joe Biden up out of his seat at a USA women's hockey game, and gave him a t-shirt. He spun around and held it up to thunderous applause. Everyone came together with the most powerful spirit and sense of global community. At the end of the first week, I received my first performance review. Mostly positive, except...

"You need to cut back on the dirty dancing with women," the producer said.

A familiar lesson: You always have to remember who hired you in the first place and respect their wishes, even though it's hard. (Plus, I knew the girl!)

Giving a big congrats to the goal scorer, "Sid the Kid" (Sidney Crosby) after he wins gold for team Canada vs USA at the 2010 Olympics. Sidney Crosby, 3 Time Stanley Cup winner, Team Canada Gold, One of the best hockey players ever.

While I was there, I said yes to everything – doing *The Today Show* (I got the entire cast dancing and twirling tees!), tons of fun TV spots with stations around the world, and several radio shows. I was having the time of my life. Sure, there were minor occupational hazards along the way, too – like having to put on special moisturizing gloves because my hands started bleeding from so much clapping! But it was all worth it.

I made it to the final weekend, where Team Canada would square off against Team USA for gold.

The committee told me, "Don't pick sides."

I laughed.

Over 10 million Canadians were watching the game. The energy in Vancouver was off the charts. And I had a front-row seat to the insanity. My hard work had truly paid off, and I was especially gratified to be hosting my pal Palmer at the game, so he could see where my focus had brought me. When Sydney Crosby buried the overtime game-winner, Canada went OFF! I've never seen or felt anything like it since. The game was over by early afternoon, and from then on it was red, white, and go nuts time.

Millions of people poured into the streets partying, playing street hockey, dancing, singing. It was an historic moment for Canada. And let me tell you, that first beer after the Gold Medal game was the most delicious beer I've ever tasted.

I'll always thank Christy for having an open mind and responding to my persistent emails. I'm grateful beyond words, and proud that I was able to be in my own country doing what I loved. Somehow all the Motel 6 nights, late check-ins, exhausted flights, and early mornings had paid off.

Oh, and I *may* have snuck into the Canada House with the team after the party…

FAN-TASTIC GIG

Sports kook paid to fire up crowds

By STEFANIE COHEN

It's the third quarter, the Knicks have been trailing all night and the fans are booing the defense and screaming profanities at the refs.

"They need the crowd behind them," says a tall redhead in section 126. "They need *me*."

He punches himself in the chest three times, jumps into the aisle and starts gyrating like a belly dancer on crack.

"Come on! DEFENSE!" he shouts. The crowd is stunned at the sudden explosion. But their shock turns to laughter as the dancing gets more spastic. Now he's doing the robot; now he's approximating Michael Jackson in "Thriller"; now he's leapfrogging down a flight of stairs, crashing into an innocent passer-by.

"How much did that boy have to drink?" a bewildered fan asks.

They're appalled, but they're also smiling and clapping along — and having a lot more fun than they were a minute ago.

They think he's a crazy fan, and he is — crazy like a fox.

He's Cameron Hughes, professional fan. Paid up to $2,000 a night to get the crowds riled up for the New Jersey Devils, the Atlanta Hawks and the Cleveland Cavaliers, among others.

Hughes, 37, makes about six figures a year for attending 80 games and doing what most do for fun.

"Having Cameron there adds just a little extra energy to the crowd, and it definitely gives the players an extra advantage," said Amanda Greco, a Cavaliers team official. Other teams, such as the Devils, don't like to discuss Hughes' work for them, believing people would be disappointed to learn he isn't a die-hard fan.

Hughes stumbled drunkenly into his life's calling when he went nuts at an Ottawa Senators hockey match in 1994.

"I'd had too much to drink and I just started going crazy," said Hughes. After the game, the team offered him a few hundred bucks to come back. And a star — er, psycho fan — was born.

Nowadays he's all business. He never drinks during games, and each of his uncoordinated dances is carefully coordinated with the team beforehand.

He teases kids, flirts with women and makes old ladies get up and dance. His signature move is wearing 15 T-shirts and pulling them off one by one, flinging them into the crowd like an overweight stripper.

"I just want people up, clapping, dancing, cheering, whatever," he says. "I want everyone to have fun at the game."

Hughes doesn't work for the Knicks — not yet. But the impromptu audition he performed at last week's game to try to land a job seemed to work in getting their attention.

stefanie.cohen@nypost.com

New York crazy at MSG – New York Post page 3 article.

David Shoemaker, sports executive, solid tennis player.

I LOVE NEW YORK! Igniting the crowd at the US OPEN tennis in NYC!

24

BIG APPLE LOVE

"Anything is possible when you have the
right friends there to support you."

Misty Copeland

Following the insanity of the 2010 Winter Olympic Games, I was *spent*. Being on the road for so many consecutive months, capped off with the epic whirlwind of Vancouver, had taken its toll on my mind and body. Late nights with little to no sleep followed by early morning wake-up calls and a breakfast of bad airplane food, followed by flights… games… hotels. Repeat. The process was a grind. I needed a vacation. So, I booked a flight to the Dominican Republic to get away from it all, making a brief stop in Florida along the way to see my friend David Shoemaker.

David and I met and worked together at the tennis club back in Ottawa. Since then, he'd made a name for himself as a top corporate and commercial litigator representing high profile sports-related clientele, before being appointed the president of the Women's Tennis Association (WTA). We played sports together (me not as well), had lots of fun in high school, and kept in touch throughout the years.

Over a round of golf, I opened up to him about my feeling stagnant. I knew I needed to do something different, even after a fun Olympic tour. That was a one-off.

"I hear the US Open might be looking for someone," he said. "Would you like me to make an introduction?"

Tennis? A sport where "quiet please" is practically the official slogan? In my mind, there was little chance they'd consider bringing me in. But I really wanted to keep pushing the envelope. Although I'd just performed at the Olympics, the phone wasn't exactly ringing off the hook. Maybe my old friend tennis *was* the answer. Plus, what David had in mind for me was an in-arena hosting gig, not a crowd-igniting one. Maybe they would go for it. I had nothing to lose.

"I'd love an introduction," I told David as we sipped margaritas. The more I thought about his proposition, the more it started to make sense. Why wouldn't the United States Tennis Association (USTA) want to take a chance on something different? On bringing in someone with very "un-tennis-y" energy? A smashing good idea, David!

QUIET PLEASE

I met up in New York with Francene Costello Thomas, the USTA's manager of entertainment, to discuss the opportunity. She was curious and friendly, but I didn't feel it was a home-run meeting.

My intuition was correct. *Wham, Bam, No-Thank-You, Cam.* They ended up going with a spirit patrol and having Andy Taylor, the beloved, long-serving US Open stadium announcer, do special promotions. While I was disappointed, I was now convinced more than ever that my presence could work well at the US Open! So I needed to find a way to get in the stands.

Ask yourself: what do you do when you want something, but they say no? Have you ever been in that situation? How do you react? Sometimes, we're told no for a perfectly good reason. *No! You can't cannonball off the condo's balcony into the pool!* Or *No! Don't do that, it's a crime.* Those are rules. Laws. But I'm not talking about breaking any rules or laws, I'm talking about breaking *the law of self-limitation.* Those times when we have the raging fire of an idea in our hearts and we're told flat out, "No. It won't work. Can't happen. You're shooting too high."

My take? Keep pushing. Find a way. Get creative. Anything can happen. With this in mind, I reached out a few weeks later with what I felt was a no-brainer proposal:

Hi Francene,

I'm going to be in NYC during the second week of the Open and I'd love to come and perform for your fans.

How does this work? One hit. Four tickets. Footage of my performance. And $1.00.

Thank you,

Cameron

(That's right: $1.00)

I'll never forget pressing send on that email. I thought, *Well, I had to try.*

Her response:

Cameron – $1.00 sounds fair. Footage on the screen – we can get that for you.

You already have four complementary tickets with your name on them.

I'm all about being paid what you're worth, but sometimes you just have to get in the door and show people what you're made of. Even when you've been doing it for 16 years. Don't limit yourself. Be open, be fluid, be creative.

What would you do for a dollar?

I'd dance in front of 22,000 people at the US Open.

You bet your ass I would.

LIGHTNING IN A BOTTLE

So there I was, sitting in the upper deck at Flushing Meadows with my dear friends Karim, Krista and Ariane, big tennis fans who were dying to see what I had in store for the crowd. When the moment finally came, a changeover with Nadal up 5-2 in the second set, I heard their whispers... "Go, go, go, you got this!"

"Everybody Dance Now" blasted on the speakers. I got up in the aisle and started to move like a fan possessed. As I shimmied and grooved in all directions, fans scurried to get out of the way. I kept going, barreling down the stairs like I owned the joint. This proper tennis crowd suddenly had permission to be rowdy New Yorkers again, and they appreciated it. *Loudly*. Things got really insane when I plopped the big fat cherry on top: I peeled off my final t-shirt, revealing the "I LOVE NY" tee I'd purchased earlier that morning. Best ten dollars I've ever spent. The crowd howled at the moon. And. Would. Not. Stop. The umpire asked *twice* for "Quiet, please!"

I strolled back to my grinning friends, and as I sat back down, my phone started *blowing up*. Unbeknownst to me, the McEnroe brothers were talking about my performance live on ESPN!

"Not something you see on center court at Wimbledon, ladies and gentlemen," John McEnroe said. "Biggest applause of the night, this crowd is abuzz right now – *that is awesome!*"

When a world-class disruptor like Johnny Mac gives you respect, there can be no higher praise.

After the match, I took the subway home with my pals and practically everybody on the train was hugging and high-fiving me. My rate had just hit an all-time low, but I was on top of the world!

What on Earth would I do with that dollar?! (Author's Note: I still have it!)

"Cameron came along at a time when we were trying to find new ways to engage the crowd, especially the more than 50 percent of the Fans in Arthur Ashe Stadium who attend the US Open and are seated in the Promenade."

Michael Fiur, Executive Producer/GM, US Open Entertainment

THE MECCA OF BASKETBALL

Whenever I flew into New York over the years to work for the Devils, or for the US Open, I couldn't help but let my eyes wander toward Madison Square Garden. Remember, the last time I performed there was over 10 years ago, I was booed out of the arena in favor of the hometown crowd favorite, Dancing Larry. But I wasn't a green kid anymore. It was time for redemption.

A mutual friend had introduced me to Stephanie, a reporter from the *New York Post*, who proposed shadowing me for a game. The plan was simple: we'd show up at a Knicks game together with nothing more than a couple of t-shirts and tickets in hand to see if I really could get the fans going.

I bought six t-shirts that screamed "NYC tourist" all over them from a nearby bodega, and off we went.

I felt like I was on a first date on an episode of *The Bachelor*. Could I impress this young lady by igniting the notoriously tough NYC crowd? I waited far too long for my liking, but I hit it. The response was tepid, at best. Stephanie certainly wasn't convinced. *Okay, fine.* I'd encountered this before; I simply had to tap in and change my energy levels to match the crowd. Shift gears. But the doubt gnawed at me:

What if she writes that I failed? That I overhyped it? That won't look too good on my résumé…

Simple, I decided. I had to make it count.

During the next timeout, I stood up and gave it everything I had. The place exploded. Tees were flying, and fans were going insane. At the end of my bit, a rep from the Knicks approached and asked for my contact.

I made Page 3 of the *New York Post*.

A few weeks later, I got the call.

The Knicks wanted me.

This was over-the-top insane for a kid from Ottawa. At long last, I was going to "play" Madison Square Garden, the world's most famous arena.

The subway ride to the Garden was a carnival of nerves. Could this be real? As the train jolted to a halt at each stop on the way there, I did that thing where you lean and subtly brace yourself so you don't topple into the commuter next to you.

Then I'd fight back a big goofy grin, because I wanted to break out in dance right there on the E train, and have the passengers follow me, like the Pied Piper, up and into the Garden in one big conga line when we got there.

Checking in at the security gate – getting that pass, those tees, and that Knicks jersey – was an out-of-body experience. Sure, I'd done other NBA teams, but this was the kid from Canada getting the keys to the kingdom in *New York City*. The Big Apple.

I had found a way. There was no straight line, I realized after so many years had passed. You don't just pick up the phone and things automatically happen. You just make sure you don't stop until they happen. You find a way. And I found a way into Madison Square Garden. I wished I could have been a fly on the wall of the meetings where they agreed, "Bring the crazy t-shirt guy in." What did they say? How in the *hell* did I get here? As I walked through the stands, the hallways, and the locker room, I looked at everything in awe. *I've made it*, I told myself.

Rising from my seat before the crowd of nearly 20,000 on my first cue, I couldn't help but tear up a little bit.

The kid who couldn't make the high school basketball team was just about to rock the house at Madison Square Garden in New York City. If you can make it here, you can make it *anywhere*.

What a thrill to go from not making my high school hoops team to performing at the World's Most Famous Arena – Madison Square Garden. Put your game face on!

EVERY TEAM I'VE SHARED THE ROAR WITH

NHL

- Anaheim Ducks
- Arizona Coyotes
- Atlanta Thrashers
- Buffalo Sabres
- Calgary Flames
- Carolina Hurricanes
- Chicago Blackhawks
- Colorado Avalanche
- Dallas Stars
- Edmonton Oilers
- LA Kings
- Minnesota Wild
- Montréal Canadiens
- New Jersey Devils
- New York Rangers*
- Ottawa Senators
- Toronto Maple Leafs
- Vegas Golden Knights
- Washington Capitals
- Winnipeg Jets
- NHL All-Star Games 2018 Tampa Bay 1997 San Jose

*unofficially :)

NFL

- Dallas Cowboys
- LA Rams

NIFL

- Louisiana Swashbucklers

MLB

- Chicago Cubs
- LA Dodgers
- Toronto Blue Jays

NBA

- Atlanta Hawks
- Charlotte Hornets
- Chicago Bulls
- Cleveland Cavaliers
- Dallas Mavericks*
- Denver Nuggets
- LA Clippers
- LA Lakers*
- New Orleans Pelicans
- New York Knicks
- OKC Thunder
- Toronto Raptors
- Washington Bullets
- NBA All-Star Game 2016 Toronto

*unofficially :)

CFL

- Toronto Argonauts
- Hamilton Tiger cats
- Montréal Alouettes
- Grey Cup 2008 Montréal

CHL

OHL

- Guelph Storm
- Mississauga IceDogs
- Ottawa 67's
- Peterborough Petes
- Saginaw Spirit
- Sarnia Sting
- Windsor Spitfires

QMJHL

- Cape Breton Eagles
- Halifax Mooseheads

WHL

- Brandon Wheat Kings
- Edmonton Oil Kings
- Kamloops Blazers
- Moose Jaw Warriors
- Red Deer Rebels
- Regina Pats
- Saskatoon Blades
- Spokane Chiefs
- Tri-City Americans
- Victoria Royals
- Memorial Cup - 2013 Saskatoon, 2014 London, 2015 Québec City
- CHL Top Prospects Games 2014 Calgary, 2015 St. Catherines

ALPINE SKIING

- FIS Alpine World Ski Championships 2015 Vail

AHL

- Bakersfield Condors
- Cleveland Lumberjacks
- Cleveland Monsters
- Grand Rapids Griffins
- Hartford Wolf Pack
- Lehigh Valley Phantoms
- Manitoba Moose
- Norfolk Admirals
- Ontario Reign
- Rockford IceHogs
- San Antonio Rampage
- Wilkes-Barre/ Scranton Penguins
- Outdoor Classic 2017 Bakersfield

MILB

- Aberdeen IronBirds
- Brooklyn Cyclones
- Delmarva Shorebirds
- London Werewolves
- Memphis Redbirds
- Nashville Sounds
- Norfolk Tides
- Normal CornBelters
- Ottawa Lynx
- Spokane Indians
- Storm Chasers
- Toledo Mud Hens
- Tulsa Drillers

UFL

- Omaha Nighthawks

ECHL

- Adirondack Thunder
- Atlanta Gladiators
- Atlantic City Boardwalk Bullies
- Bakersfield Condors
- Charlotte Checkers
- Cincinnati Cyclones
- Colorado Eagles
- Evansville Icemen
- Fort Wayne Komets
- Idaho Steelheads
- Indy Fuel
- Iowa Steelheads
- Kansas City Mavericks
- Las Vegas Wranglers
- Mississippi Sea Wolves
- Norfolk Admirals
- Odessa Jackalopes
- Ontario Reign
- Orlando Solar Bears
- Pensacola Ice Pilots
- Phoenix Roadrunners
- Rapid City Rush
- Reading Royals
- San Diego Gulls
- South Carolina Stingrays
- Stockton Thunder
- Toledo Walleye
- Tulsa Oilers
- Utah Grizzlies
- Victoria Salmon Kings
- Wheeling Nailers
- Wichita Thunder
- ECHL All-Star Games 2005 Stockton,

2009 Reading,
2011 Bakersfield,
2013 Loveland,
2015 Orlando

CENTRAL HL/WPHL

- Amarillo Gorillas
- Arizona Sundogs
- Denver Cutthroats
- Lafayette Ice Gators
- Lake Charles Ice Pirates
- Laredo Bucks
- Memphis Riverkings
- New Mexico Scorpions
- Quad City Mallards
- Rapid City Rush
- Rio Grande Killer Bees
- Rocky Mountain Rage
- Shreveport Mudbugs
- All-Star Games Arizona, Lake Charles, Rapid City, Rio Grande, Shreveport

NLL

- Buffalo Bandits
- Colorado Mammoth
- Edmonton Rush
- Ottawa Rebel
- San Jose Stealth
- Saskatchewan Rush
- Toronto Rock

NCAA FOOTBALL

- Buffalo
- Old Dominion University
- VCU

MILB

- Aberdeen IronBirds
- Brooklyn Cyclones
- Delmarva Shorebirds
- London Werewolves
- Memphis Redbirds
- Nashville Sounds
- Norfolk Tides
- Normal CornBelters
- Ottawa Lynx
- Spokane Indians
- Storm Chasers
- Toledo Mud Hens
- Tulsa Drillers

U SPORTS CANADA

- 2013 Men's Basketball Final 8 Ottawa
- 2014 and 2015 Panda Game – University of Ottawa versus Carleton University Football
- 2014 Men's Hockey David Johnston University Cup Tournament Saskatoon

ROLLER HOCKEY INTERNATIONAL

- Ottawa Loggers
- LA Blades

AF2

- Corpus Christi Sharks
- Oklahoma City Yard Dawgz
- Rio Grande Valley Dorados
- Stockton Lightning
- Tulsa Talons

EIHL

- Belfast Giants
- Cardiff Devils
- Not the EIHL Finals :)

WOMEN'S SOFTBALL

- USA versus Taipei

RUGBY

- Friendly Game England versus New Zealand
- Leeds Rhinos Super League
- Singapore Sevens
- Vancouver Sevens
- Wigan Warriors Super League

TENNIS

- US Open
- Match 4 Africa

BARBADOS CRICKET T20 TOURNAMENT

NCAA BASKETBALL

- LSU
- Notre Dame
- Old Dominion University
- Syracuse
- Temple
- University of Buffalo
- VCU
- NCAA Division I Men's Basketball Tournament 2000 Buffalo

WOMEN'S HOCKEY

- Canada versus USA Exhibition 2009 Victoria
- IIHF World Women's Championships 2000 Ontario

OLYMPICS

- 2002 Salt Lake Men's and Women's Hockey (Official-ish)
- 2010 Vancouver Men's and Women's Hockey

INTERNATIONAL HOCKEY

- 2010 IIHF World U20 Championship Saskatchewan

Clockwise from top: ODU band camp.

Cubs magic.

Scaring Leafs fans.

Golden Chico.

CBU Eagles night.

First night with my dear friend Ariane.

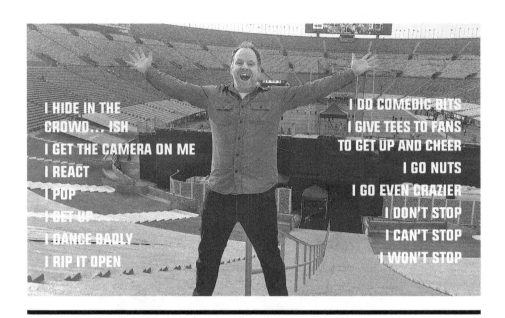

I HIDE IN THE
CROWD... ISH
I GET THE CAMERA ON ME
I REACT
I POP
I GET UP
I DANCE BADLY
I RIP IT OPEN

I DO COMEDIC BITS
I GIVE TEES TO FANS
TO GET UP AND CHEER
I GO NUTS
I GO EVEN CRAZIER
I DON'T STOP
I CAN'T STOP
I WON'T STOP

I GET INTO FANS' FACES AND ENCOURAGE THEM TO PARTICIPATE

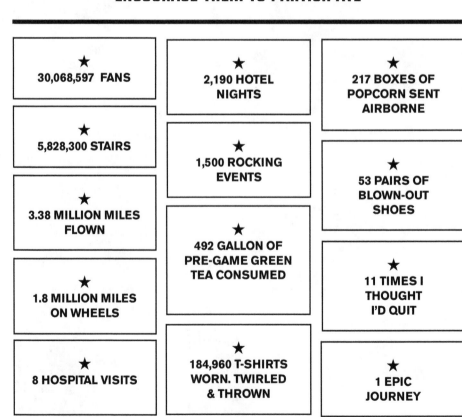

★ 30,068,597 FANS

★ 5,828,300 STAIRS

★ 3.38 MILLION MILES FLOWN

★ 1.8 MILLION MILES ON WHEELS

★ 8 HOSPITAL VISITS

★ 2,190 HOTEL NIGHTS

★ 1,500 ROCKING EVENTS

★ 492 GALLON OF PRE-GAME GREEN TEA CONSUMED

★ 184,960 T-SHIRTS WORN. TWIRLED & THROWN

★ 217 BOXES OF POPCORN SENT AIRBORNE

★ 53 PAIRS OF BLOWN-OUT SHOES

★ 11 TIMES I THOUGHT I'D QUIT

★ 1 EPIC JOURNEY

Whooping up the Toronto crowd at the NBA All-Star game, 2016.

PART 2

OKC Thunder Hoops magic.
Photo: Richard Rowe.

Colorado
Avalanche game.

THE GIGS. THE ROAD.
THE CRAAAZY. THE FUN.

The random stories that HAVE to be shared

Congratulations! You made it to Part Two, and this section of the book, like a good t-shirt twirl, is meant to be enjoyed when you're feeling the need for a smile, a little treat for the cheap seats.

When I was putting this project together, part of my plan was to share the best stories from my career of cheer. The way I was able to connect the dots was important to me in bringing you from the team list of doom on my high school gym door all the way to the exhilarating heights of the Olympics and Madison Square Garden.

I showed up, danced, put myself out there – believed. While creating this incredibly gratifying career, I shared so many magical moments with fans around the world. This part of the book is a heaping helping of those memories, plus, some golden nuggets of insight and experience I picked up along the way.

Did I mention:

I'm not a big fan of rules. (How do you think I ended up here, and writing my own book?) and I have ADHD, which I contained in part one but I am letting out, full force, in Part Two.

When you look at your own story, you begin to see common themes. For me, a few stick out: People have to believe in you in order for you to get the shot. Work hard so people will give you that shot, and then pay it forward when you can. Work the room hard, follow-up, and follow-up again, and send thank you notes. Be a little different, or a lot. Push it and do whatever it takes to be *your* best you.

And don't stop getting up. Trust it! Easier said than done, but it's a muscle. The more you get up, the more you'll *want* to GET UP!

For the second half of this book, let's turn up the volume and have some fun. There are no rules. We didn't ask for permission to get up that first night in Ottawa, so let's not start asking now. Y'all ready for this?!

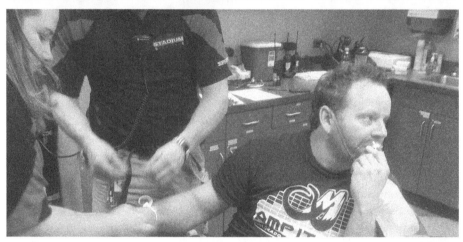

Clockwise from top: With Kroenke Sports & Entertainment team Steve Johnston, Camden Kelley, Kerry-Anne Keogh and DJ Craig.

Avs All-Star Nathan MacKinnon.

Needing some oxygen and an IV after doing two games in the same day at high altitude – oops!

Hockey Hall of Fame player and GM of the Colorado Avalanche Joe Sakic.

Working the crowd at the Avs game with my pal, Brooks!

AN AVALANCE IS COMING

I called Cam to come in and do a game for the Colorado Avalanche in 2009. The Avs were struggling that season, and we needed some help getting the crowd going. I remember how Cam had brought the SaddleDome to life back in Calgary (where I started my career) and knew he would be able to do the same in Colorado. The catch was, we needed him to do a doubleheader... an Avs game followed by a Mammoth lacrosse game. You know, to make it "worth" it to spend that kind of money on a hype guy.

I had been asked by a couple of higher-ups before booking Cam, "Can't we just find someone local who does the same thing?" and "Aren't there better ways to spend your budget than on a hired hype guy?" The simple answers to these questions are "no," and "probably not." Of course, these questions stopped once they saw Cam in action. Cam brought a combination of infectious energy and crazy happiness to the games that no one else could even come close to matching. It's not the dancing – he's not all that great at that – but his motor was endless. More importantly, he really connected with the fans and made them part of the show.

So, in the thin air of Denver after doing a three-hour Avalanche game there was Cameron... lying on the floor of Dressing Room #2 with an IV and oxygen mask and a team of attendants monitoring him. Like a true psychotic professional, he still had the energy to engage with everyone and bring 100 percent to the Mammoth game a couple of hours later.

I'll never forget, legendary Avalanche player Joe Sakic walked by as Cameron got his oxygen. "Everyone okay in there?" he asked with a big smile. Cam and I have been great friends since then, and we've had him back for Nuggets, AVs and Mammoth games. Joe gives Cameron a hard time at each game, but I know Cam loves it.

Steve Johnston, Executive Producer, Game Presentation KSE

YOU OUGHTA KNOW...

The date: March 9, 2007. *The location*: The Townhouse bar in Venice. *The occasion*: My birthday party. *Translation*: Tequila. Lots and lots of tequila. One of my hometown pals, Heather, brought along her superstar friend, Alanis Morissette, another Ottawa native. I'd never met her before and we hit it off right away. The party turned into a regular hoser fest – take off, eh? Tons of Canucks tore up the dance floor, and I acted exactly like a professional party-starter does on their b-day! And let's just say, Alanis and my Heather definitely held their own.

A few weeks later, I got a secretive call from a third party. *"Show up at Alanis's house."* No details, just "be here" kinda thing. I went (duh) and was asked to get dressed in some cheesy '80s men's wear. Hey, no problem, that's my go-to. The next thing I knew, I was on a music video set. Wait, *whaaat?!*

Alanis was doing a top-secret project – spoofing the "My Humps" video by the Black Eyed Peas. Being the *provocateur* she is, she wanted to have a little fun with Fergie's infamous video. Myself and five other gentlemen were preening, posing, dancing and desperately trying to flirt with Alanis as she sang a deadpan piano-ballad version of the club hit. I had a feeling it was going to be something special.

Within a few weeks, it had *10 million views*. Was it because of Alanis's sultry, funny ways or was it because of my incredible dance moves? Who can say for sure? Ok, fine, my moves had nothing to do with it, but however you slice it, it will go down as one of the original "viral videos." It made headlines everywhere. Alanis brilliantly chose not to do any interviews about it, which only made the media froth even more. The next week, she threw a party to celebrate. It was fun to mix it up with more LA Canadian transplants, like Matthew Perry, Elisha Cuthbert, Chantal Kreviazuk. Fergie herself sent Alanis a cake in the shape of – what else – lady humps!

CONDORSTOWN MAGIC

I absolutely LOVE when I get to work with an organization that pushes creative engagement and disrupts expectations, that wants to deliver unique experiences for the fans. Case in point: the Bakersfield Condors. My kind of outfit, all the way! Our relationship is now 65 games and going strong.

THE FLIGHT OF THE CONDOR

The team brought in an actual condor for the opening-night puck drop. One little, teeny weeny problem though – the broad-winged bird (a kind of vulture, I found out) took off from his keeper and flew all over the rink. And he wouldn't stop. The crowd was eating it up and, frankly, so was I. Can you say "ESPN

Celebrating Alanis's magical video –
My HUMPS in 2007.

Condors fans fun at the outdoor game.

highlights for a year"? Men with toupees ducked for cover. The best part was when it swooped over the Condors bench then winged it down the tunnel into their dressing room. Hey, what was it supposed to do, fly into the visitors' dressing room? Of course not, he was a Condor!

FREE THE BEARS

Every Thanksgiving weekend, 8,800 fans in the sold-out arena celebrate the Condors' first goal of the night by throwing teddy bears onto the ice. Watching that many cuddly bears fly through the air – including the one that I heave with my golden arm – and knowing that they're all going to local kids in need is a heartwarming sight. I loved it so much the first time that I made sure I've been there on at least seven different "Teddy Bear Toss" weekends. Minor league teams all across North America do the same thing, too, so you should find a game near you and toss a Teddy! Free the Bears!

WE DON'T NEED NO STINKIN' UMBRELLAS

Taking the lead from the genius marketing move of the NHL, the Condors set up a promotion where they played an outdoor game. Unfortunately, it took place in January 2017, during the middle of a two-week rainstorm. We were at the Memorial Stadium of Bakersfield College, and when I say "we," I mean me and thousands of drenched, hockey-loving fans. The teams were literally skating in a slushy pool. Legend has it the refs wanted to call it off, but both teams wanted to finish the game. The celebrity game the night before was coached by hockey icons Wayne Gretzky (husband of my friend Janet) and Luc Robitaille and featured a ton of former NHL players and celebs. Once again, it was the creativity of Condorstown that shined brightly on ESPN and all the sport highlight reels!

Magical nights with 3,000 comedy fans at Just for Laughs Gala's with Jim Jeffries, Trevor Noah, Montreal's own Sugar Sammy, Adam Hills and Andy Nulman co-founder Just for Laughs and former president. Thanks for flying Southwest!

HA HA HA

I'm often asked by people intrigued by my story, "How do you get all these crazy gigs?!" It really does vary. From just showing up unannounced in the early days, to hiring editors to make VHS promo reels, to traditional word of mouth, there have always been an assortment of ways people hear about me and then hire me.

Sometimes it can be in the works for years without me even knowing it.

Take the summer of 2011. I was sitting at a coffee shop in Venice, California, when I saw a note pop into my inbox. I read it, and almost spit out my coffee.

Dear Cameron: I am the President of the "Just for Laughs" Comedy Festival in Montréal and I like what you do. Perhaps we can find a way to integrate it into our shows next year. Looking forward to hearing from you. Andy

What?! HAHAHA.

The "Just for Laughs" Comedy Festival in Montréal is the largest of its kind on the planet. Having grown up just a few hours from Montréal, I knew it well, but had never attended.

When I started out in television back in '01, I had a fleeting thought that maybe I'd be there one day but hadn't considered it since. Why on *Earth* would they even have me there, anyway? I wasn't a comedian. Maybe my dance moves were so bad they were funny?

Curious, I emailed Andy back.

He wasn't 100 percent clear on what I'd do, either, but he knew he wanted me to be a spark and bring in energy to light up fans before the big acts, or whenever the festival needed it. Andy was *looking for something different* – and that's usually where it all begins for me. So, we struck a deal.

Montréal, here I come.

Before the show opened with the big-name acts, I sat in the crowd of 3,000
waiting for my cue. My knees bounced. My heart raced. As the anticipation
started to build, I could feel sweat dripping down my back – I was nervous but
I was also wearing eight t-shirts. Then my song started.

Go time.

I jumped out of the crowd and lost my mind. Comedy fans had no clue what
was going on, but they came along for the ride, and we energized the room for
some of the best comics in the world. I ended up doing gala shows for the likes
of comedians Trevor Noah, Howie Mandel, Joan Rivers, Russell Peters, Sarah
Silverman, The Muppets, John Oliver, Jim Jefferies, Jimmy Carr, Orny Adams, and
Dane Cook, who when he walked out, asked, "What the fu*k is that guy on?!"

One of the coolest things I've learned from these top acts is just how hard
you need to work to reach their levels of success. I'd see them year after year
working their craft. After a show where Orny Adams got a massive standing

Clockwise from top: On stage at Just for Laughs.

With comedy rock-star Sebastian Maniscalco.

Comedian Jennifer Hsiung and British comedy legend Jimmy Carr.

Orny Adams hardest working comedian around & Canadian comedy legend Mark Critch.

ovation, I said to him, "I'll see you at the hotel bar later tonight." He laughed and replied, "I'm going back to the hotel to work on my material."

Incredible, the level of commitment from these top acts. That's what it takes to become the best in the world.

But how did I get that gig in the first place? How had Andy even heard of me? Why did I nearly spit coffee all over my laptop? Well, that story is proof that you never know how or when the positive energy you put into the universe will come back and pay you a nice dividend.

In 2008, I received an email from Mike Darling, a writer for the in-flight magazine for Southwest Airlines. He wanted to do a feature on me for an upcoming issue. Intrigued, we discussed a plan.

Then, a week later, I got an email from *another* airline magazine asking if they could do a story on me. Huh? Confused, I shared this with Mike. He couldn't believe it. Turns out he'd had a beer with the guy from the other magazine and told him about doing my story – and the other guy tried to steal it! I felt like the homecoming queen before Prom! In a bit of a panic, Mike said that he would offer me the cover, 5,000 words, and two big photoshoots, and that he really hoped I'd say yes.

In shock? Yes.

In? Also yes.

"To this day, mentioning the adventures of the professional 'super fan' who travels the world getting paid to pump up crowds is one of the easiest ways to make people stop what they're doing and start asking questions."

Mike Darling, former Senior Editor, Spirit Magazine

The magazine came out on April 1st, 2009. I figured, "Why not fly SWA today?" The flight attendants and I had a good laugh about it. Then, out of nowhere they announced to everyone that they should grab the magazine and said the guy on the cover will be handing out peanuts. *Hey, since when do cover models work for free?!* I even signed a few copies! (Yes, wise guy, they asked.) As it happens, "Just for Laughs" honcho Andy was a Southwest passenger that same month and read the story! Intrigued by my unique skill set, he kept that magazine in his creative drawer for a rainy day. Eleven months later, that rainy day came and I got pinged at a coffee shop with a dream opportunity. Funny how the small things we don't see coming can lead to big things we don't see coming.

I LOVE NEW YORK

From Live Interview ESPN @USOPEN

Brad Gilbert, ESPN: *"At the end of the first set — I notice you notice everything — the t-shirt guy got up does his whole shtick then you waited and you changed your t-shirt. Did he inspire you to change your t-shirt at the end of the first set?"*

Roger Federer, Tennis Superstar: *(Laughs) "As I was doing it, I was like it's the wrong moment to do it, I'm having a face-off with the guy." (Laughs) "Anyway, he did a better job than I did. He's the Man!"*

The US Open – the single largest two-week sporting event in North America, in case you forgot – called me back for year two. The USTA booked me for five nights this year, so that one-dollar bet I made on myself last year had really paid off.

We did the games every other night. I was wearing US Open tees but would always end on the big reveal of the "I LOVE NEW YORK" shirt as I leapt to the landing area in the bottom of the upper deck. The crowd would roar and roar as play was about to resume. If I didn't get a "Quiet, please!" from the umpire, I felt I hadn't done a good job.

One Thursday night, my buddy Chris showed up to support me in the stands. We met up after the match in the concrete underbelly of Arthur Ashe Stadium. As I was packing up my white Reebok Pump tennis kicks in my makeshift locker room, he said, "Novak Djokovic is talking about you on live TV."

I glanced up. "Huh?" I was so confused.

Next thing I knew, Open executive Michael Fiur suggested I meet Novak after his press conference to say hi and bring him an "I LOVE NEW YORK" tee. Michael was always trying to push the fun factor.

This was beyond cool. Moments later, there we were in the hallways of the Open with a few media people, waiting for Novak Djokovic, one of the greatest tennis players on the planet. And there he was.

We shared a hug and a laugh, and then of course we had an impromptu dance-off! And that was it. It blew up. It was everywhere. From *Good Morning America* to Australian TV to flooding YouTube, the unlikely pair caught people's

US OPEN 2011 | MEN'S SINGLES QUARTERFINAL | IBM
3 Roger FEDERER | 6
11 Jo-Wilfried TSONGA | 4
Match Time: 37min

A huge smile on Roger Federer's face after watching
'SuperFan' Cameron Hughes dancing at the 2011 U.S. Open

Roger Federer at Match 4 Africa Event.

US Open Tennis ✓
@usopen

Through the years...
🕺 1990s: Macarena
🕺 2000s: Soulja Boy
🕺 2010s: ...This?

#USOpen

Michael Fiur the entertainment maestro of the Open!

Rafa Nadal post game debrief.

Friends supporting at the Open.

Federer's agent, Tony Godsick at the Match 4 Africa.

eyes. Novak was a big, charismatic tennis star, but the previous years, he'd said some things about the NYC crowds that didn't go over so well.

Then we danced.

I had him sign my "I LOVE NEW YORK" tee, and it was all love. He would continue to dance on his own after matches, and the fans were loving it. No doubt buoyed by our dance-off, he went on to win the US Open that year.

The same year, Roger Federer was playing a match when he was caught looking up at me during a changeover. As he got to his starting position, he could be seen laughing in disbelief at my uninhibited shenanigans. The video has over five million views.

A few years later, Federer's agent Tony Godsick called and said I was the only person ever to make Roger laugh during a match, and would I like to come and surprise him at his charity event in Seattle for Match For Africa?

"Uh, let me check my sched – YES!!!"

In the celebrity doubles match for his great cause, Federer was partnered with some "Geek Squad" wannabe named Bill Gates. Roger and Bill played against tennis star John Isner and lead guitarist for Pearl Jam, Mike McCready.

Roger didn't know I was coming. Tony knew a surprise was needed at his own event.

During one of the timeouts, I leapt out of nowhere, and hit it hard. Roger was shocked. He and Bill were howling on their bench, watching me go nuts. After the match, Tony brought Roger by to introduce us. He appreciated how much energy I brought to the event and thanked me for being there. A true gentleman. As he was going out to play Isner, I asked what he wanted me to do with the crowd.

"The more you do, the less I have to do," he joked. "Don't hold back!" You got it.

The next year I was invited to San Jose for another "Match for Africa" event. I'll never forget starting the wave that year, because Roger ran on the court and joined in. Then, when it seemed like it might never stop – he swung his arms and motioned to me with a huge smile to stop the wave so he could resume the match. Which I immediately did. I mean, it was Roger Federer!

What a thrill and honor to be involved. In those two years, these awesome events raised over $4.5 million for the noble work of the Roger Federer Foundation.

At the 2013 US Open, ESPN host Brad Gilbert (love him), told Rafael Nadal after a winning match that he thought he noticed the champion sneaking a glance or two up at the dancing t-shirt guy in the bleachers during the changeovers. Rafa admitted it was true. "That guy is amazing," he laughed.

Once again, Open exec Michael Fiur shook things up and had me connect with another world-class champion. In front of a row of photographers outside a stadium elevator, I asked Rafa to sign my "I LOVE NEW YORK" tee, and presented him with one of his own. Then I asked him for some dancing advice. He said he'd need some tequila for that! Congrats to Rafa for winning the tournament that year. Anyone notice the trend?!

I'd have to say my biggest US Open moment came at the 2015 tournament, my sixth consecutive year in Flushing Meadows. After bringing the crazy to the fans, I decided to stick around to watch Brad Gilbert interview the winner, Novak Djokovic, on center court.

Holy shit. They're talking about me again. Is Novak a stalker?!

"He has done well, you know," Djokovic said. "He entertained the crowd. It was phenomenal. Thanks for dancing! Keep it up man, wherever you are."

Uh, I'm right over here.

Suddenly "Mony Mony" began to blare, the stadium DJ acting like my ultimate wingman on a night out. My mind raced with excitement.

Is this really about to happen?

Then Michael, my official US Open cheer whisperer, gave me the green light. Gilbert and Djokovic were waving me down to the court.

No.

Freaking.

Way.

It's happening!

Sprinting down the aisle towards the court, I leapt over the barricade and onto the famed playing surface, two white XL "I LOVE NY" tees holstered in my belt like I was some kind of bizarro cowboy, heading to a mysterious showdown with the world's top tennis player.

What!?

I could sense the security guard's disappointment as I floated past him. Typically, a trespassing fan would be greeted by a punishing tackle, but not this time. *Stand down, fella.* The crowd was roaring. I was in shock! I mean, c'mon – all I ever won at my tennis club was the sportsmanship award – and I just made it to center court at the US Freakin' Open!

Skipping my way up to the net, I locked eyes with my old dance partner, three-time Wimbledon champion Novak Djokovic. He'd just beaten his opponent

Novak Djokovic post-game celebration dance at center court. Thanks Brad Gilbert!

in straight sets, so he was ready to celebrate. I ripped one of the tees from my waistband and handed it over to him – he started to put it on, but I stopped him.

No.

Pump the brakes, Djokovic. Not yet.

Then I raised my arm at a 90-degree angle, t-shirt gripped firmly above my head, orbiting around my hand like planets around the sun. Djokovic did the same. I twirled my tee even faster, as if to hypnotize him. It worked. He locked his right leg in place and kicked his left leg up, madly twirling his shirt in unison with me.

The crowd went nuts. The camera guy's gum fell out of his mouth. Gilbert was giggling. This spontaneous act of cheer was being broadcast around the world, live on ESPN.

The dance ended. Novak and I embraced. A smile pervaded his face as I pulled the "I Love NY" tee over his head.

My work here was done.

At my friend's New York City loft, nobody was home. I sank back into the mattress and flipped on the television; cold beer in hand, smile as wide as Broadway.

There I was on SportsCenter. It was exactly the break David Shoemaker said I needed. I couldn't believe it, or maybe I could. The hustling, the showing up, the GETTING UP – it had all collectively led to this magic playing out on the screen before me.

It was always about the fans. About showing them something they'd never seen and making them feel part of the Open magic. The dance-off with Novak, the hang with Nadal, and being part of Federer's charity events – well, that was pretty cool, too.

By the way, I saved that dollar. Never spent it.

Amazing how a kernel of an idea led to so many magical moments.

Thank you, New York.

I love you.

OKC Thunder Basketball
Fun Santa photo courtesy
of Richard Rowe.

Merry Christmas.

HOOP DREAMS

FEEL THE THUNDER

"Hey Dad, I'm in Oklahoma City. Off to a Thunder hoops game." By morning he'd tell me about the Sooners, the size of the energy sector and why the team is called the Thunder (yes, it's storm-related).

OKC is a great sports town, and I'd worked there quite a bit already. I became a regular for the OKC Blazers – the CHL hockey team – for over 20 games. I also had done some Hornets games in town when they had to relocate due to Hurricane Katrina. My girlfriend at the time was convinced I had *another* girlfriend in OKC. I swear, I didn't! I just loved the energy of the Oklahoma City crowds.

Tonight's game was going to be huge. The Thunder, with Kevin Durant and Russell Westbrook, were on the verge of closing out the mighty San Antonio Spurs in the Western Conference Semifinals. From the sea of Thunder blue t-shirts and the buzzing sold-out pre-game crowd, I was once again reminded that OKC was without question, one of the best fan bases in the NBA. I had flown in that day next to a producer from *American Ninja Warrior*. My new friend was a big hoops fan, and told me the top bosses and hosts, Matt Iseman and Akbar Gbaja-Biamila, were going to be in attendance. After we landed I called the team and was able to surprise him with some seats, too. The game that night was electric, and the crowd roared to new heights when I did a "LOUD – LOUDER – LOUDEST" three t-shirt reveal. Later, as I danced down the aisle, who did I cross paths with, but a 6'6" former Oakland Raider who just so happened to be one of the "Ninja" hosts! Akbar and I had a spontaneous dance-off, much to the fans' delight, and the Thunder went on to an epic playoff series victory.

"I'll admit I was a Cameron Hughes skeptic... only took one game! One of a kind crowd master. You had OKC in the palm of your hands instantly."

John Leach, Director of Events & Entertainment, Oklahoma City Thunder

---

THAT'S GOTTA HURT

Game 1 of the NBA Playoffs in 2008. The New Orleans Hornets were playing the mighty Dallas Mavericks. I was going out of my mind as usual, but this time, I slipped doing a particularly awkward dance move, and immediately knew something was wrong with my knee.

Breathe, Cameron. The show must go on.

Mark Cuban himself was a few seats over. He gave me an *oh shit* look, followed by a *you'll be okay* nod. That's what I hoped, too.

Should I have stopped right then? Of course. But I didn't know how bad it was, so I forced myself up and kept on grooving. I finished the game as best I could, fueled by adrenaline and the crowd. No more dancing for me, but I gritted my teeth and tossed out tees until the final horn blew. Exhausted, I then turned to my helper, and made a request I never thought I'd have to make – I needed a wheelchair. I later found out that it was a sprained MCL. Yikes. I still feel it from time to time, mostly when I jump off a railing or into a large man's arms.

DA BULLS

I've always loved the Chicago Bulls, so when I got the call to perform for them in the 2017 playoffs, I was thrilled. The team front office suggested that I start my performance from center court during a dance contest. This had never been done in my career, but it was Michelle and Emily, executives who I'd worked with in New York at the Knicks games. I trusted them.

They said I'd be competing against an older gentleman and a young woman. My stage manager told me that I'd win easily – then the plan was for me to go nuts and ignite the crowd from the stands. Something didn't feel quite right about this, but I nodded and let it go.

During a TV timeout in the first quarter, the dance-off began, and the senior citizen, decked out in his vintage '70s tracksuit, went first. He absolutely CRUSHED IT. Like, I mean breakdancing, pop-and-lock, off-the-chain amazing. The entire arena went berserk – including me and the other contestant.

Then I remembered, *I was supposed to dance, too!* All of a sudden, I felt like I was standing in front of a firing squad... of 20,000 fans. The other contestant and I should have both walked off the court right then and there. This was *not* what I'd signed up for. But, valuable lesson – it's what I agreed to. The plan of me winning and storming into the stands had just gone up in flames.

I'll admit it now, I was having a bit of an ego moment. Of course, the b-boy grandpa won the contest in a landslide – and I felt like I had not been set up to succeed. The stage manager didn't know what to say or do. I was rattled. I didn't really see how I would be able to win the crowd over for the rest of the night after what I'd just gone through. *How was I supposed to get intro'd now?* In the second quarter, they sent me into the stands, and I felt like it was going to be a

NHL All-Star Game Tampa Bay 2018.

Lake Charles Ice Pirates WPHL 1997.

struggle. Yet instead, some very valuable lessons were about to break-dance into my stubborn brain. As the camera settled on my face, everyone recognized me as the poor guy who just got his butt whipped in the dance contest. We had, *all of us*, been swept up in the joy of his dancing heroics, and the Bulls crowd was still in a great mood, primed to have even more fun.

So when I got up and went insane, much to my surprise and delight – the crowd was RIGHT THERE WITH ME! After all, to them, this was just the next phase in a crazy party that had been kickstarted by the electrifying moves of the older man.

They wanted me to win this time, because *we were all in the fun together*! Big thanks to Michelle and Emily for an unforgettable lesson: Sometimes you just need to let go of your ego and run with the BULLS!

HEY NOW, YOU'RE AN ALL-STAR

It's simple math. If I'm working a game, there's a good chance someone from another team will see me or hear about me. But the very best way to put my face in front of ALL the teams at the same time is to work at an All-Star game! (Cue Smash Mouth.) CHL, ECHL, AHL, NHL and NBA – if you're throwing an all-star event, guess who's going to find a way to be there, working the crowd *and* the room?

Unlike my VHS promo tapes from the early days, which may or may not have ever gotten into the hands of the right exec, *these* were my live auditions that were impossible to miss. Let's face it, most all-star contests are low energy, so this was my best marketing tool of all time. I take great pride in how hard I work the room at all times, putting myself out there both in the stands and at the networking cocktail parties… Your pal Matt Riley from Bakersfield is there and suddenly introduces you to Jason Siegel from the Orlando Solar Bears. And now – boom, just like that – you're going to Disney World!

★★★

Being in Toronto for the NBA All-Star game in 2016, where I'd done my very first NBA game, was a huge thrill. I remember Steve Nash saying how proud he was to see me still rocking it. (No rollerblade pub crawl that time, but it was great to see him, too!)

And for a Canadian kid like me, who'd once scraped ice at local rinks, getting invited to the 2018 NHL All-Star Game in Tampa was quite a significant moment. I'd worked for more than half of the teams in the league, 19 by that point, and a lot of the players recognized or even knew me. In the social setting of the weekend, they had a good laugh wondering how on Earth I even ended up doing this... still! I often do as well.

MUDBUGS AND GREEN TEA

Back in '04, Jason Rent, the GM of one of the hottest franchises in minor league hockey, the Bossier-Shreveport Mudbugs, hired me to do a few games. For my first game, I showed up late. That was the first – and only! – time that's *ever* happened in my career when it was purely my fault. I blame it on the nap I needed because of the crazy travel schedule I had.

Helluva first impression. Jason was a guy's guy. Friendly with a splash of *No BS*. After the game, he was sitting in his office poking fun at me for putting green tea on my rider list. "We all thought it was a bit weird you had green tea and didn't want beers!"

Fast forward to 2007, when Shreveport hosted the CHL All-Star Game. I was excited to perform at the big game on Wednesday night. The night before, the CHL was planning an awards gala ($100 per ticket, minimum) for about 500 fans. A couple of months out from the event, Jason asked if I knew anyone who could host.

"Let me connect you with my friend," I said. Sure enough, my friend Jonathan, who represents major acts and speakers, was able to help Jason book comedian Jim Breuer. It would be a win for all involved. Jim was an SNL alum, great touring comedian, and perfect for a hockey crowd.

Then, just hours before the big event, I got a call from my friend Brad Treliving, the CHL President. "Hughesie, do you do stand-up?"

I frowned.

"Pardon me?"

"Well, Jim Breuer can't make it to Shreveport," he said. "At this rate, we don't know if the Stanley Cup (which was an attraction for the gala) will even make it."

Turns out Breuer was set to fly from Houston but didn't love the icy conditions coming into Shreveport. So, he turned around and went home.

Shite.

"I've done a lot of speaking stuff...", I said hesitantly. "But not comedy, per se."

"Perfect! Talk to Jason and sort out a deal. We'll see you tonight."

What?!

My heart pounded. Pulse was off the charts. Was it too late to say no? I mean, this was a little out of my arena, to say the least...

My friend Jason Rent (team GM) who brought me into Shreveport with the Mudbugs, All-Star Games, and years later the Rapid City Rush. And he paid up!

But, what was that I said earlier about saying yes?

"Okay, Jason, but here are my terms."

I knew Jim would have made a pretty penny for the event, so I told Jason I'd go on stage for $2,000, and if it went well, another $2,000. He had no one else – so we had a deal.

I sat in the lobby bar for an hour trying my material on every GM in the league. I had to get in the zone. As the gala started, I was nervous as heck. Heart roaring in my chest to the beat of the crowd, all talking at once. But as soon as the sweet sounds of "Everybody Dance Now" floated my way, I got fired up.

Making my way to the stage, I said into the mic: "Something is definitely wrong." Then I ran off, grabbed three cases of beer, and brought them on stage, passing them out to the all-stars at the head tables. The players were psyched and the crowd cheered. The ice had been broken.

"Cam absolutely killed it!" Jason said. "It was like he never left the barstool he was at two hours earlier, as we were all sharing funny stories from this crazy business. It was like those 500 or so people were sitting right there with us."

With my freshly earned bonus, let's just say I looked after the team GMs that night.

"After I introduced Cameron to a crowd that was expecting an SNL star, I hurried to stand by the back exit. Part of me didn't want to watch – as you know, there are not many things worse than watching a family member or friend crash in front of a crowd. But I stood there with one foot still in the room in support… After that event, not one person who was in attendance felt shortchanged."

Jason Rent, GM, Shreveport Mudbugs

Wigan Warriors Rugby
Super League.

Guest speaker, Project 11
Winnipeg Jets Bell Let's
Talk Day.

I'VE BEEN EVERYWHERE

've performed in 40 states, nine provinces, and just about every small arena in North America. I've even performed in a converted barn! I love being a part of the team fun backstage and in the dressing rooms, and connecting with people of all stripes across the continent. Management and players always made me feel like I was part of the town during my short stays. I joke that I don't have a hometown, I have hundreds of hometowns. Ripped from the pages of my road trip journals, these are some of the best stories, full of blood, sweat, beers and cheers!

SOUTH CAROLINA STINGRAYS – "THE HUMAN SPRAIN DELAY"

I came to beautiful Charleston, SC, to perform in Game 3 of the ECHL Finals for my pal Darren Abbott, the GM. With a crowd of over 10,000, I went for a big physical, leaping dance move, and let's just say, uh, I didn't stick the landing. Like not even close. Everyone thought it was a joke. It wasn't. I slowly got up and I think the crowd actually moaned with me. Fans weren't sure what to do. I got helped into the locker room, where I found out it was a horrible sprain. The team duct taped me up with ice packs big enough for an offensive lineman's quads. I went out to the Zamboni tunnel and led cheers, the wave, and got everyone going for the last period of the game. They won! I stayed off my feet for the next 53 hours and actually came back for the final game. It was the most intense tape job of my life, and the Stingrays went on to win the championship! Let's just say, ever since that game I tape my ankles, wear a brace – or both.

ODESSA JACKALOPES – "WERE YOU RAISED IN A BARN?!"

They play in a barn. No seriously, this minor league hockey team plays in a converted cattle-rodeo barn. The owners are the nicest people in the world – Tracey and Bill Nyborg. On some nights, they pack 3,000 people in there, but when the local HS football team is playing, they're lucky to get 200. Can you say "Friday Night Lights"? It's about this town! I have a lot of strange memories from Odessa. One night in particular, I hadn't even started dancing yet when an errant puck went screaming into the rickety bleachers. Guess who speared it one-handed? *Big Red in the barn, baby!* The crowd went apeshit, and I took that puck as my cue and launched directly into my opening act, flinging Jacks tees and burning down the barn... On the quieter nights, I'd hand out all the tees I had and then kick back and watch the rest of the game with the Nyborgs, sampling some of the local beers. Only in Odessa.

AUSTIN ICE BATS – "BURN AFTER CHEERING"

Cam's Pro Tip – Get a cool sponsor who will give you the same high-top shoe in eight different shades – that way, you can match just about every team's colors. Cam's Problem When He Landed in Austin – The airline lost my bag, the puck was going to drop at 7:30 p.m. and I had *nothing* to perform in. *No shoes, no jeans, no service.* And maybe no cheer?

Oops. To help out, the team owner lent me his Wrangler jeans, belt buckle, and running shoes from approximately 1965. Then he said, "Throw it all out when you're done." *Jeez guy, thanks for the compliment.* Even the belt buckle?! It must've been a lucky outfit because the team won and they soaked me with Bud Lights. So yeah, I definitely chucked his stuff.

RIO GRANDE KILLER BEES – "NOT SO TINY DANCER"

One night I had a dance-off with a 400-pound fan... and lost. This guy was good. Pound for pound, the most nimble man in America. He won "Fan of the Game," and saw me as a bit of a rival. I ended up coming back to do five more games in Rio Grande, but never danced against him again. You've gotta know when to hold 'em and know when to fold 'em.

CORPUS CHRISTI RAYS – "LA BAMBA & THE ROCKER"

More hockey in Texas! Yep, part of the early days of the CHL. The arena had the worst view of the ice I'd ever seen. It was like a roller rink. La Bamba himself, Lou Diamond Phillips, a local resident, dropped the puck for the first game in team history. I want to thank the Rays for sending me their limo to get me at the airport and putting me up in a nice hotel... well, at least the cockroaches seemed to think it was nice. Strange side note: I ended up partying with the lead singer from the band The Verve Pipe on his tour bus until 4 a.m. Long story. Let's just leave that one there. We were only freshmen.

LAFAYETTE ICE GATORS – "RAGIN CAJUN"

This Louisiana franchise in the mid-'90s was as hot as any team in the country. Every game was NUTS – 11,000 hysterical fans cheering their faces off. I came back a few years later and was a bit confused to find just 748 people at the game. *Um, hey y'all, what happened to the old Ice Gator gang?!* Gotta admit – it was hard to get excited for this one. Yikes. But I dug deep and found a way to give everyone the best show I could. This was one of my first "aha!" moments, where I realized it's not who *doesn't* show up, it's who *does* that matters...

> ## TIMEOUT
>
> "Life is one big party down here," says Ice Gators coach Doug Shedden, an Ontario native who played center in the NHL from 1981 to '91. "If a player wants to drink 10 beers the night before a game, why not? He'll sweat it out on the ice."

BRANDON WHEAT KINGS – "SUNDOWN IN THE PARIS OF THE PRAIRIES"

I rolled into Manitoba and it was a crisp minus 38 degrees. Oh joy. I was there to do my first game for the Wheat Kings, one of the most famous Junior Hockey League teams around. My face was frozen. I couldn't feel my feet. I was definitely not "feeling it." When I got my shivering self into the arena, mistakenly entering through the players' entrance, the whole team was right there in front of me, warming up with the "sewer ball" hockey tradition. (Kind of like hacky-sack with a soccer ball, if you don't know it.)

Rather than razzing me for coming in the wrong door, the young Wheat Kings gave me a big welcome cheer and invited me to play with them! Incredibly gracious. Even though I was more frozen than Olaf, I threw off my parka, put on my kicks and got into the game. (Btw, I came in second, believe it or not – my first and only game of my career) And they won that night. Coach Kelly McCrimmon even let me in the room to do a pump-up and celebrate with the boys! Ya gotta love that prairie spirit – it warms your frozen heart.

IDAHO STEELHEADS – "IS THERE A TAILOR IN THE HOUSE?!"

How best to put this? If the Idaho fans read their "Farmer's Almanac," they'd know there wasn't *supposed* to be a full moon that night. Yet, my jeans had other plans. I needed two rolls of duct tape to finish the game. Before I performed the next night, I had to make a quick stop to a men's clothing store. Let's just say that "let 'er rip" has more than one meaning.

YEARS OF FUN! Planes, trains, automobiles, late nights, early mornings and millions of smiles!

ROCKFORD ICE HOGS – "ONE FOR THE FILES"

They sent a stretch limo to pick me up from O'Hare! I thought I was being *Punk'd* and refused to get in at first, but finally I did. Probably the first time in history someone got a stretch limo ride to a Holiday Inn Express. This game was also memorable because a couple of fans got married during intermission. I offered to officiate but they said no thanks – shocker! Safe to say few teams have ever looked after me as well. Thanks Bernie!

COLORADO EAGLES – "WHEN THE SHIRT HIT THE FAN"

This game was insane. Energy boosters on turbo, I got up just as I had hundreds of times before, ripped my jersey off, twirled a tee like a weapons-grade blender ready to make an epic toss... and accidentally nailed a fan in the head. Like, hard. In full view of the entire arena. It was all caught on video, too, so if it had happened today, we'd be viral, for sure. The shirt-shocked guy's reaction was natural – his eyes went red and he pulled his fist back, ready to knock the daylights out of me. Luckily for me, nearby fans told him I was just "firing up the crowd" – and not trying to start a fight. I got him some ice to wrap around the shirt and press to his ouchie.

HALIFAX MOOSEHEADS – "POW! RIGHT IN THE KISSER"

I was in town for a few days, performing for the premiere team in the Canadian Hockey League that featured future NHL stars Nathan MacKinnon and Jonathan Drouin. After my first game, I made friends with Mia, a local actress who said she liked my act. I asked her if she'd want to do something fun at the next game. She said you bet.

So the next night, during the "Kiss Cam" segment, I faked like I intended to kiss a few fans, then found Mia. I begged her for a kiss on the cheek. The crowd was cheering me on, hoping this lovely young woman would play along. Mia was very coy, holding a beer, minding her own business. Finally, she gave in. But instead of an innocent peck on the cheek, we locked lips and kissed for a good ten seconds. The place went NUTS. Instant classic. I never told Nathan and Jonathan, or the 9,484 fans, that it was staged. And hey, why would I? Check it out – CameronHughes.TV.

LAREDO BUCKS – "HOCKEY NIGHT IN MEXICO"

The Bucks were a CHL hockey team on the border of Mexico and Texas. The predominantly Latino crowd was new to the game of hockey and still trying to figure out the rules. The fans were full of spirit and cheered insanely, but not always at the right times. They were also a tad shocked to see Big Red, a 6'4" Canadian gringo losing his mind and tossing tees. We were all fish out of water together that night, and it was a thing of beauty. After the game, as I was heading back to my hotel (table for one), they graciously invited me to postgame tailgate with them, which, of course, I did. For hours. *Gracias, amigos.* Gotta connect with the locals.

ALEXANDRIA WARTHOGS – "ON THIN ICE"

This one, I'll never forget. Right after the game, I asked the team rep to drive me to the local "Money Mart" to cash my check. Like, immediately. The team had so few fans come out, and rumors were swirling that they were in trouble, so I had to do it. I'm glad I did – they only lasted four more months.

SIOUX FALLS, SOUTH DAKOTA – "TARDY TO THE PARTY"

Nothing like "D League" hoops, baby! These towns aren't in the middle of nowhere, but they're pretty darn close. Sometimes, like with this Sioux Falls game, it requires three separate flights to get there. So when you miss your first flight, as I did, it's a domino effect that would give even the best travel agent a migraine. I had briefly considered bailing, but decided to honor my commitment and pull a *Trains, Planes & Automobiles* to get there. Still, my final connecting flight didn't land in Sioux Falls until just *after* the opening tip. Frantic, I changed into my game gear in the taxi on the way to the arena. My driver got a great tip for not bringing me straight to the police station, or posting the totally hot video on YouTube. Obviously, no rehearsal with the game day crew. I burst into the arena during the second quarter and just dove in. It was a whirlwind of a day, but I think the crowd picked up on my manic energy and we had an absolute blast. The team must've been happy because I got paid in full. Only the second time EVER that I was late. Man, what a crazy ride…

CHARLOTTE STING WNBA – "FLASH PANTS"

This was the first and last time a woman has put cash down my pants while I was performing. Hey, it was a different time back then…

A NIGHT FIT FOR A PRINCE

Who doesn't love a good chick flick? Come on, you do, don't deny it. My friend produced *The Sisterhood of the Traveling Pants* 2 and invited me to the premiere. As my old friend Jay (of "making the basketball team when I didn't" fame) had recently moved to LA, I invited him as my plus one.

We were a bit reluctant to go. As dudes in our late thirties, we thought we might be out of place among the teenage girls the movie was certain to attract. Plus, Jay had just sprained his ankle playing basketball and was hobbling around on crutches. But we pulled up our big boy socks and ventured out.

The first surprise of the night is that we both really liked the movie. Afterwards, there was a small reception in the theatre. Jay and I laughed as we saw people ten years younger than us – okay fine, 20 – with their parents. Let's just say we weren't the target audience.

Just as we were about to call it a night early, our producer friend asked us if we wanted to go to the after-party.

"Where is it, an American Girl store?" Jay asked.

She replied: "Not exactly. It's at Prince's house."

A beat of silence.

I said: "At *a* prince's house, or *Prince*'s house?"

"The latter," our friend said.

It turns out, the director of the movie doubled as a music video director and was tight with His Royal Purple Highness.

As I tried to keep my cool (*Prince!*), she gave us the directions to his place up on Mulholland Drive. Soon, Jay and I were pulling up to the 20,000 square foot palace in my Ford Focus station wagon, which we parked between a Maserati and a Lamborghini. Fitting right in already. Two Canucks trying to make it in show biz were suddenly being escorted into the home of one of the most legendary recording artists of all time.

The first thing we saw when we walked in was a massive purple portrait of Prince. I assumed this was the closest we'd get to seeing him. He was famous for having huge parties but never making an appearance – part of his mystique. As we followed the yellow brick road to the kitchen, filled with producers and beautiful people, we ran into my friend. The next thing we knew, we were getting an impromptu tour of Prince's home and being ushered into the basement by his band mates.

A magical night with the sisterhood and artist known as Prince.

That's when it happened. 12:38 a.m.

Prince graced us with his presence.

Now, I'm not a religious guy, but laying eyes on Prince felt… otherworldly, maybe? And it only got better. Prince took to the stage in his own private nightclub to act as DJ, and of course a full-on dance party broke out. Jay was sitting on a couch in the corner, nursing his ankle, when Prince yelled at him: "Hey, you on the couch. Get up and dance. You're bringing down the vibe!"

When Prince tells you to dance, *you dance.* Or hobble, as Jay did.

As you might guess, nobody had to ask *me* to dance. I was out there on the floor, going full-tilt, busting some moves next to some of Prince's most gorgeous friends. As I stepped away to take a bathroom break, Prince zeroed in on me. "Hey, take it easy out there with my ladies, my man," he called out. Pretty sure I blushed.

When Prince tells you to take it easy, *you take it easy.*

Still, the rest of the night was, well, crazy. Let's just say that we partied like it was 1999.

The next day, Jay and I compared notes and could barely believe what had happened. *Was it real?* It sure was. Only in Hollywood…

DON'T BE BLUE SANTA

After a few beers one night my pal, Shawn Bennett, who ran the Knicks entertainment, came up with this crazy idea to have me wear a Blue Santa suit to the always-famous Christmas Day game at MSG. It seemed like a genius idea at the time, but I didn't hear from him for a while, so I thought it was off. Then

Rocking Blue Santa at Madisson Square Garden – HO HO HO!

I get a note saying: "Blue Santa suit is in. See you 25th?" Although I thought my costume days were over, for three years in a row I was Blue Santa at MSG. This was too much fun not to do. I'd lose my mind and bring the blue cheer, then I'd rip off the outfit, flag a yellow cab and hop up to Ottawa in time for dinner with my dad and sister. And, no, you can't breathe in those things (almost passed out three times). Good laughs sitting beside some celebs having chats – I wonder if John McEnroe recognized my moves from the US Open!

THE SUPERFAN

"I was sitting at my desk in Kamloops working for the Blazers prior to the 2012 Season. An email popped up on my computer with a link to a YouTube video of this crazy fan out of Ottawa who gets up and cheers during games and tries to encourage others to do the same. As a former player, I loved it. When you have passionate fans who will do anything to cheer and make noise for your team that literally fuels off this energy, you have to love it. When someone has a good shift, blocks a shot, beats the shit out of someone, or simply just makes a play that has no stat, we feed off that. Fans who pay for a ticket have every right to cheer or boo their favorite team on whenever they want. That's the reality of being a fan.

I fell in love with this knucklehead long before I got to know him. His story is real. His heart is as big as any player that plays the game, and his energy is contagious.

We were in the playoffs that year against the Portland Winterhawks in the third round of the Western Conference Finals. We were down 4-0 or worse and the building was dying for something. We brought Cam in for this game to see firsthand what the energetic "Super Fan" could offer.

Down this bad halfway through one of the biggest games of our playoffs, Cam absolutely electrified the building. You can ask anybody that was in the house that night and they will not only remember Bronson Mashmeyer's game tying goal late in the third, but they will remember the energy this quirky, goofy, semi-bald, out of shape 40-year-old virgin from Ottawa brought to the table.

Cam helped mandate a win that night. He brought energy to our fans who transferred that energy to our kids on the ice who really just needed a push. I strongly believe that we would have never come back and forced a game seven had Cam not been there. I love the guy!

From the Desk of Dave Chyzowski – Former Director of Marketing, Kamloops Blazers

RETURN OF MELONHEAD

The phone rang. It was my *alma mater*, Bishop's University. Seven years after I earned my degree, they asked me to come to campus and speak to the incoming freshmen. *Wait, they know I wore a watermelon and was asked to leave for a year, right? Yes? Alrighty then.*

After my epic journey from Los Angeles all the way to Lennoxville, Québec , I met with the 20-year-old student leader to go over my speech. He knew that the new students would gravitate to someone who had tried a lot, failed a lot, and learned a lot. I would be relatable to them because I made mistakes. Yeah, I said it. My message to them was this: when you're knocked down by your failures and challenges, *keep getting up!* Of course I showed up with my trademark watermelon and rocked that theatre full of 600 students, 600 fresh faces, 600 new dreams. I challenged them to build a foundation, to *carpe* that *diem*, to grow in ways they never saw coming. I said "Don't be afraid to try!" Build your community. I said *eat* watermelons, don't wear them – that's *my* thing. I told them: "Say YES."

Giving that talk was one of the best, most rewarding things I've ever done in my life. In fact, I loved it so much, I did it for 10 years in a row. Raise a toast to Bishop's!

CARLETON NORTH HIGH SCHOOL

I made a surprise visit to Florenceville, New Brunswick, which bills itself as "the Potato Capital of the World" (the famous Canadian food company McCain is based there). I spoke at an assembly and both the students and I had a fantastic time. Next-level school spirit mania.

As I was leaving, the school hockey team lined up in a row to give me a "slow clap" out of the building. It was their way of saying thanks. I'd never gotten my own "Rudy" slow clap!

A few months later, I was shocked when I read that two tragedies struck the school within a short time of each other. Two horrible highway accidents, that no community should ever have to deal with. I called the principal and said: "What can I do?" I had to be there.

A month later at the last assembly of the year, they announced a fake name as the last speaker of the day. No one came out on stage. The students were like *huh*? Then I bolted into the gym and said, "I'll do it!" They didn't know what hit them. They went wild. That day, because of the sad events that occurred that year, I gave a very different talk (but always random dancing!), going deep on what they were all facing. That day, I gave them my heart. And then I gave them

Hanging with my Star Friend, Ashley Taylor at CNHS Grad.

even more. I spoke about loss, real loss. About how we need to let go and feel it all in order to heal and properly grieve. I shared a few examples of how I had spoken with a therapist after losing my mother during high school, and how everyone in the room needed to feel they could talk with anyone at any moment. And, I said it's okay to be angry, to feel it all, to be less strong in the moment... because it is. You need to be brave enough to admit you're hurting. They needed a friend. We all do in these moments. We need a lot of them.

Half a year later, I was boarding a flight when I got an email from Ashley, a Carleton North student. She wrote that, before I showed up, she was having a hard time processing her grief and needed help. She needed an outlet, something to open her up. She was stuck, lost, and scared. She told me that my surprise appearance gave her the opening she needed. Either someone was peeling onions around me on that flight, or I cried.

A few months later, I was asked to give the graduation commencement speech for the class of 2012. Hmm, let me think about it... YES! The day before, I surprised Ashley at her house. She almost fell over. It was a great reunion.

At the commencement ceremony, I shared a story of how, when I was in university, I asked a few close friends to write down what drove them in life. Then I challenged the graduating class to do the same. Then I reached into my blazer pocket, and pulled out a piece of paper that said:

Make a difference.

I told them I wasn't always sure I was doing that. But then one day I got an email from Ashley. :)

HE'S NOT GOING TO BE EVERYONE'S CUP OF TEA

"You know, he's not going to be everyone's cup of tea."

That's what I was told before I brought Cameron over for his first game in the British Elite Ice Hockey League. Yup, we call it ice hockey over here, because "real hockey," I have been told many times, is played on a field.

To confuse you even more, I brought him to Belfast, Northern Ireland, which really isn't quite British and isn't quite Irish – but that's a whole other book to read.

I had shown the video of Cameron entertaining crowds across North America to a few colleagues and volunteers that worked for my team at the time, the Belfast Giants. The reaction was a bit pessimistic to say the least, which if you know British people, is, well, very British of them. They aren't exactly open to dancing in the aisles and swinging t-shirts. Don't get me wrong, we have amazing fans over here, but there are still some traditionalists who prefer to clap for a successful penalty kill or sing a song that they've sung every game for 30 years rather than be pushed to get out of their seats when "Mony Mony" comes on the loudspeaker.

Telling me that he wasn't going to be everyone's cup of tea is basically what made the decision for me, because I have always wanted to show people here that sports are about more than just the game itself – it has to be about the whole package. I'm a huge believer that the game night experience is as important as the scoreline in making sure people come back every week. And for any pro sports team that relies mostly on bums in seats, that's even more important. We don't have TV money or big league sponsors – we have to eat what we kill. Ticket income pays the bills.

I knew the majority of people were going to love Cam. So we brought him over and sat him in the stands. Three or four whistles into the game, up he got. It took a solid eight seconds to get a reaction from the crowd, and man, was it a long eight seconds – but then the crowd went nuts. He had them.

I mean, he really had them.

For the rest of the game, he was electrifying and engaging and fun and hilarious and everything else I hoped he would be – and so much more.

The lady who told me he wasn't going to be everyone's cup of tea couldn't help herself when he was there in her section, face to face, and asked her to join him. She let her guard down, laughed out loud, and did what sports fans across the world want to do every time they hear a great song at a live event.

She stood up and danced.

I've brought Cameron over to Belfast and now over to Cardiff to the new team I run. I have met up with him in New York, gone to fan engagement conferences with him in London and shared many nights of laughs and stories over beers to remember.

Over here in the UK, we don't have "Three Stars of the Game" – we give out the "Man of the Match." That first game in Belfast, Cam became the first non-player (must be the only one) to ever win the "Man of the Match." He got one hell of an ovation when he knee-slid out to centre ice to pick up his award. I guess that night he was everyone's cup of tea.

From the Desk of Todd Kelman, Hockey Executive, Belfast Giants, Cardiff Devils

---

Having Cameron in the crowd for a game in Belfast and meeting him before for his first wee pint of Guinness really helped create a buzz and an incredible atmosphere for our fan base!

Adam Keefe, former player, coach, Belfast Giants

FEELINGS, NOTHING MORE
THAN FEELINGS

I love how people in my industry turn each other on to great new ways of connecting and innovating. My Ottawa Senators colleague Glen introduced me to a British gentleman, Mark Bradley, a genuine force in the "fan experience" business. Shortly thereafter, Mark helped get me invited to the "Stadium Summit & Fan Experience Forum," which travels around Europe. In 2014, it was taking place at Wembley Stadium in London. Executives from around the world would gather for two days to attend seminars and exhibitions and exchange ideas. I was asked to speak at the fan portion of the event. I flew over from North America, and although I wasn't paid a cent, had a gut feeling I needed to show up. I had to walk my own talk. Show UP!

My mission statement for the talk was to *"Remove the barriers to create an emotional experience that makes your fans come alive."* In other words, stop all the fluffy things at events and do things your fans will *feel.*

In sharing my story, I wanted to put each of the executives in the position their customers were in. Teams get so caught up in using social media and technology to entertain their fans, they lose sight of the important human interaction.

The driving force behind everything I do is the idea that when it comes to an audience, it's all about creating a feeling. Make people feel something. Make them come alive. When you feel something, you talk about it, you share it, and you ultimately want to do it again. People won't remember the tweet of the game, but they'll remember getting up to dance, cheer, let loose, being pushed, and connecting with the community.

After my talk, a dozen team and league officials approached me. *Giddyup!*

I ended up having inspiring conversations with executives from Arsenal, Manchester City, various cricket and rugby teams, and some random associations that run global events. It made me realize there are so many more opportunities outside of North America – the fan experience was truly universal. So, when Rob Porteous, the Rugby Football League's head of marketing, asked on the spot if I'd be keen to stay in the UK and do a game for the Leeds Rhinos and the Wigan Warriors, I was blown away. The next day we had a deal. My strategy of not booking a return ticket had paid off.

Bet on yourself. Show Up.

Rocking the teal with the Giants fans in Belfast.

Todd Kelman, President of Hockey Cardiff Devils (formerly Executive with Belfast Giants).

Team Cheers with Cardiff Devils after a big win!

TRY

Longest its ever taken me to get a reaction from the crowd: Leeds Rhinos – 90 seconds plus.

For almost two solid minutes, I was out there pumping my legs, swinging my arms like an over-caffeinated air-traffic controller, and the British fans couldn't even be bothered to yawn. But then… my persistence somehow won them over. (Watch the painful scene at CameronHughes.TV.) After that awkward staring contest, it was game on! My very first rugby match ramped up in a hurry – we went from zero to the rowdy fans hoisting me on their shoulders like a 230-pound hot potato. Happily, after that slow start, I went back to raise the roof with the Rhinos and Wigan Warriors a few more times.

P.S. Wigan, your meat pies are my favorite stadium snack of all time!

"We knew he could win the fans over, just didn't know what that looked like. English fans are notoriously set in their ways. Could this crazy Canadian really impact them? We have to try new things with our fans, even when they prefer traditional moments. It was worth the mini heart attack before he went on… the fans loved it… eventually!"

Rob Porteous, former Marketing Director, Super League Rugby

Working the Kensington Oval with Colin Gray. From Lisgar to Barbados! Thankfully the rain finally stopped and we got our shots!

Olympic Stadium in London – New Zealand All-Blacks vs England. WOW.

Singapore Sevens Rugby – Unbelievable to perform in Asia with 30,000 fans!

A thrill to hang with Australian rugby legend George Gregan. Thanks for the crowd tips!

MORE GLOBAL CHEERS

BASEBALL – DOMINICAN REPUBLIC

We shot an episode of *Game Face* down in the D.R. The local baseball game was incredibly animated and featured the most beautiful cheerleaders I've ever seen. However, that didn't make up for the scene in the 8th inning, when the hard-partying crowd was so revved up to get free t-shirts that *they literally chased me out of the stadium!* I ran like Forrest Gump for half a mile, before they gave up...!

CRICKET – BRIDGETOWN, BARBADOS

Here to shoot the pilot episode for *Planet Fandemonium* at Kensington Oval. It was a T20 tournament with countries from all over the world. There had already been five rain delays by the time we showed, but because of our schedule, we just had to make it work. The national Barbados team was playing against Team Canada, so there was no way a little rain was going to dampen this guy's spirits. I may or may not have gotten into the rum with a few of the fans. That *might* have been what inspired my wild dance-off with a local. He killed it, but the crowd took my side when I threw out almost 20 tees to the shocked fans. Hey, a little bribery never hurt anyone, am I right? Oh yeah, I also rode a wild bronco, danced with the cheerleading squad on center stage and pulled my groin. I was on the DL for a week, totally worth it.

RUGBY – SINGAPORE SEVENS, SINGAPORE

After performing at the Vancouver Sevens rugby tournament, I was contacted by Singapore officials to go over and shake things up for their rugby event at the stunning National Stadium. I couldn't believe it. My flight was delayed by a day, so after 17 and a half hours in the air, I got there the morning of the event. Luckily, the organizers flew me business class, so I slept like a baby and was raring to go when I landed, ready to fire up 25,000 passionate rugby fans.

The organizer, my man Ben Bartlett, had 600 extra-large t-shirts waiting for me, just as I had requested. *Perfect.* Unfortunately, not one of them fit me. We quickly figured out that in Asia, XL doesn't mean the same thing it means here. *Not so perfect.* Ben was horrified. But we took a deep breath and I figured out a plan B – I'd just stuff a bunch of shirts in my pocket and access them that way. The fans in Singapore didn't know me, which meant that they didn't know that I usually wear t-shirts and then strip them off. No harm, no foul! When I unleashed my performance on the unsuspecting crowd, they went bonkers! The intro bit had over three million online views within two weeks, and the best part is – those 600 shirts found a home.

RUGBY SCRUM – LONDON

I had serious jitters for this gig. I was so nervous, it brought me back to my first time performing as a young pup in high school, wearing a goofy painter suit as I cheered on the basketball team. I was in the UK to shake things up at an international rugby match between England and New Zealand at the Olympic Stadium. Oh, and it just so happened my girlfriend, a cousin and a bunch of friends showed up, so that contributed to the jitters.

As I walked into the building, I got goosebumps. It was packed and the fans were buzzing. This great city was home to bands like The Clash and The Sex Pistols, and I wanted to rock the crowd in that same spirit, but my enthusiasm was quickly curbed when the producers told me: "You can't go here," "You can't do that," You can't do this," "You can't..."

Frustrated, I blurted out: "What *can* I do?"

The Health And Safety Board in London has tons of rules. At least three-quarters of the stadium was off-limits to me. I wasn't allowed to throw shirts more than three feet. And I had to be fun but not "too crazy," whatever that means. Suffice to say, I was bloody well frustrated.

So what do you do in a situation like this? I knew there was really no choice. I sucked it up, said "ok," and did everything I could within the rules. And you know what? I went out there, gave it my all, and the proper British crowd came along as far as the number of pints allowed them to.

The next day, my girlfriend surprised me with tickets to go to the Paris Open to see my dancing partner, Novak Djokovic. A rock star move. She gets me. She really gets me.

INTO THE WILD

Minnesota has 10,000 lakes, as you might have heard. So, when they freeze, that's 10,000 free hockey rinks! Thus, its cool designation as the "State of Hockey." I had always wanted to perform there, and in 2013 after a friend in the NHL reached out to the Wild on my behalf, I got the call. Score!

Paul Loomis, the executive who brought me in, wanted to shake things up for the fans. And after the team clocked a big win during my first appearance, I was invited back. Soon, St. Paul became a regular destination. One night I was at the local bar after another big win, having drinks with Paul. I started chatting with the extended group of the team executives, one impressive yet unassuming gentleman in particular.

He told me what he thought about my performance, recounting specific details, which then turned into an involved and highly perceptive chat about fan engagement. I asked how he was involved in the team.

"Um, I own it!"

Sure enough, it was Craig Leipold.

Thank you to the Minnesota Wild owner, Craig Leipold for having me over the years, Devan Dubnyk for stopping so many shots, and Zach Parise for scoring when I'm there.

As I continued to work with the Wild, Craig and I would occasionally resume our chats about sports, entertainment, and even my personal story. I found him to be not only a great listener, but a true leader. A devoted family man, I learned he was not only dedicated to fielding a championship-caliber team, but was intent on creating a welcoming, high-energy experience for the hockey fans in the Twin Cities.

Seven years and over 30 Wild games later, Craig remains one of the most approachable and generous owners I've met in sports. He is somebody who sincerely understands that connecting with his fan base is crucial to improving his product – on the ice and off. Fortunately for me (and you!), he was kind enough to agree to answer some of my questions about our business.

Q & A WITH CRAIG LEIPOLD, OWNER – MINNESOTA WILD

What Does Fan Experience Mean to You?

The primary responsibility of a sports franchise is to provide the best fan experience possible. A large part of that experience is winning, but fans today look at the total experience to determine their satisfaction. That includes having the best food and beverage possible and engaging our fans during the entire time they are on our campus.

What's Changed in Fan Experience?

Improved technology in the past decade has greatly enhanced the fan experience. The quality, size and flexibility of the high-definition video boards in today's arenas enable game operations departments to be very creative and entertaining in engaging our fans. The non-game experience is a very important aspect of the total fan experience. I take fan experience very seriously with my great team. Our loyal hockey fans deserve the best of what we can bring them. GO WILD!

Why Bring Me In?

Our fans just love having you in the arena, creating excitement and fan engagement to support the team. It's real emotion and fans respond really well to that. You fit in well to our team strategy to provide the best fan experience possible. And fans don't really care how you are introduced – they just love when you appear!

HI, REMEMBER ME?

Getting close to a yes is a great feeling, but the rejection does wear on you. As noted, I've auditioned, created, shot and worked on enough shows that I lost count. At times you just want to throw in the towel. But I've always believed I have what it took to bring the magic on screen. I always keep a shirt ironed for the next lucky meeting, idea or pitch.

While I was in and out of NYC, I would get introductions to TV executives. One in particular, Abra Potkin, liked me and definitely got me. She was awesome. I mean, she had a Ms. Pac-Man arcade game in her office – how cool is that?

Then an old friend from Canada – let's call her Kathleen, because that's her name – was working on a syndicated talk show called Katie (hosted by TV powerhouse Katie Couric, of The Today Show and CBS News), which was in its first season. One day out of the blue, I stopped by her office to visit and grab lunch. While I was there, she suggested we go say hi to, you guessed it, Abra. She was now a senior producer on the show. Lo and behold, Abra said she wanted me to do something on the show.

This was my TV career summed up: "Yes, we love you, but what should we have you do?"

I didn't get my hopes up, but definitely celebrated the drop-in.

A few months later, the call came: "We want to use you for a big campaign around Sweeps Week." Now we're talkin'!

They pitched me an idea that was fun, but felt forced. They wanted me to do an "ambush-style" dance in various cities.

I suggested we do something that had a timer on it, that had some fun emotional stakes and that "wrote itself." We tweaked it together, and the rest is TV history.

A few weeks later, I'd be shooting segments called "Challenge for Change" on TV icon Katie Couric's show.

What?!

They sent me to five cities in nine days. In each city I had a challenge I needed to meet. For example, in Phoenix, my challenge was to collect one million cans of food for the local food bank in 24 hours. Think Jack Bauer meets Oprah! Picture me with a megaphone going through a grocery store, getting people to donate! We pulled out all the stops and called everyone I knew in sports and life in each city. The producers worked their magic. In Denver, we delivered 5,000 coats for

So fun to be part of the Katie Show and host "Challenge For Change!"

Thank you Katie, Abra and Kathleen! We made a difference :)

Colorado. In Detroit, we helped dramatically upgrade a youth center. In NYC I wore a turkey suit around town to help us get over 1,000 turkeys and a ton of food for the River Fund.

The first time Katie and I actually ever met was on live TV – a smart idea because when you watch it, it's completely authentic. And yes, I shed a few tears talking about the power of the segments and people wanting to help out. It was one of the proudest moments of my career – we were making a difference.

A few years later, I was back in LA and was set up with a woman who wasn't sure she wanted to go out on a date with me after watching all my "Sports YouTube" videos. But she said she saw the work I did on the Katie show and realized I had a bit more range. Super glad she made that extra click.

Thanks, Katie, not only for the big assist to me, but for making a big difference in thousands of lives.

Clockwise from top:
Mascot Moondog.

Cleveland Cavaliers magic
2015-2018 Cavs Fans.

Cavs Legend Kevin Love.

I LOVE THE LAND

In 2015, the Cavs went to the NBA Finals. I was at most of the games during the playoff run, having the time of my life. After nine years, LeBron and I were *back*. It was the big story.

BROTHERS IN ARMS, ONCE AGAIN. BUTCH CASSIDY AND THE BAD-DANCE KID

Okay, who am I kidding? But it was a thrill to be asked to be part of the playoffs. Unfortunately, the Cavs lost to the Warriors. I saw Steph Curry and company raise the trophy – good for them – but my heart was deep in "the Land," now. The next season I could feel the team coming together in new ways. They seemed to be having more fun. They were gelling. The Land was hungry for a championship. The Cavs were rolling in the first few rounds of the playoffs, and I was right there in the middle of the madness, whipping the crowd into a frenzy. In between doing Cavs' games, I was flying across the country, lighting up other playoff crowds for the likes of the Raptors, Hornets, Thunder and Clippers. After waking up from my naps on the planes, I would have to press the touch-screen flight map to remind myself where I was going to be landing, and then figure out what color shoes to put on that night!

As we were waiting to see who the Cavs would play in the Eastern Conference Finals, I decided to meet my girlfriend in Cabo for a much-needed few days of chill. I'll never forget sitting at the hotel bar having a few margaritas watching the Raptors beat the Miami Heat and earn the right to square off with LeBron & Company again. I was excited for them. I had done Game 3 in the first round for the Raptors. My first game back in years, and it was off the shizzle.

That's when things got interesting. The next day, the Raptors emailed, asking if I'd do Game 3 of the Eastern Conference Finals.

NOW, LADIES AND GENTS, WE'VE GOT A PICKLE ON OUR HANDS

Both teams wanted me to cheer for them. The only other time something like this had happened in my career was when I did a CHL game in Wichita one night; they played against Oklahoma City. The next night I was in Oklahoma City, cheering the team on *against* Wichita. But fans tend to be a little more forgiving during regular season games, and plus that was minor league hockey, where I was less likely to be seen on any highlight reels.

Unsure how to proceed with the offer, I called two of my trusted mentors to get their take on the situation. Not surprisingly, they were unanimous: "Call Cleveland first. They're your biggest client. Ask them if it's okay." So I called up Adam, the Entertainment Manager, to fill him in on the situation. After he consulted with Conrad, the Director of Entertainment, the verdict was in.

"Of course it's okay with us if you do the Raptors game," Adam said. "We can't dictate who you can and can't perform for. That would set a horrible precedent."

Yes!

There are a ton of performers in the world of professional sports who work at any game they please, regardless of the team. The thing with my act, though, is that it is specifically designed to bring out the passion of fans as they cheer for their home teams. I build emotional relationships with the crowd. When I put that jersey or tee on, I become part of the team for the night.

Like I've talked about, I don't favor any one team. I'm out there to fire things up for everybody, not Team A or Team B. If they're at the game, they're just as much a part of it as anyone else.

But I decided not to say anything to Toronto just yet and to let things play out. I had a weird gut feeling about it. Maybe I should let Toronto know. But part of me felt that they would – they *should* – know that I was already tearing it up for Cleveland. Buyer beware. So I rolled with it. The series kicked off in Cleveland, where I lost my mind before a raucous sell-out crowd.

The Cavs took the Raps on a ride that game, and I ran into a bunch of visiting Raps fans who said, "Hey, didn't we just see you in Toronto?"

Needless to say, there was some fun banter. "I just love connecting with people," I would say. Always leave them with a smile. After the game, icing my knees and brain, I was in my Cleveland locker room when I opened up an email from the Raptors:

"Hey Cam. We are going to need to cancel on Saturday. I didn't realize you were in Cleveland tonight. We had a large group of fans and staff down there for the game. This takes away from the show here in Toronto. Wanted to let you know early as I know you have travel plans."

Steve, Toronto Raptors

I showed the email to Conrad, who then told his boss about it, who then shared it with *his* boss. Whoa. Within 24 hours, I was summoned to a meeting with the Cavs executives.

"Stay in Cleveland for every game and every watch party," Conrad said. "Do some Monsters games, too, while you're at it! You're our guy now!" *Hallelujah.* I *was* their guy.

From that point on, I was ALL IN with the Cavs. I mean, I should have bought a condo in downtown Cleveland. It was magical to be part of the Cavaliers' quest for a championship. I began living, breathing, and working toward the next Cavs win. They took out the Raptors in six games, and moved on to another heavyweight rematch with the Warriors in the Finals. This was incredible athletic drama!

During the Finals, we were constantly trying to come up with new ways to introduce me. During one meeting, Adam shared how someone wanted to propose to his girlfriend at a game. I asked if we could work that in somehow. Hard no; it was the NBA Finals. Fair enough. But at the next game, I was about to get up for my dance, and some guy sitting right in front of me dropped to one knee and started proposing to his girlfriend… it was the same guy! There were 20,000 fans in the stadium that night, but I just so happened to sit behind *him, of all people.* Needless to say, that night was a little more memorable than most. (She said yes, by the way.) The Land was undoubtedly living its best life. Fans all got free shirts on their seats when they arrived, and some nights my helper Tyler and I were throwing 300-plus different tees into the crowd. It was an epic, seven-game series, and this time, LeBron and Kyrie and the guys would not be denied. They won the title 2,000 miles away in Oakland, 93-89, while yours truly and a stadium full of crazed Cleveland fans had a watch party for the ages!

TIMEOUT

In 2019, since LeBron had moved on to LA, I guess the Raptors felt like I would be available now, too! As Kawhi Leonard, Pascal Siakam, Kyle Lowry and the rest made their title run, guess who got the call to come back to Toronto! There I was in Jurassic Park, rocking the house in Game 1 of the NBA Finals. My hit went viral, they won the game en route to the championship, and I even gave them my 2016 rate!

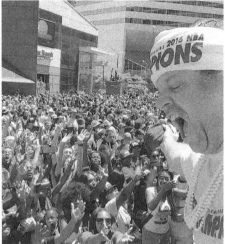

Cavaliers Championship parade with 1.3 Million OHIO friends.

Working the float with local legend, Machine Gun Kelly.

With former Cavs coach Ty Lue.

WE ALL FLOAT ON

After the Cavs won that 2016 NBA Championship, I attended an amazing after-party at the Q. Naturally. I ran into my old friend Kerry Bubolz, the team President, who I'd known since I did a game with the Cleveland Lumberjacks back in the day.

"You have to come back for the parade!" Kerry said. "We'd love to have you work it."

Parade! It was ON!

Even better, the Cavs agreed to my requested fee. It's a number I'd always said I wanted to make in sports. The energy in Cleveland was pure bliss. They'd finally won the championship! You could feel the love everywhere you went.

CLEEEEEEEEEEEEVELAND!

The night before the parade, Moondog called me and asked if he could stay in my hotel, because it was closer to the arena (and no other hotels in the city!). *Of course, Dawg!* Just picture that visual for a minute. I got to the parade before the true insanity hit, but things were already popping. People had started to line up in the streets, and it was damn early. I was told I'd be on a float with Bernie Kosar, the legendary Cleveland Browns quarterback, and Machine Gun Kelly – *Who?* As I was getting set up on the float, this skinny dude with tattoos everywhere tried to jump up on the back of the truck. I casually pushed him back. "Nice try, buddy." Turns out it was Machine Gun Kelly himself.

Oops. My bad.

I learned he was a rapper, and that he and his entourage were ready to seriously, mind-bendingly party on this insane float. Okay! Over the next three and a half hours, I threw out over 2,000 t-shirts, danced, cheered, and partied with 1.5 million of my closest friends. It was a celebration, to be sure, but I've never in my life performed so hard for so long. Without a doubt, one of the coolest days of my career.

THERE'S NO SUCH THING AS BAD PRESS... RIGHT?

In 2018 I was hired to perform at the Elite Ice Hockey League Finals in Nottingham, UK. I'd already worked with the Belfast Giants and the Cardiff Devils for several games and had a great relationship with both fan bases. They were very welcoming. A week before I arrived, a reporter wrote a story that mentioned I'd be attending the event to "add some atmosphere." I'm not a big fan of promoting myself before any events, but I felt this was harmless.

I landed in London ready for a day or two of chill before heading to Nottingham. As I was taking the train into the city from the airport, I checked my Twitter feed. The reporter's story had been posted on Tuesday, and within an hour, the tweets about it had started rolling in. Someone asked who I was, so I replied that I couldn't wait to be part of the magic and meet them. Seemed innocent enough. I replied to a few more tweets in a similar way. By that night, I had blown up in the Twitterverse.

But not in a good way.

People were beyond angry that I had been hired. How dare the league insult the fans by implying they needed help to create a better atmosphere? Then word got out that some of their beloved local mascots wouldn't be coming, and fans were pissed. The last thing you want are the home town mascots as enemies. This had gone south very, very quickly.

"We arranged to bring Cam, and one of the owners thought leaking the story would stir up the excitement. What a mistake. It sent fans into a tailspin. They were mad at the league for thinking that the weekend needed more of an atmosphere – the tradition of the playoff weekend was the atmosphere itself."

Todd Kelman, Managing Director, Cardiff Devils

Meanwhile, I was scratching my head, wondering what on Earth just happened. My friend Todd, who'd spearheaded the hire, was furious. He wasn't happy the article had been written at all, but he was more upset about the reaction to it – definitely a case of headline hysteria, a term that hit home for me like never before. These people didn't know me, but they didn't care. By this point, everything had been blown way out of proportion. The tweets were decidedly, un-Britishly impolite and wouldn't stop.

"Piss off, Tosser!"

"You are all deluded in that boardroom if you voted for this being a good idea."

"You fly this guy over and pay him. What for?"

"It could be the first time in EIHL history that the whole crowd chanted in unison: "who are ya, who are ya, who are ya, who are ya...'"

"Oh god why??? Between the fans singing and the mascots and the cheerleaders (and us with our #PlayoffPomPoms!), we don't need some cringeworthy nobody to create artificial atmosphere!"

Nobody calls Baby a tosser! Cringeworthy, maybe... But still, I wouldn't respond. There was nothing to gain. It was a no-win situation.

I assumed I'd still be taking a train to Nottingham in a few days. But read those warm words of welcome again and let me ask you: What would you do?

We spent the next 24 hours debating our move. It was clear in my gut that I shouldn't go. But then I'd have this sharp pain in my heart, saying, "Go and bring the magic." There was so much hate being flung at me. What if I got my ass kicked by some hostile fan? That would make for some headlines. This just in:

CHEER GUYS GETS BEATDOWN FROM FANS!

So all parties slept on it and made the call in the morning. There were also a lot of positive tweets from the two fan bases I did know, but it seemed obvious – the well had been poisoned. I did not go.

I don't regret it. Did it affect me at the time? 100 percent. This was the first time in my career I'd seen any reaction at that level. I mean sure, I was used to getting rejected by women, but not by fans. Especially fans who hadn't even seen me do my thing. I'm a very emotional guy who cares so much for everyone. I would have been okay if it was after I'd performed, but they didn't even give me a chance. Did I get over it? Sure did. On Friday, I met up with very good friends in London and went out on the town. If only the teams hadn't promoted me, I would have been partying with fans for the next two days instead of getting insulted and run out of town.

This experience highlights in capital letters why teams don't promote me. Let my bad dancing, my energy, and my passion for connecting with the fans surprise them. No matter where on the globe I am performing, I AM one of the people, not an outsider. That's always been the key to my success in connecting with crowds all around the world.

Ottawa Senators magic a few years later. I'll never forget the sound of Stuntman Stu's voice welcoming me home. And, to all the Sens fans – THANK YOU! Photo credit Jean Levac.

Sens' superfan returns

Ottawa native Cameron Hughes has made a career for himself by cheering for sports teams and getting paid for it. He got his start after being noticed at a Senators game in 1994.

JESSICA BEDDAOUI
Ottawa Sun

Friday night will be a homecoming of sorts for Cameron Hughes.

The Ottawa native launched his career at a Senators vs. Jets game in 1994.

The Sens were down by a goal with eight minutes left in the game.

"Nobody was cheering ... but I could feel something in the arena," said Hughes.

There was a routine pause in the game and the song *We Are Family* started blaring.

What happened next was crucial — he got up from his seat and started "dancing and gyrating" to the music.

Initially, fans were confused and unsure of how to react to his antics, but eventually they cheered him on.

"I did it, I sat back down and there was a buzz in the arena," he said.

After the game, Hughes was approached by the Senators organization. In exchange for tickets, jerseys, and hockey paraphernalia, he would have to attend home games and be responsible for getting the fans riled up.

Immediately, he accepted the team's offer.

"The second year they even paid me," Hughes recalled.

In 1996, he moved to Toronto and opportunities started to flourish.

He was hired by sports teams across North America to boost fan morale.

"I was getting kinda discovered by other companies, too. They loved what I was doing," he said.

Hughes was also approached by school boards and corporations to encourage and motivate students and employees.

At the 2010 Vancouver Olympics, he was hired by organizers as the official crowd animator for 25 hockey events.

"If it wasn't for the Senators organization and the fans, I wouldn't have this amazing life," he said.

Hughes will be attending Friday night's Sens vs. Penguins game as part of the Senators' ongoing 20th anniversary celebration.

As for what fans can expect, he remained coy.

"All I can say is that there's a video involved ... and then I'm going to be an ass."

jessica.beddaoui@sunmedia.ca

FULL CIRCLE

Have you ever wished you could time-travel back to an unforgettable party that happened back in the day? Your epic high school graduation blowout, maybe, or even just an awesome hang with your friends where the soundtrack was flawless, everything flowed and you had the time of your life? Of course you have! We've all been there and we all want to go back, even for just one night. Luckily for me, I got to experience that in Ottawa.

I hadn't been back in twelve years, so it was definitely a surprise when the Ottawa Senators reached out to see if I'd perform at their 20th anniversary celebrations. When I did my two-year stint as the "Dancing Guy" for the Senators, I'd had an exclusive deal with the team, and when I moved on, "I went from totally chic to totally geek," to paraphrase a favorite movie quote from that era. (Bonus points for whoever can name the flick? Hint: Classic McDreamy)

Getting that unexpected call from Glen Gower, the Director of Entertainment, made me so happy, it's hard to describe. I'd always hoped things would come full circle with the Sens, but I didn't know how or when they could. I mean, it's not like I beat up Spartacat or something, but still it had been a *long* time.

The team had always had such a special place in my heart, so this call was huge. I was never happy to cheer against them, but it was always a performance, and the fans in Ottawa certainly got it as the years went on. This was the team, the city and the fans that gave me my start, and I genuinely believe the ones that knew my story were happy for me. I've been proud to boast where I got my start as I've traveled the world.

Glen wanted to create something magical for the fans. Everyone I knew in Ottawa was coming to the game and the after-party. It would be the first game my dad would attend in years – he hadn't seen me perform in almost a decade. *Bonus for him*: He didn't need to call me before the game with any factual tidbits! This was a homecoming I'd never thought would happen. And it was another reminder to be grateful for each gig, for each opportunity to share my energy with people. It was 48 hours of goosebumps and gratitude.

This was just the third time in my career I was introduced over the PA, and the first time I was happy about it – not only happy, but I couldn't have dreamt up a more full-circle moment even if I tried. I was nervous as all hell. My dad was there, my sister, my childhood friends. I'll never forget the section, my helpers' cheers, and the moment before it happened.

"Ladies and gentlemen, heee's back. Twenty years ago, he took the Civic Center by storm, and hasn't stopped dancing and cheering around the world since," Stuntman Stu said. "We're thrilled to welcome back Ottawa's own Cameron Hughes... Let's hear it for him!" Such a powerful moment to be acknowledged like that in my hometown. It was a night I'll never forget, and testament that we really *can* do anything we dream of doing. I mean, just by getting up and dancing all those years ago at a Senators game, I had taken my first steps toward building the most unlikely of careers. And it *happened*. Somehow I'd created a career that took me around the globe, and here I was, back where it had all begun.

"From an authentic beginning as a very animated fan in Ottawa in 1994, Cameron has continued to inspire enthusiasm, shift momentum, and has won many fans of his own. Our fans were excited to see him back over the last few years. He's never forgotten where it all started, that's for sure."

Emily Knight, Director of Game Production, Ottawa Senators

Two years later, I would come back for my 1,000th game. Where else on the planet would you want to be but the city that gave you your start? Ottawa will always be my home, and there is nowhere I'd rather be for my 2,000th. They were stuck with me for my 25th anniversary game in 2019, and with all the gratitude one could ever ask for. We did it, Ottawa!

DID YOU WHEELIE SAY THAT?!

It was the second period of a home game for one of my favorite AHL teams, the Lehigh Valley Phantoms, owned by brothers Jim and Rob Brooks. Over the years, I'd done many games with the various teams they owned, but this one was special.

My stage manager was super fun and we were all over the arena, lighting up the night in a close game. I was flinging t-shirts at the top of the stairs in the lower bowl, when I heard a voice calling out for me. "Hey Sweetie?" she said. "I'm with the girls over there and we'd all love a t-shirt." I turn around to find a woman in her 70s sitting in a wheelchair. I looked at her with a stern face and dry smile and said, "I'm sorry, but I'm not a big fan of people in wheelchairs, especially senior citizens…"

My stage manager and the usher were about to drop, shocked by what had come out of my mouth. Dramatic pause. The woman blinked and looked at me

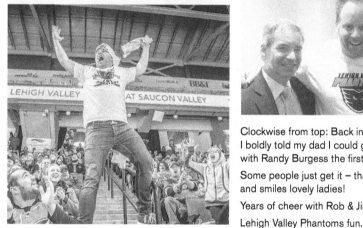

Clockwise from top: Back in the stadium where I boldly told my dad I could get the crowd going, with Randy Burgess the first to hire me to do so.

Some people just get it – thank you for the laughs and smiles lovely ladies!

Years of cheer with Rob & Jim Brooks.

Lehigh Valley Phantoms fun.

in awe, before losing her shit, laughing so hard she almost cried. "Come over and meet my girls... oh we love you, we love you so much!" She got it. She wanted to play. I could just tell she had a sense of humor. So, we celebrated the moment.

I've learned that fans want to be pushed – they want to be challenged. It's not every day you encounter a sweaty t-shirt slinging beast, so why not make the moment one to remember? People are often filled with joy during my interactions, because they know my *sole purpose* in that moment is to put a smile on their face. You either get it or you don't, but one thing's for certain: I'm sure Granny slept well in her free tee that night.

FRENCH TOAST

On January 7th, 2015, I woke up to a bunch of voicemails from a few friends. My friend Brian had called and left word that my best pal Marc had died in the night. I was in the deepest state of shock ever.

On a business trip in Norway, Marc asked the waiter (like he'd done thousands of times) if the chef could make sure there was no poultry involved

My dear friend Marc Lucas the day after his wedding.

At my dear friend Marc's celebration of life with Jay Shore, my father and Bill Knowlton.

in the making of his meal. Marc had some very serious allergies. He was allergic to chicken, eggs, and more. I'd been with him many times when he needed his magical EpiPen. He and his colleagues from the mining world went on to have their dinners, but then suddenly Marc wasn't well. He started hurrying back to his hotel room, and from there, I'd rather not go into details. It was too late. My best pal died from a chicken in an elevator in Norway. I don't think there's a joke in there, but if you knew Marc, you'd know he'd want there to be one.

Just three months earlier he'd married the mother of his two young boys, a lovely ceremony where I gave a toast. He also had two beautiful daughters from his first marriage. He was so happy that he'd made it to this point in his life. We were all thrilled for this next chapter. The joy in my heart seeing such a dear friend be that content was overwhelming.

The funeral was held on a snowy day outside of our hometown where Marc and I first met as young kids. My eulogy was appropriately titled "French Toast," after the names we called each other as kids. It was the hardest talk I've ever done. As I hit the midway point, I said, "Something's not right…" I held a long pause to the curiosity of the room, and then went to the pulpit. I grabbed a Montréal Canadiens Jersey, I turned around, and everyone saw his last name, LUCAS, on the back.

Marc loved the Montréal Canadiens, also known as *Les Habitants* or simply *Habs*. I mean *loved*. And, wouldn't you know it, they had a game that night. So, we started the chant that I'd heard so many times as a kid from Marc.

"GO HABS GO! GO HABS GO! GO HABS GO!"

For the next two minutes, everyone in the room let it all out. We gave it our all, in the spirit of Marc. It was the greatest cheer I'd ever led.

Following the proceedings, I walked my father to the parking lot, tears in my eyes. We embraced tightly.

"I'm so proud of you, son," he said. "Marc was proud of you, too. I love you."

"I love you too, Dad."

SKI BUNNY CHEERS

A few weeks after Marc's memorial I was in Vail, Colorado, performing at the Vail World Ski Championships. Because if there's anything a professional ski race needs, it's a sexy male cheerleader. I know what you're thinking: Did I bring "Rocky the Raccoon" back and fire up the ski hill in between races? Not exactly, but I did get in the stands at the bottom of the course and light up fans during breaks, get on the snow and do insane improvised dances with the cheerleading teams, and anything else to rev up the fans. They thought I was dancing to show enthusiasm, which I was, but I was also just trying to stay warm.

It was definitely a unique gig for me. The organizers had seen me in Denver doing Avs and Nuggets games, and wanted to bring the same fun to the slopes. Seeing fans from around the world cheering on their favorite racers was quite familiar. By the last day, not only had my feet froze, but I broke down and had my moment of grief.

I left the hill early and sat at an outdoor patio toasting Marc. When the organizers heard what I was going through, they understood. Cheering people on can be tricky when you're going through your own stuff. It certainly is a powerful and yet difficult feeling to make people smile when you need one yourself.

CALL TIME

AND WE'RE LIVING HERE IN ALLENTOWN

March 7, 2015, I was back in Allentown performing for the Lehigh Valley Phantoms. I was in bed exhausted, thinking about how I hadn't heard from my father the night before. I wanted to tell him where I was. It was strange. Then a text message came in. It was from my cousin, instructing me to call my sister as soon as possible. My stomach in knots, I got the bad news from Andrea.

My father had suffered a stroke. He was in the hospital. I was nine hours away, alone in a hotel. What was I supposed to do?

Once my sister got to the hospital and checked with the doctors, she called and told me he was going to be okay (which was total BS, but a smart thing to say). She told me to do my game and drive up in the morning. *Yeah sure, no problem.* No sarcasm here.

The team president and owners were supportive – they told me to go be with my family. But, bolstered by my sister's words, I was going to do the game, and I was going to kick some ass and keep my commitment. The next morning, I rushed home – it was the longest drive of my life. I immediately went to the hospital to see my father. Walking into that room was one of the worst moments of my life. My dad was attached to what seemed like hundreds of tubes. My heart dropped right into my stomach. I was allowed to be there for all of ten minutes. When I got back into my car, I lost it. I couldn't drive. Couldn't move. Couldn't function. Over the next few weeks, my father would fight for his life. He was severely weakened, drifting in and out of consciousness. He would fight and fight. With our only living parent on the ropes, my sister Andrea and I bonded deeply.

There was nothing more we could do.

STATE OF HOCKEY SHOCK

A few weeks after my Dad's stroke, as he battled in his hospital room, my family and I agreed it would be a good idea for me to get out and do a few events, to get my life going again. I needed a deep breath of my oxygen – the crowd.

And so I was off for three games in four days. First stop, Minnesota, to cheer on the Wild. I was so excited to connect with fans again. As I was about to take my gameday nap, I got a call from my sister.

"You need to come home, now." Andrea and I had been worrying, wondering, crying, scared and shattered together as one for a few weeks. Hoping for a miracle, no matter how unlikely. Her words punctured that possibility for good.

Time froze in that St. Paul hotel room. I'd felt this before, but not quite like this. Not really.

It was 2 p.m. That night the Wild had a big game with playoff implications. I called my friend Paul, who ran the game day entertainment.

"You need to be with your family," he said. "Our organization supports that. Go."

Then I called a few friends while checking flights to get home – of course there weren't any that evening. My support network was incredible, offering words of comfort, but one friend couldn't have said it better: "Cam, you have a chance to put 18,000 smiles on people's faces tonight. 18,000 people will have more fun, a few extra laughs, because you're there. You know your dad would be so happy for you. He'd be so proud." The words hit home. It's as if my father had asked him to call me. The next flight out wasn't until pre-dawn tomorrow morning, anyway.

I had a not-really-napping nap, then went out and performed one of the best shows of my life. I was raw and vulnerable, feeling desperately like I wanted to connect with the precious gift that is the human spirit. People were tuned in, feeling it, loving it all. I kept the last drenched t-shirt.

Afterward, I grabbed a beer with Paul to talk about life... and death. His friendship was invaluable that day. I shared how my dad was never sure what I was doing with my career – all the highs and lows – but that he had come aboard and supported my passion, nonetheless. What would I do without those calls? I guess I'd have to find out.

"This guy is on the road all the time – maybe he doesn't have as much opportunity to lean on someone when he needs it. The fact that he opened up made me realize he really needs to know someone is listening. And I was – I wanted to. I couldn't even imagine the level of pain, fear or anxiety he was feeling – especially since he was on the road. To hear the devastating news from him hit me to the core; I really felt an overwhelming sadness for him, as well as his father. So I just did what any good friend would do; I first listened, then I gave him some words of encouragement – to savor the memories, to know the value a good and decent father brings to the world."

Paul Loomis, Executive Producer, Minnesota Wild

Thank you Paul Loomis for the Wild magic and friendship.

The night I had to dig deep after hearing news about my father. I dedicated the game to him.

A few hours later, at 4 a.m., I was up and off to Ottawa. For the next few days, 24 hours a day, I was on call for my father, who had taken a turn for the worse. He couldn't talk, but he registered with us, what was going on. So I brought the old stereo system from his place and played his favorite classical music. I held his hand. We had his favorite team, the Senators, on in the hospital room. I walked home each night after the nurse told me to go home and get some rest. There wasn't anything else I could do. I was just there.

The night that he passed, just as I had on the night my mother passed away, I had made a conscious decision to go out and be social, to be with my good friends and sister. After that night of trying to be normal, I saw I'd missed a call from the hospital.

I knew.

I drove over to the same parking lot at the hospital I had been in 28 years earlier. I kissed his forehead, and told him I loved him.

I believe my father was proud. He knew how hard I tried, that's for sure. It wasn't always the smoothest relationship, but my dad taught me a lot about being a great person, having strong integrity, and caring for people. He raised Andrea and me to be kind, respectful and loving towards all people.

So there I was in the Colorado Eagles' parking lot, a couple hours before my first game back after his passing. All I wanted was the phone to ring and my Dad to ask me where I was and who I'd be cheering for tonight. I'd tell him I was in Loveland, population seventy-eight thousand, seventy-six miles from Denver, a beautiful outdoorsy city. And he'd tell me he'd be keeping track of the score, and then I could go inside, knowing in my heart he was with me all night.

That timeless tradition, like so many we have when we grow up, was now gone. But there are things we take with us when they go; we take their memories, their lessons, and their eternal spirit, which are ours to cherish. And when we lose a parent, even though they aren't there to tell us, we always know they are in our heart. Having learned this lesson the hard way now, twice, I know one thing is certain: we should never take those moments, when they can actually tell us that, for granted.

When I ended my dad's eulogy, I shared the story of his parting words to me after Marc's funeral a few weeks earlier. When he said, "I'm proud of you son. I love you."

That's all I ever wanted to hear.

TIMEOUT

MY FIVE FAVORITE PERFORMERS

Krazy George

He created the wave (no big deal) and inspired me to push the boundaries and be a lot more crazy.

Youppi

First mascot I ever saw as a young fan of the Montréal Expos. A mutant muppet who really got the crowd going..

Moondog

My furry friend and I shared a locker room for over 30 games (and one hotel room!). A true team player, he pushed me out on center court often to do bits at Cavaliers games.

Max Patkin, Clown Prince of Baseball

A former minor leaguer knocked out of the game by injury. A skinny, rubber-faced, double jointed clown with a "?" on the back of his jersey, Max cracked up crowds for 51 years, and got to dance with Susan Sarandon in Bull Durham!

Dancing Gabe (Winnipeg Jets, Manitoba Moose, Winnipeg Blue Bombers, Goldeneyes Baseball)

Big heart, hilarious moves, and shows up at every game.

THE BUSINESS OF HUMAN INTERACTION

MOUTH TO MOUTH!!

I've never done CPR at a game, but I guess maybe this one was close? Of course it was in Bakersfield. I'll let my pal Justin tell you what happened...

"Just this year getting a phone call from a fan that felt really ashamed of herself because she took a shirt out of your mouth with her mouth, said she just got caught up in your fun and excitement. News stations had that on camera and showed it during our game highlights. The conversation with the lady was pretty entertaining. She realized she was more to blame than you, and she shouldn't have had so much to drink. And then she asked us nicely not to show the footage"

Justin Fahsbender, Bakersfield Condors

WHOOPS, I HAD TO DO A 'TAKEBACK'

Team Entertainment Director:
Hey Cam!
Got a complaint from Sunday...
Do you recall this?
FAN: *While we were at the game the man that runs around and dances and throws shirts came around our aisle. He took a shirt and threw it to my son who is 11. My son was so excited he got a jersey. Once the man saw that my son received the jersey he said wait give that back to me NOW. My son looked confused and threw it back. The man threw my son a t-shirt and then he said to my son HA HA YOU ARE A SUCKER! Are you kidding me!? That is so rude it is unbelievable! Me and my husband cannot believe that you have someone like that working for you. He is a kid and doing what he did upset him so much! This is not expectable in our eyes. Being rude to a child when you are a grown man, come on!*

TRUE CAM CONFESSION: Uhhh.. guilty as charged? But please allow me to explain (he said somewhat sheepishly). Hey, in the heat of the moment, sometimes when I'm going for "fun," it might not always land perfectly.

I remember this incident well. I had an NBA jersey with me, and instead of a t-shirt, threw it to the young man by accident. Since the team (sometimes) wants the jersey back after the game, I asked him to please toss it back to me. And, when we made the swap, I made the joke, probably going a bit too far on the sarcasm level. He even said thanks for the tee, but I shouldn't have teased him. I usually only do stuff like that when I sense the fan is in on it. It was definitely in the heat of the moment, and I thought it was fun and light. Apparently *they* didn't. I owned up to it and offered to buy the kid a new jersey and send it to him. But the team understood what had happened, and said they'd look after it... :)

HOW TO GET A FREE T-SHIRT. YOU'RE WELCOME!

If we've ever interacted because you want a t-shirt, you probably know I like it when fans say "please" and "thank you" for a shirt. I almost always stay around until a fan says "thanks" – especially kids, which makes for some fun moments no matter the age. It's not like I want them to kiss my butt for a shirt – it's because I want them to be appreciative of the moment, and the connections we make in these situations. Before one game, the director of a team told me he had to let me know about a recent complaint – he said "fans called in and complained you made their kid say 'thanks' after giving him a shirt." He paused, waiting for me to reply. I paused, so we could consider what he'd just said. I finally said, "Okay... did you tell them he *should* have?" Silence. Ha! I won't change that policy!

Team Indeed spirit with fearless leader Nolan Farris and the crew!

The SPARK Conference with apartmentlist.com, Matthew Woods, John Kobs, and the most beautiful spirited group!

ON STAGE

The VP has let you know attendance is mandatory. *Great*. It's like the days of being in high school when some lame speaker is going to lecture you about generic topic X. As you get settled, the host in this case gets up, welcomes everyone and starts the program. Within a few minutes they start to bore you with their monotone and scripted presentation. Then you hear somebody pipe up…

"This is lame. This isn't what I thought it would be!"

"Excuse me?" says the host to the crazy redhead in the back corner.

"Yes, you heard me. Spice it up, let's go."

"Ummm… I'm in the middle of a meeting."

"I know, let's party!"

The host challenges this ginger to make it more fun.

"Play some music!" he yells.

The audience is dumbfounded. How is this happening? Should they run? Call security? Should they back him up or just pray it plays out? The host agrees to music. Music plays, Big Red gets up like he has hundreds of times at games. But now he's going insane in your boardroom conference hall, sales event, etc. *What* is going on?

Then the shirts fly, a jersey flies, layers of clothing expertly flying off, and now your company's name is emblazoned across his chest, like Superman! "Cameron Hughes, ladies and gentlemen!" A video, a powerful talk that leaves them laughing, crying and/or ready to dance. And ready to take more chances and have more confidence.

Guess what, businesses are teams, and I LOVE teams. I've been shaking up corporate events and conferences for years now, and I love it!

BE PREPARED

When I left the "Just for Laughs" comedy festival in 2017, all I could think about was how some of those top comedians prepared, how they mastered their craft and were always so consistent. I had worked hard on many keynotes over the years, but I knew I had to do more if I wanted to build that part of my career.

I had to become a reliable wild card, if that makes sense – to harness the raw emotion and human connection of my game performances, and combine those with useful lessons and challenging group interaction.

So, I sat down, worked my ass off and did just that. My "Power of Cheer" presentations aren't, nor will ever be, a memorized TED talk – they're more Will Ferrell meets Tony Robbins with a touch of Brene Brown authentic. :) I'm thrilled to report that audiences are responding very positively to this approach – at the 2018 Spark conference in San Francisco, I was rated #1 out of 29 speakers!

Speaking of speaking events: People often ask, "What's next?"

My answer? I'm just going to do more. I have so much more to give, and branching out to other kinds of groups feels right, feels organic. I love to see people shine, and I want to make a bigger difference on different stages.

I'm going to keep asking for volunteers like Michelle, a woman who was originally too shy to get up at a recent corporate event, but wound up dancing and twirling tees for a room full of hundreds of people!

She stepped up and showed her peers that there's more to her than meets the eye, that they don't know what she's capable of. Maybe she even discovered some of that herself!

What I know for sure is that people are tired of boring meetings, and now Zoom meetings present a whole new challenge! Sure, I can't fling a t-shirt your way through the internet (yet!), but there are countless ways we can connect better and send cheer to our colleagues and loved ones.

So, we shake them up and bring that spark! I'm just getting the mic warmed up.

We have invited Cameron into several events to celebrate our teams and acknowledge their incredible work helping people get jobs, and had a blast doing it. And yes, he shocked the room! It takes a few seconds of courage each day to thrive in today's business world, but it also requires a positive tone, direction and care for the people around you. Cameron has helped my leadership team think about who they are cheering for each day, and also take a moment to cheer on themselves!

Nolan Farris, Indeed

NO FEE TOO HIGH, NO JOB TOO WEIRD

Just a Few *of the Strangest Side Gigs I Have EVER Done*

The Blobfish Classic

What's a "Blobfish Classic"? Oh, just a one-on-one basketball contest between Jimmy Kimmel and Senator Ted Cruz. Yep, yours truly was the Cheer Guy of this bizarre match-up, with ESPN's Kenny Mayne doing play-by-play and hoops legends Ralph Sampson and Isiah Thomas (my Toronto guy!) doing commentary! Honestly, if I didn't have the check stub, I would probably say it had just been a weird dream. Thank you, Jill.

Dancing For The Sitcoms!

Back in the '90's, my Ottawa pals Brian and Chris Murray came to LA for a visit. They were childhood friends with some guy named Matthew Perry. We all went to a taping of *Friends*, and when legendary audience warm-up man Bob Perlow asked for audience volunteers to show off a skill, guess who shook their moneymaker for the people?! Bob was so kind and generous that when he found out my career goals, he had me dance for some tapings of *The Single Guy*, too.

Blades Girls

Every young sports-crazed kid growing up in Canada dreams they will one day get to fire up the crowds at an indoor, rollerblading hockey game in Los Angeles. *Oh, what's that??* Only me? Huh. Well, I did it, and it was a gig I'll never forget! Jeannie Buss hired me to work an LA Blades game at the Forum in 1996, and the best part is – I shared my locker room with very special halftime guests, THE LAKER GIRLS! My hair and makeup has never been so on point.

Take off, EH!

Whenever you finish your big documentary project, and are looking for a theatrical cheer man, look no further! When my friends Rob Cohen, Colin and Megan Raney (Colin's sister! Remember, from pitching the TV show?) made a hilarious and fun documentary called *Being Canadian*, I was enlisted to fire up the crowds. Draped in red and white, I did so at the world premiere in Toronto and also at an LA screening, where Jimmy Kimmel and his exec producer, Jill Leiderman, were in attendance – so yes that's how I got the Blobfish gig! Check it out eh!

BEHIND THE CHA-CHEER

GREEN SKITTLES

A t each event I ask for a stage manager, intern, or game day staff employee to help guide me around the arena, help with my cues, and carry a pack or four of t-shirts, water, and a fresh towel. I've had so many interesting and wonderful characters help me over the years, it's hard to keep track. Each person taught me something and helped me give the best performance I could. Some wound up acting as emergency therapists, offering relationship advice as I was on the road, others I cheered on and helped with their careers, and some have become lifelong friends. And most would probably tell you at some point, "Cameron's a bit nuts," or that "this guy cares too much about making sure it goes right" – but hey, I get paid to care. :)

Most entertainers have a rider that outlines their hospitality requests. I keep mine simple (I swear). I learned in the early days to be as easy to work with as possible, plus I'm not that big of a diva! I was doing a game for the Washington Capitals where my friend Scott was producing the game. Scott is quite the joker, so I added a ton of wacky stuff to my rider that I sent with my invoice – fancy hand soaps, colored towels, drinks at certain temperatures, a steak sandwich, even a ping pong table with a right-handed intermediate player to be available one hour prior to the game. And green Skittles, of course.

By the time I arrived for this game, I'd probably done five others in between, and had totally forgotten about my outrageous requests to Scott. But not so for a new intern named Chris. When I showed up, this bright-eyed youngster had it all spread out on a long table. His boss, my friend Scott, had never looked at my note and just sent it to Chris to "look after." Which he did, to the max! (Unfortunately, the Caps were using "my" pong table!)

So, that's the true "Behind the Cheer" story of how Chris earned the nickname "Skittles"! We've kept in touch over the years and worked together, and he's killed it.

"My first encounter with Cameron was when I was at the very beginning stage of my career with the Washington Capitals. I was his assistant for a game and I was told that he'd requested a few items and a specific color of Skittles for his dressing room.

I found this odd, but I separated the Skittles so that Cameron only had that flavor in his room. Come to find out that it was just a joke in his contract and he was very surprised that I did that for him. I have always kept the same mindset of treating people how you would want to be treated and giving them respect. Maybe one day I'll have a pong table for him! "

Chris Cunanan, Director of Entertainment, Los Angeles Lakers

SPEAK DIRECTLY INTO THE POPCORN, PLEASE

My helper at a few Colorado Avalanche games was Kerry-Anne, a young, enthusiastic assistant with the organization. During one game as we were having a quiet moment between the chaos, Kerry confided in me that she wanted to be an in-arena host.

So, after the game we went to the locker, I grabbed a funky bag of popcorn that could double as a mic, and encouraged her to do a mock interview with me. I threw a towel around my neck, water all over my face, and had another stage manager film it. Landing that Cam Hughes exclusive was huge for her career! Or at least, that's what I tell myself now that she's hit it big in Colorado! When's our follow-up, Kerry-Anne?

"I had been working for the Colorado Avalanche as an intern when I volunteered to follow Cam, and boy-oh-boy was it an adventure. What I took away from the experience more than anything was that you never know when a silly interview with a bag of popcorn and some crazy t-shirt guy could turn into me getting an on-camera job with the Colorado Mammoth that led to me now being a full-time in-game host, producer and game presentation manager for the Denver Nuggets (my dream job!). I have definitely been told "no" more times in the sports industry than I have been told "yes," but it's all about getting the right "yes" and working hard every day to get there."

Kerry-Anne Keogh

"Working with someone so passionate about their work can be a very rewarding – yet taxing – experience. Cameron embodies that fully. A quote that he has reminded me of, that has continued to drive me is, "The day that you lose the jitters is the day that you have to stop showing up!" It's stuck with me since the first time I've heard it. Through the stairwell hype and vent sessions, the hundreds of tees everyone wants, and the countless children that he demands a please and thank you from, no one can ever say, "Cameron doesn't care about what he does."

Zack Frongrillo – Stage Manager, Vegas Golden Knights, 40 games together

PUMP UP THE VOLUME

I can't tell you how many times I showed up and wasn't feeling it. I was exhausted from travel or the game the night before, sick, or just out of sorts... but I always found a way. Mostly because I've learned to listen to crowds, and feed OFF them.

I have an internal switch I turn on that puts me in the right state and then a moment happens that gives me the adrenaline I need to rally. Yes, I have a wacky warm-up routine, but it works! (Picture a wingnut running around the bowels of an arena doing weird moves and stretches!) And it helps to have the right music pulsating through me! I get to work with some truly talented and inspired DJs, like Jake Wagner of the Golden Knights, and many, many others...

TIMEOUT

TOP 5 PARTY-STARTERS

1. Billy Idol – "Mony Mony"

Best call & response song – definitely the most-used song of my career. One day, I vow that Billy and I will perform it live.

2. Steve Aoki – "Delirious (Boneless)"

Playhouse Magic. No one has more fun, and when you hear this song... good luck not dancing.

3. Guns N' Roses – "Welcome to the Jungle"

Unreal after a slow clap. Next question.

4. The Killers – "Mr. Brightside"

Crowd-surfing and water-fighting with thousands of fans in Singapore at the 7s Rugby tournament during a timeout. "Coming out of my cage" indeed!

5. C+C Music Factory – "Everybody Dance Now"

Every time I hear this song, I think of wearing a pink shirt in front of 66,000 screaming Canucks at the Grey Cup game, dancing like a runaway jackhammer. And also my first US Open hit, and many more!

HAT TRICK

F or the third straight year, I was off to the Memorial Cup, basically the Stanley Cup finals for the Canadian Junior Hockey League. That year it was being held at the same time I was trying to have a third date with a woman I couldn't wait to see again. (Good things come in threes?) I was sponsored by BMO for several years running to bring the spirit to each city and fanbase. This particular year, the 10-day event was being held in Québec City, a gorgeous French-speaking city nestled in the hills with a European vibe, great restaurants, and a lot of history. *Tres romantique!*

Right before this 2015 event, I had moved back to Los Angeles to start a new chapter. My father had just passed away and I needed a change of scenery from New York City where I had been living. I was staying with my dear friends Katie and Glen who I was fortunate to have crashed with over the years and who were once again hosting me during my transition back. One night, as I was leaving the house for a first date, their youngest daughter Payton said, "How do you get all these dates?!" I mean, I had to keep living and I was on a good roll since I'd been back in the city, trying to focus on living instead of grieving.

That night, I had just landed home from the NBA playoffs in Cleveland and had a wrist sprain. I didn't want to go anywhere, but I had a first date planned. A good mutual friend had suggested I meet a woman from Canada who was living in Los Angeles, and our date had been on the books for several weeks. She was a successful filmmaker, with a bent more towards the arts than sports.

As a matter of fact, she had resisted going out with me because she didn't think we had enough in common – until I told her with some insane confidence that I had actually been ranked the third best kisser in Canada. She was intrigued enough to put the compatibility interests aside and agreed to meet for a cocktail. (And yes, seeing those Katie Couric clips on her YouTube dive helped my cause, too.) It had taken a little coaxing and I didn't want to cancel, so despite the sore wrist, I rallied.

When she arrived on her skateboard, I was damn glad I had. Our first two dates in LA went really well (she held an ice pack on my wrist, for god's sake!) and we planned to meet again soon. My life was insane during that time, and because of my plentiful back-in-LA dating mojo, I wasn't in my usual "hurry up and do something to scare her" mode.

Clockwise from top: Being on our 3rd date, and meeting these future NHL Stars- Alex De Brincat, Connor McDavid, Dylan Strome.

Love doing Pink in the Rink nights.

Thank you for the breath work, Champion.

Harvey the Hound magic, in Calgary.

Cut back to: Québec City. I was there for the Memorial Cup, staying at one of Canada's most infamous hotels, the Château Frontenac, and I found out my two-date friend was going to be in Toronto on business. I asked her how she'd feel about me flying her to Québec City for a 48-hour third date – she could come to my game, and then hang with me and a great group of friends who'd also be in town. She said yes and we had her flight booked within the hour. This woman knew how to seize the moment, which made me even more excited.

As our small group, including my lovely date, was enjoying a fun meal in a funky restaurant in the historic old city, three young hockey players – in town to receive major JHL awards – walked into the bar. Dylan Strome, Alex De Brincat, and the number-one selection in the NHL draft, Connor McDavid. The bar was quiet that night, and these guys were fired up. It was the first time they could legally drink.

I went over to say hi and started some fun banter. My pal Jeff Jackson was Connor and Alex's agent so we had a mutual friend. Plus, they had seen me perform, so there was a great frame of reference for us to start a super fun conversation. I said, "See that beautiful girl over there? I'm on a third date with her."

They thought it was pretty cool that our third date was in Québec City even though we both lived in Los Angeles. The young players thought it was even cooler that she produced movies they had grown up watching on their bus trips – they wanted to meet her! She had no clue who they were, but was excited to hear Connor would be off to her hometown to play for the Oilers. It was fun to hear them chat about her old city and his new future. She was charming and curious and this chance meeting gave an already magical night an extra splash of magic dust. Over the next two days, we ran into the guys at every turn, which definitely gave our whirlwind weekend that little extra *je ne sais quoi,* and I had a very good feeling there'd be a fourth date.

Thank you for the assist that night, Connor, Alex, and Dylan!

FIRST STAR

A year and a half later, the roof of the new arena in Edmonton was about to pop off – the team was on fire and the city was pumping. It was like the glory days of Oilers hockey all over again. That kid from the Québec restaurant, Connor McDavid, was leading an exciting team, and I wanted to be part of it. I texted my pal, Oilers CEO, Bob Nicholson: "Let's light it UP." He responded within minutes. "Can you be here in a week?" Next thing I knew, Big Red was in Orange and Blue, going nuts at my very first Oilers game. There I was in the home that Gretzky built, going nuts with the hockey-mad fans, and ready to surprise Connor. He was the first star that game, scoring a game-winning beauty in OT.

As I headed back to my locker room, I had to pass by the team locker room so I was asked by the PR guys to wait until the team got settled. Connor was coming off the ice after getting the first star. He saw me, stopped and gave me a big sweaty hug, saying how stoked he was that I had the place buzzing at epic levels. I corrected him – *he* had the arena buzzing, and I was just a lucky bystander. Talk about a humble athlete. The PR guys were confused by the interaction and I told them, as anybody would: "Hey what happens in Québec City, *stays* in Québec City." Doing games in Edmonton after such an auspicious trip to Québec was full-circle magic.

An opportunity to connect and be part of a community is never lost on me. I often remind Connor of one of the best assists of his life, that little extra spark on that third date way back when, which led to a beautiful relationship with the love of my life. It's been a total blast going back to Edmonton over the years to fire up the fans on big nights and cheer on #97 and the boys!

I've probably spent the equivalent of five years in stadiums and arenas. That's more than most pro athletes. I spend most of that time in the stands, either planted in my seat or roaming from section to section. But, just like the players, I need a pre-game space to put my stuff, go over my props and get my head right. But as you probably know, most arenas have cozy home locker rooms and visiting team locker rooms, but NOT "Roving One-Man Cheer Brigade" locker rooms. The indignity of it all! All you want is to be in the right state to give the fans the best performance. Sometimes you get to share a locker room with a Moondog, and Sir CC Mascot in Cleveland, anthem singers or even jugglers. My accommodations have ranged from sharing lockers with sweaty mascots and

Rocking the Orange in Edmonton.

NHL All-Star Awards hang with Connor McDavid, and Wasserman hockey execs Adam Phillips and agent, Jeff Jackson.

Great to fire up Connor McDavid and the guys at several games over the years.

My pal, Bob Nicholson, President of Hockey for the Oilers who gave me the shot.

suits that haven't been washed in weeks, or even drunk mascots (in the early days!), to the corner of executive offices, basements, hallways and twice even a taxi on the way to the event. One time in Cleveland for a big game, they ran out of space and I wound up sharing a locker room with Marv Albert and Steve Kerr! The Big Three, together again! Talk about a funny pre-game banter. They were so confused, but kind. You show up, and make it work.

I NEED 100%

At one point I knew a few executives with the Chicago Blackhawks, and even a few players. It was the 2015 season and they were riding high in the Stanley Cup playoffs yet again. I'd done a ton of games for their AHL team, but always wanted to do a hockey game at the famous United Center.

After the Memorial Cup, I was driving from Québec City to the Montréal airport to head to London to perform at a massive international cricket event. Yes, a cricket event!

I checked my email after pulling over at a truck stop. The Chicago Blackhawks emailed asking me to perform at games three and four of the Stanley Cup Finals! This would be huge for me. I couldn't believe it. I took a few massively deep breaths and called AJ. He said he was pretty sure he wanted it to happen.

"How sure a thing is this?" I asked.

"85 percent."

"I need 100 percent."

"What?"

I don't think he understood until he could hear the planes flying overhead. "I'm on my way to London for a gig, and it would be logistically difficult to make it happen if I took off." He told me to sit tight while he tracked down his bosses.

I ate 212 Timbits while waiting. He called back in 10 minutes, and five days later I was ripping it at the NHL Finals. (I was able to give the cricket organizers 72 hours notice and a rain-check.)

In Chicago, my opening hit was insane. AJ had an idea to put me deeper into the crowd to make it feel even more "real." I was farther in a section than I'd ever been before. Sure enough, as I started to dance in my seat and the camera panned to me, the crowd was mildly alarmed. Dancing like a possessed descendant of the hometown Blues Brothers, I made my way to the aisle, and no one could believe it: *What's he doing?! Who is that guy?* Twenty thousand fans were now locked in on the ride as I ripped off my jersey and then more Blackhawks tees. It was so loud, I couldn't hear myself think.

AJ was right.

It worked. It was a hit I'll never forget. Ever.

TIMEOUT

YOUR DRIVER IS HERE

After performing at the Stanley Cup Finals in 2015 in Chicago, I threw my crap into the back of an Uber on my way to O'Hare. I was zonked. My driver, Tony, was an energetic man in his late 40s who had just lost his job and was excited to be working again. We made small talk, and he asked where I was heading next. "Off to Cleveland, my friend."

"No way, what's happening there?"

"The Cavs game."

"So you're telling me that you're going from the NHL Finals to the NBA Finals back to back? That's bananas!"

We had a laugh. Then I somewhat sarcastically asked how much he'd charge to keep driving all the way to Cleveland.

"Give me a minute," he said.

Wait, what?

He called his wife, who said, "Go, go, go!"

Amazing. I mean, I did have a flight booked, but Tony called my bluff! Why not just roll with it?

A few miles after we committed, I told Tony I was hungry. So what does he do? Calls his wife back and asks her to fire up some breakfast sandwich specials! Twenty minutes later I was in his kitchen enjoying breakfast with him and his wife and son. Tony dropped me off in Cleveland five hours later. Unfortunately, I wasn't able to get him a ticket to the game, but he called me at halftime to make sure everything was going well. Every few months I get a note from someone on Facebook saying they're in Tony's Uber and he says hi!

GO TONY!

TIMEOUT

5 DREAM GIGS, ANYONE?!

Super Bowl

A Pro Team In Every US State

10 to go, and one Canadian province (Help me get there! "C'mon New Brunswick, the phone lines are open!")

Australian Open Tennis

National Hockey League

Outdoor game – dead of winter, 10 feet of snow!

Any Big Event in Africa

Rugby, Soccer, Tennis, Other!

Kerry Bubolz, president of the Vegas Golden Knights, Richard "Boz" Bosworth CEO of the Virgin Hotel Las Vegas, and Jim Frevola SVP VGK.

THE GREATEST TWIRL

"It takes a lot of practice to be spontaneous."

Heinrich Nüsse

Vancouver, Canada, is host to one of the top stops on the Rugby Sevens global tour, with over 40,000 passionate fans from around the world converging to turn the city into some kind of Halloween meets Mardi Gras meets Miami Spring Break situation. This is no humdrum scrum, people!

During my second year of performing, we had the crowd fired up in every way possible. It might have had something to do with my outfit: A purple unicorn costume. I looked insanely sexy. Like, next level unicorn sexy. We shot unicorn videos around the city a few weeks earlier with some Team Canada rugby pals. At the event they showed the video, then cut to me in the stands, rocking the solo forehead horn. Even though I almost tripped and flew down the stairs, fans loved the creative intro. Maybe the six beers they had all had by 2 p.m. helped too.

I'd been performing on and off for about seven hours, and I had to get up one more time, for the final timeout. I was zonked, but the fans always give me energy – and I could feel that they sensed something was coming. It was my birthday weekend, and I dug deep to end as big as I could. Go time.

The song was "24K Magic," by Bruno Mars. My plan was to cut the song and start a slow clap with the 25,000 or so fans in the house. Then I felt something behind me. When I turned around, I saw five young boys dancing along with me. *Beauty! Teamwork makes the dream work.* I kept going. When I turned around again, there was only one teenage boy. He wouldn't stop. Couldn't stop.

I moved out of the way to give this young dance master the room he deserved. He was having the time of his life. The fans were transfixed by him. I tossed him the last of my shirts, and he started to twirl and throw them out like a pro! Then he ripped off his jacket. The crowd got louder and louder. His incredible smile was infectious. It was electric. He was born to do this. If you EVER need a feel-good boost, just watch this video… you're welcome!

We all waved our arms along with him, and then he, now totally in control of the show, closed off his performance with a majestic Usain Bolt dab. Perfect punctuation! The crowd roared. I looked at him in hopes that he'd follow me with the slow clap. No problem. He caught my cue and elevated it. Soon, the whole stadium was clapping along.

Canada Sevens Rugby magic with my pal Malcolm. You took a moment and made it your own with 35,000 fans. So proud of you for your incredible spirit.

With Mike Fuly and Nate Nate Hirayama Team Canada Rugby Sevens Legends.

Unicorn on the loose!

"Impossible not to take notice of your surroundings when you're running into the field and the crowd is going nuts. From a grown man in a random unicorn outfit, to the incredible costumes, you feel that energy. You thrive off it. One of my favorite memories was seeing Cam and Malcolm getting the crowd going at our home tournament in Vancouver."

Nate Hirayama, Captain Team Canada Sevens

His name was Malcolm. He was an 18-year-old with Down syndrome. And he has more energy and infectious passion and joy than anyone I've ever met.

Later, I met his mom (she's in the video, hiding!) and took a few snaps with my new pal. I couldn't stop smiling all weekend. Watch the video – I bet you won't be able to either.

It was a truly magical moment.

All my career had been about getting others to be more in the moment, to let go. When I got up in Vancouver, I was tired and ready to end my day. But then, I felt it. Malcolm was ready to take what I had started to the next level. He was fun. Fearless. On his face was a look that said he was being naughty but didn't care.

He was breaking all the rules. Basking in the glory of life. Watching this young man dance, it felt as if every moment of my career had led up to this. His joy was my joy. His happiness was every fan's happiness. That five minutes perfectly encapsulated the reason I do what I do. Thank you, Malcolm, for the greatest moment of my career.

The next year the organizers of the tournament asked Malcolm to do a few dances. Of course, he had that crowd with him every step of the way!

"I was so happy that my dream to be at the Sevens' game dancing for everyone came true. I hope every kid's dream one day comes true like mine did."

Malcolm Gendall, Canada 7s Superstar

"I promise you this wasn't staged. It was a truly pure moment of joy for the entire stadium, and Cameron. There was some destiny involved, but the relationship Cameron has built with audiences around the globe enabled him to realize the situation and prioritize the audience over his own performance. Magic."

Bart Given, Torque Strategies

WHAT HAPPENS HERE, ONLY HAPPENS HERE

"We wanted to be sure to give the community of Vegas something that was theirs. It was an absolute no-brainer to bring you in to help establish the bar of what a passionate, unadulterated dancing machine and super fan could be. We knew if we raised the bar to a 10 with you, then fans who might've been coming in at a 5 would be fine coming in at a 9, because it was less crazy than that massive, sweaty "t-shirt" guy. The rising tide lifts all ships, and you helped elevate the allowance of the fans' fury in The Fortress."

Jonny Greco, former Head of Fan Experience, Vegas Golden Knights

---

It was 5:30 p.m. on game day. I entered the T-Mobile arena. I walked down the hall in the middle of the arena into the stands. The arena was practically empty. Within seconds, a fan who had gotten there early came over. Grabbing my hand, he looked me in the eye and said, "We need you tonight. Whatever you do please don't hold back."

It was October 10th, 2017. Ten days after the worst mass shooting in US history.

But first, let's back up.

If you're a big hockey fan like me, you probably remember thinking how cool it was, hearing that Las Vegas was getting an NHL team. Right? Crazy – hockey in the desert. And who knew what it would *even* look like? A bunch of tourists in Hawaiian shirts chugging jugs of Bud Light and cheering on their favorite team?

I was at the NHL All-Star Game in LA in 2017, when I ran into Kerry Bubolz, the new team president of the freshly announced Vegas franchise. Last time I'd seen my old friend was at the Cavaliers' championship parade! Kerry asked if I'd have any interest in possibly working exclusively with his new team, the Golden Knights. *Hmm… It had been 24 years since I did that, back in Ottawa.*

A few weeks later, I was on vacation in Hawaii when I got a follow-up call from yet another old Cleveland pal, Jonny Greco. He had been hired by Kerry as Head of Fan Experience, and was keen to not only have me at a bunch of games but get me more fully involved with fan engagement. It was a ground-floor opportunity, and I was so excited by the possibilities that when I got home I immediately hopped on a plane to Vegas to go meet with Jonny and his team. What was even more special about this situation was that I was reuniting with so many familiar faces from my long and winding road of a career. Not only Kerry and Jonny, but the team's assistant GM that year (now the GM) was Kelly McCrimmon, the old Brandon Wheat Kings coach who'd had me do pump-ups for his team! And then there was Ayron Sequeira and Tyler Cofer, too! I'd worked with Ayron at San Jose Stealth games, and Tyler was an OKC Thunder alum.

Our brainstorming sessions were super productive. We loved the prospect of introducing Las Freakin' Vegas to hockey! I hit the town with a camera crew, doing silly "man on the street" videos at the Fremont Experience, mixing it up with tourists and locals alike, asking them about their new team! We rolled the funny, engaging clips at the NHL Awards, then online. It was such a rush. Doing those spots made me like a community ambassador not only for the brand-new Golden Knights, but also for hockey, the national sport of my homeland, Canada.

As the season approached, we made a deal for me to do 22 games during the regular season and playoffs (*Ha!* I thought, *fat chance for an expansion team!*). Still, though, I'd be working Vegas more than a Cher impersonator!

I was ready to dance in the desert, and the city was ready for the puck to drop.

Then, October 1st, 2017 hit.

The tragic shooting in Las Vegas took 59 lives, and rocked the world.

At that point, the home opener was a week and a half away. Obviously, the Golden Knights had to scrap the planned pre-game hoopla and figure out a way to respect and honor the horrific event that had just occurred. The team had to help the community heal. Deryk Engelland, a Golden Knight who lives in Vegas, took the mic during the opening ceremony. It was one of the most powerful speeches from an athlete I'd ever heard. He ended with these simple words: "We are all VEGAS BORN."

This set a new tone. We all need community to survive tragedy – and this city now needed its brand-new team in a way nobody could ever have imagined.

I'll never forget my first hit at that game. It was a wild dance song, and the timing was perfect. Most of the fans had no clue who I was, or what to do. But they went with it. Then the team went wild and started the game off 3-0. The Knights went on to win, then they surprised the league and kept winning. The city was starting to heal, and hockey was a big part of it.

★★★

As the Cinderella season rolled on, we were doing different intros, doing three big timeout bits a game and firing up these passionate fans who had dubbed their new home 'the Fortress.' My locker room was a hallway with a sexy Golden Knight, a Big D, a Shunock, a mascot named Chance, the Golden Girls cheer squad, the Drumbots, the spirit team, and the production crew. It was manic, intoxicating, and one of the most exciting times of my career. I met fans from everywhere and ran into old friends from different teams everywhere I turned.

Cameron did many trips to Brandon where I was coaching the Wheat Kings, we always won when he was there! I even let him talk to the team before a game one time to fire the boys up. Imagine my surprise when I got to Vegas and Cam was a regular with the Knights as well. Great person, a ton of fun, passionate about entertaining fans!

Kelly McCrimmon GM, Vegas Golden Knights

Before I knew it, it was playoff time. The Knights swept the Kings. No biggie. Then they took down the Sharks *and* the Jets in the next two rounds (Hello, *West Side Story* fans!). WHAT?! Yes, this brand-new squad made it to the Stanley Cup Finals in YEAR ONE. I'm not making this up.

Coach Gerald Gallant had them playing world-class hockey. The city was consumed with Knights fever. The sports media was amazed. *How could a first-year team do this? Where did this miracle come from? And why are the fans so off-*

Photos courtesy of L.E. Baskow, Daniel Clark,
Tyge O'Donnell, Al Powers

the-charts engaged and energized? As somebody who had a front-row seat to the unlikely success story, I have some thoughts on the matter. Obviously, the team was great, but this was a clear example of creating an atmosphere of engagement that many organizations – both sports-centric and not – could learn from. *What was the secret sauce?*

Well, the Golden Knights came in with a *mission* to let their fans be fans and have a stake in this thing. There were no rules. This was all-inclusive. Permission to be themselves at new levels. The team, including yours truly, was out on the streets, helping spread the good word, and people were responding. The locals bought in, had true sweat equity, and the Black & Gold was hot hot hot. They didn't win the Stanley Cup, but the bond had been forged. I learned a lot about the power of the Vegas mindset.

GOLDEN MAGIC

"I like how he gets people cheering and on their feet between whistles. His crazy dancing and energy makes me laugh and relax throughout the game – when the play is not going on, obviously."

Marc-Andre Fleury, Goaltender, Vegas Golden Knights, 3-time Stanley Cup Champion with the Pittsburgh Penguins

---

Season Two was equally loud and fun. I did 10 games over the year and worked hard to keep it fresh. The fans didn't lose an ounce of interest in their beloved team. I started to meet more people, the regulars, in each section and build great friendships. Memories were made every game – kids on my shoulders, tossing popcorn everywhere, jumping into grown men's arms, losing my mind with a Wolverine, even getting complimented by Vegas icon Wayne Newton for my passion! Doing big intros with the Blue Man Group, dressing up as an usher and anything else we could come up with, was the Vegas way. I'd get invited to have a beer after every game with random people. I'd often go. I met broadcasters, local media folks, wonderful bar and restaurant promoters, and on and on... We were all so connected.

The Golden Knights had become the unofficial NHL ambassador team. Whether you were from Nashville or Toronto, of course you wanted to come to Vegas to have some fun and cheer on your team. And the Vegas fans knew how to welcome each one of them!

One game in season three, we were down 3-0 vs. the defending Stanley Cup champion St. Louis Blues in the second intermission. (Notice how I said *"we"*? Guilty. This town, this team, this crowd really got me.) Most teams would fold. They'd give up. But this is Vegas, baby! Luck is something you generate, that people believe in, and sometimes that formula seems to actually work. It was 3-1, fine. At least we won't get shut out. Then 3-2 – oh, hey, wait a minute. The decibels cranking up in the Fortress! Then it was 3-3, and it sounded like Elvis's private jet took off! After that... no freakin' way, 4-3 Vegas with four minutes to go!!! Storybook ending, right?!

Except then the inconsiderate Blues tied it back up! *What?!* I was going out of my mind. We were all on a roller coaster of emotions that night. I was so hyped up that I fell off a railing doing a bit I've done a million times, cutting my elbow open.

My trusty stage manager Zack said sternly, "Take a minute. You need a break, Cam."

There was blood all over my jeans and shirt. Whatever! Wiped it off and kept dancing.

It was overtime. The Fortress was shuddering with energy.

Vegas stole the momentum back and won in a stunning comeback. The biggest comeback win for the team, ever. 18,393 fans went INSANE. Hugs, high fives, you name it. The place exploded. Popcorn was flying. Everyone was so connected. A community came together, celebrated together. It was Vegas. I was so proud to be a part of a community that had used the power of community to heal. It was such a life lesson in perseverance and the importance of positive human connection.

The last game I did before COVID-19 changed our world forever was a Vegas Golden Knights game. We held a special tribute to one of the ultimate Vegas superfans, John Baratta, a.k.a. "The Hulk," who'd passed two days earlier. He was a prince of a man, and quite a character. The emotion of the event inspired me to push it to new heights. The Knights won, 3-0 – and as I walked out, star player Jonathan Marchessault gave me an extra hard fist bump and said how much he loved the energy that night, wondering how I was still walking. I wasn't. I was floating.

When a fan base is that charged, it makes you go deeper. Pushes you to be more present, to give more. When celebration is celebrated, and people are rewarded for cheering, the cheer gets even more powerful. The team gave the fans permission to be the best versions of themselves, from the very first puck drop – and the fans responded. Thank you all for the Golden moments.

Flying Vegas style.

UNDEFEATED

I haven't kept track of "my" teams' win-loss record for the entirety of my career. But I know for a fact that over the first eight years, the home team won around 65 percent of the time. Think about that. (Not only was I there for the Knights' glorious season, but I also had the tremendous 10-0 streak in Buffalo when the scoreboard was down. Not to mention, the Cavs' great runs, and many, many others...) NHL home teams usually win around 55 percent of the time, and it's closer to 60 percent for the NBA.

So I would wager my "record" is above the norm. (This is *not* me claiming direct responsibility for that success – after all, I record my wins and losses on the basis of smiles and claps, so I'm pretty much undefeated :)) All I'm really trying to say is – I have one of the most unusual, but rewarding careers in the world, because I get to help unlock positive human energy on a daily basis. And folks, it really *works*. I am not only deeply grateful and humbled for that opportunity, but awestruck by what we can accomplish when we connect and cheer each other on. I'll see you all at the parade!

FINAL CHEER

Putting this collection of stories together, I was continuously reminded of what I already know so profoundly – the importance of taking chances, trusting your gut, doing the work, asking for help, offering help, connecting the dots, and surrounding yourself with people who believe in you. Not to mention how lucky I am. Writing this book was another iteration of the journey of my career; a lot of "no, thank you's," to get to the "yes, thank you's!"

At the end of the day, the greatest thing I've learned is this: share your spirit and joy for life, and it will come back to you. My mom taught me that years ago, and it's been my North Star. I am who I am because of my Mom's wisdom, and also the wisdom I gained by losing her so young. Dealing with that loss head-on, with the support of close friends and family, made me a stronger person. It was difficult, and it hurt – it hurt really bad – but it left me no choice but to grow up fast (yes, I know, I know – I haven't in many ways!). She won't be there to spoil my little girl rotten or find out what kind of a woman would ice my wrist on our first date. And there's nothing I can do to change any of that. It's how I live today that matters, and carries on her legacy.

Back in my hotel after a game, I'm pumped full of adrenaline roaming my room. What goes through me isn't just the blood flow, it's the smiles, energy and magic we just shared. How we connected in powerful and fun ways. I can't stop smiling. I lie in bed for a few hours wondering if I'll ever come down from this. And after 26 years, the answer is no!

I often wonder what stops people from getting up in life. From just being themselves. Why we seek permission far too often when we know the answer. What stopped me? Was it that mascot mask, costume, watermelon, or facepaint, hiding something? I don't know if there's such a thing as "perfect" timing, but everything came together that first night for me in Ottawa – when courage, or at least the "Screw It!" moment, won. The opportunity was there, and I showed up. The melons were gone and never to be carved again. It was showtime!

I was asked in a docuseries on people with interesting careers in California if I felt I had made it. I grinned, and without missing a beat said, "I'm here aren't I?" A group smile ensued. I might not have been rolling in a Porsche 911 to my Malibu mansion, but I *had* made it. I was doing what I loved. If that producer had instead asked me what it was like to face a mountain of rejection, I probably would have answered the same thing. "I'm here, aren't I?"

And here's what all these stories show me about my wacky, unlikely career. Do something that ignites you and eventually your heart will glow. I didn't make the basketball team, but I ended up at center court at the NBA Finals. That's it. That's the one sentence I hope you will really take away from this book. If I have any wisdom to espouse, there it is. *There are other ways to contribute to the team.*

If somebody who could barely dance to Phil Collins as a chubby little redheaded kid with a speech impediment can do it, *you can too.* What have we really got to lose?

Just.

Get.

Up.

Trust me – your crowd is ready to cheer you on!

Thank you for being part of the best CHEER of my life!

WOOOOOOHOOOOOOOO!

THANK YOU

- Every usher, for letting me in your aisle, for your smiles. For getting it.
- Every Assistant/Stage Manager: you helped me get ready for the big moments, were patient and celebrated the fun.
- Every mascot, character, spirit team, host, and producer: thanks for your passion and having me in your house.
- Every DJ who listened to my plans and then listened to the crowd, then took the tunes to a new creative place.
- Every full circle adventure from coming back to do Leafs games 23 years later, (thanks Steve Edgar!), LA Kings (thanks RB & GM), Ducks, and many places in between. What a thrill. And, I'm cool a few teams are copying my schtick outright. I'm flattered, just work on the twirls more, please.
- Every passenger I've sat beside on the way to a gig and you were going to the same game and I didn't warn you that I'd visit you in your section, or on the way back from a gig, for understanding why I'm so wired and tired. Those I shared laughs and inspiration with and who were there at the right time on the right trip. I think we can all agree the open and powerful chats one can have on a flight, etc. Next time I'll have a book for you.
- Every teacher who helped me grow, pushed me and marked a shit-ton of red ink on my assignments. And, Mr. Fraser, thank you for cutting me from the Hoops team and putting up with me in English class. And, Mr. Laughton, for being my extra voice and ears when I needed it most. And, to all the teachers out there who believe, who encourage and ignite sparks in their students.
- Every fan who caught a tee. Yes, all of you. I don't know what you did to get it, but as long as you didn't rip it out of a kid's hand I'm glad we had that moment. I hope you washed it a few times!
- Every team executive who said, "Yeah, let's do it. Let's do something different for our fans, let's shake things up and try something new." Never stop pushing the fun factor in the human-connection department. Your desire to keep improving and trying new stuff is appreciated by fans around the world. And for the meals, the laughs, beers, hugs and epic friendships.
- Every supporter behind the scenes over the last few years – David, Kelli, Michael,, Viv, Bob, Adam, Jax, Scott, Woody, CJ, Oren, Boz, MB, Anna Maria, Ariane, Riley, K2, Rob, Cols...

- Every Superfan who got up, who went for it, who got it, who danced, who twirled tees at whatever age, who came along, who said hi, who asked for tees in the weirdest places, who just wanted to celebrate life. What a blast connecting with you. You are the real Superfans.

- Every athlete who I've met in the halls, locker rooms, or on my travels, for being so kind and gracious, and who became friends. And, for those who took me out with them and made me feel extra welcome! It makes me want to go crazier knowing you may increase your energy.

- Every Randy in your life, who sees something in you and gives you the shot.

- Every person who gave a shout out in the book – I'm so grateful for your passion, support, and friendship.

- Everyone named David Elmaleh and Michael X Ferraro for their hard work, spirit and creativity in helping me make this dream of writing a book come true.

- Every friend and it's a long list. The ones who played hide and seek as kids, grew up together, went through puberty together (still are!). MY HS Gang. The ones I raised a few toasts with, met on the road, who came to games, who let me crash with them, who funded me financially and emotionally when I needed it. The Venice Crew. The friends I over-texted (and still do—it gets lonely out there!). The Gaiter Family. The friends that pushed my creative spirit. The Pong crew. The friends I reconnected with over the years. The friends who showed up and believed. And to all my friends who cheered me on. Wow, am I so grateful for all of you. Every single one of you!

- Everyone who added some extra spice to make this book and project possible - Rachel Small, Maya Berger, Emily Knight, Scott Modrzynski, and Steven Cook.

- My "mom" influences. Momma Langley, since the hug. Karen, Penny. Sheila. Sandy. And the ones I've met along the way who I so admire.

- My father, for his love and warm spirit.

- My cool and kind big sister Andrea, who is always so proud. I hear you. I feel it. I appreciate it. We got this.

- My aunts and uncle, cousins, thank you for the meals, the hugs, the visits, the love. Thank you for playing charades with me, games with me, and allowing me to just be me. Thank you for making me part of the family, even though I was clearly the cutest cousin.

- My Nana, not just for her chocolate chip cookies, but also for her years of meeting me at the Rough Riders games when I was a kid. She taught me about integrity, about caring for people. She was always there for me. I miss her rubbing my head at night. Her calm and class have guided me.

- My love, for your warmth, love, kindness, my birthday do-over, and all the love and spirit that led us to beautiful Spring. She is the truest form of a miracle I've ever witnessed. She gives me joy beyond measure and makes me cheer harder than I ever have. I'm so happy you iced my wrist that night.

"As for our losses and gains, we have seen how often they are inextricably mixed. There is plenty we have to give up in order to grow. For we cannot deeply love anything without becoming vulnerable to loss. And we cannot become separate people, responsible people, connected people, reflective people without some losing and leaving and letting go."

Judith Viorst, *Necessary Losses*

Thank you, Mom. I miss you. I miss your heart. I let go the best I could. But, I never let you leave me. Your love will always fuel me. I work every day to make you proud.